TEN GREEN BOTTLES

NINI KARPEL IN THE FRONT ROOM OF HER HOME
AT 56 LICHTENSTEIN STRASSE, VIENNA 1936.

TEN
GREEN
BOTTLES

THE TRUE STORY OF ONE FAMILY'S JOURNEY

FROM WAR-TORN AUSTRIA

TO THE GHETTOS OF SHANGHAI

Vivian Jeanette Kaplan

ST. MARTIN'S PRESS 📖 NEW YORK

TEN GREEN BOTTLES. Copyright © 2002 by Vivian Jeanette Kaplan. All rights reserved. Printed in the United States of America. For information, address St. Martin's Press, 175 Fifth Avenue, New York, N.Y. 10010.

www.stmartins.com

Library of Congress Cataloging-in-Publication Data

Kaplan, Vivian Jeanette, 1946–
    Ten green bottles : the true story of one family's journey from war-torn Austria to the ghettos of Shanghai / Vivian Jeanette Kaplan.
        p. cm.
    ISBN 978-0-312-33055-2

    1. Karpel, Nini. 2. Jews, Austrian—China—Shanghai—Biography.
3. Refugees, Jewish—China—Shanghai—Biography. 4. Austria—Biography.
5. Shanghai (China)—Biography. 6. Holocaust, Jewish (1939–1945)—
Austria. 7. Jews, Austrian—China—Shanghai—Biography. 8. Jews—
Persecutions—Austria.

DS135.A93K375 2004
940.53'18'092251132—dc22
[B]   2004048690

First published in Canada by Robin Brass Studio Inc.

First U.S. Edition: November 2004

*T*his story is dedicated to my parents, Gerda and Leopold Kosiner, whose heroic lives were my inspiration. The constant love and support they gave me throughout my life have enabled me to write this book.

To my grandparents, Johanna and Solomon Karpel and Bluma and Bernard Kosiner, whom I was not privileged to know during their lives but whose spirits I have somehow discovered through this work. Deep within me is the bond of blood and of love from them to me.

To my relatives, still living as well as those now deceased, whose names are here mentioned and preserved as part of a remarkable account of perseverance. Each one has a voice that should be heard, to bear witness to a shred of history that ought to be remembered.

To my husband, Barry, who has given me unquestioned love and encouragement in every endeavour I have pursued.

To our three sons, Cary, Randy and Darryl, who have brought enormous pride and happiness into our lives and who amaze us constantly with their ability, integrity and heart. They will carry their heritage forward to future generations. And also to my new little miracle grandson, Jackson Leo, who is my late father's namesake and who, born three months prematurely, has already demonstrated his inherited strength, determination and fortitude and the relentless will to live.

CONTENTS

INTRODUCTION

Ten Green Bottles can most accurately be categorized as a memoir in the creative non-fiction genre. I have written the work in the voice of my mother, Gerda Kosiner, who lived through a series of almost unbelievable experiences and survived. The events are as true and accurate as I can make them. The characters are real people, many of whom I know, who crossed her path or whose lives became entangled with hers. I have made every effort to verify scenes described in the book, including the exchange of words and thoughts that are expressed, although recreating verbatim dialogues would be impossible.

I feel myself more than a chronicler of detached circumstances. I was born in Shanghai, my mother tongue and cultural heritage are German, or more precisely, Viennese, and I became familiar with the story while listening to my mother's telling and retelling of the tales that are included. I am so intimately aware of the facts of this life that it seems almost as if I had experienced it myself. After numerous consultations with the people who are named in the book and additional corroboration with outsiders who were able to add their accounts to my research, I feel confident in the veracity of the events I describe. Where my description of an event differs from the experiences of others who lived during the same period, I can only say that this is a personal account, filled with vignettes told to me throughout my lifetime. I have included descriptions of pieces of memorabilia that I have in my possession and treasure to this day, inanimate objects that travelled the course of the journey.

Vivian Jeanette Kaplan

ACKNOWLEDGEMENTS

My gratitude to all those voices, past and present, alive and deceased, family and strangers, that echoed in my mind and guided the thoughts in my head. To my father, Poldi Kosiner, whose spirit has filled every page, whose words of wisdom and encouragement are an integral part of me. To my mother, Nini Kosiner, née Karpel, who struggled to retrieve memories, distant and painful, to aid in my understanding of her most guarded emotions and allowed me to reveal them within this story.

To the Shanghailanders, a select group of refugees who, like my family, followed the path from oppression in Europe to an uneasy haven in Shanghai. Of those who shared reminiscences, a special thanks to Kurt Fischer in Sydney, Australia, whose correspondence was invaluable in refining and confirming historical details. To those who helped in background research, my thanks particularly to Helga Embacher and Margit Reiter in Salzburg.

In appreciation to Wendy Thomas, my editor, for perseverance and an inquisitive nature, who prodded me onwards whenever I faltered or to new discoveries if I imagined that all had already been said. To Robin Brass, my sincere thanks for first respecting my writing and subject matter enough to publish this book and then the disciplined drive to perfection and precision in form and detail that made the process an education and a pleasure.

V.J.K.

TEN GREEN BOTTLES

CHAPTER 1

PAPA 1921

Kneeling on a high-backed chair, my face propped on my open palms, I wait by the window and watch as the rain clatters against the glass and the cobbled streets below. Shutters are rattling in the wind. The streets of Vienna are wet and puddled. People are rushing about in the cold downpour, and there are so many round black umbrellas darting in and out of doorways that they look like crazed turtles. I can see only the fluttering domes, not the people beneath them as they flit about, zigzagging, colliding and parting, each in search of his own shelter.

Brownstone apartment buildings stand in rows on both sides of the wide street. Our home is in one of the spacious flats at 56 Lichtenstein Strasse. Our parents have lived here since their wedding day, and it is in this home that Mama has given birth to each of her children. We are three girls, of which I am the youngest. "Nini, you must come now. It's time for bed," my mother calls.

My older sisters, Erna, who's thirteen, and Stella, who's ten, don't have to go to bed yet. They call me "Baby" although I'm five already. Good Austrian names have been chosen for each of us to connect us firmly to our homeland. My real name, which no one uses, is Gerda. My father has nicknamed me "Kindi," meaning "Little Child," a term of endearment that I cherish. In my baby version of this, however, they say that I used to repeat "Nini" and that is the version that has stuck. My sisters are always teasing me about my silly name. I'm the only one who is not called by a given name, and although I hate their taunting calls, secretly I think that I am the special one, the one that Papa loves best because of his pet name for me.

He is my protector, the source of all wisdom and strength that holds the family together. His skill as a businessman is widely extolled as he has established three large department stores of considerable repute in Vienna. He is proud to announce that his wife and children will always be well cared for and will want for nothing, living in this perfect world. He is a patriotic Austrian and reminds us often of our duty to the beloved country of our birth. My favourite time of day is the moment when he arrives home from work and swings me up in a tight embrace. I feel his prickly face rub against my cheek as I inhale his aftershave cologne, a mixture of wet wood and spice. His robust laugh starts deep in his belly and erupts, rippling in bursts, filling the room with spontaneous joy. We gather around his big deep chair where he plops in weary contentment at the end of the day to listen to our stories and to give us the benefit of his advice. He has discovered many things about the world, about human nature, and these he uses in business to his advantage. He often tries to share his thoughts with us, punctuated with colourful detail.

"There will be times, my children, remember my words, when you will rely on the help of a stranger, perhaps even an enemy. At that moment you will have to walk away from your own pride and make a deal, if necessary, even with the Devil, himself. If the need arises, you must be brave and search for any means, no matter how harsh. Don't be afraid to fight for your rights, and never lose the courage to save yourself, or to rescue someone in the family. In this world you will meet obstacles of all kinds. Search for the help that you require, no matter the source. If necessary, put pride aside and cut the hangman's rope from around a murderer's neck, even as he is strung on the gallows. If he is the one who can preserve you, you must free him. There is nothing that you should not do to survive. Only the strongest of us will succeed in life. You, my children, will have that strength."

We always listen to his words in rapt concentration and confusion. We try to memorize these stories and morals but can neither understand their meaning nor imagine any possibility of their use. As I look at my older sisters, I can see that they have no greater comprehension than I do. Their mouths agape, they try to absorb the bizarre imagery and hidden message but can't truly comprehend the mysterious words. Still, I know that this advice will be repeated again and again, as are many other stories, each told in grave consideration, weighed and measured, then offered as tiny treasures to be safeguarded and tucked away for use some day.

"And how are my young ladies today?" he asks in a tone of mock seriousness. My sisters and I curtsy and reply, "Well and happy, dear sir."

Then we abandon all pretext of etiquette and run to squeeze him in our arms. Mama laughs and scolds, "Leave Papa in peace. The poor man is exhausted and can't contend with you all."

Mama is getting rounder each day and now her belly is so full that she can't lift me. Anyway, I am too grown up to be carried around like a baby. My sisters have told me that Mama has a new baby inside her tummy and that I will soon be displaced as the youngest. At first I don't believe them but Mama says that it's true and she has let me touch the spot where the baby is alive, hiding where we can't see it deep within her expanding body. I have felt it kick my hand as if it knows I am there.

Reluctantly I kiss Mama and Papa and am bundled off to bed by the nanny. I don't like the dark and pull the covers close up to my nose for warmth and security and close my eyes to block out the demons that seem to haunt the shadowy corners and creak in the floors at night. I hate the rumbling thunder that starts growling far away, moving ever closer until it becomes a booming roar that shakes the walls. Lightning fractures the sky and suddenly illuminates the room, casting eerie shadows of fairytale witches and ogres.

When I scream Mama rushes in to reassure me that the storm will soon pass and that good little girls will be kept safe in their beds until the morning light. She sings a lullaby, an old tune in Yiddish, and hugs me in her arms until I can shut out the monsters and settle into the soothing depths of a child's sleep.

A lady comes to our home to visit sometimes, carrying a small leather bag with her. She spends her time mostly with Mama, in her room, with the door closed. Mama says that she is called a midwife and that she will help to get the baby out of Mama's belly. I am mystified by this notion but not frightened because Mama tells us that we each came into the world this way and that everything will be fine.

One day the lady arrives as usual but Mama is in her bed and not feeling too well. Her face is flushed, with drops of perspiration on her forehead, and she begs us not to disturb her. When I creep into the bedroom to see her, she looks so different to me, just a head with a huge mound attached, concealed beneath the covers. When the midwife arrives, she appears more serious than usual and hurries in to see Mama without her usual greetings to us. I am hustled out of the room.

The two women are closed away for a long time. The midwife has a white apron tied neatly around her middle and her hair is tied back with a kerchief. She is very serious and snaps orders to everyone around. A maid dashes about, carrying in tubs of steaming hot water and piles of clean towels, and rushing out again with soiled ones. Papa has come home early today looking pale and worried but he doesn't go in to see Mama. He is fidgety and impatient, unable to sit still or listen to our stories. We can hear some noises from the room that sound like Mama crying and talking at the same time, punctuated by the midwife's stern commands, followed by softer words. Then there is silence alternating with sobs and wails. We are frightened by all the strange sounds but are hushed by the nanny and told not to ask questions or to bother anyone.

We are all sent to bed at our regular time but the midwife is still with Mama and the muffled sounds coming from her room are getting louder. I can't fall asleep because of the agitated voices that fill the house. For many hours I try to lie as still as possible in my bed, hugging my rag doll close to my face and concentrating on the sounds in the other room. Hurried footsteps click on the wooden floors of the hallway. There are long periods of silence. Finally my eyelids feel heavy and I rub my sore eyes and drift off.

In the early morning, Papa, his face lit with excitement and joy, awakens us with the news that we have a new baby brother. We scramble out of our beds and run to see the newest family member, cradled in Mama's arms. Propped up by plump white pillows, she is sitting in her bed, holding a very tiny bundle wrapped in blankets and announces that the small red face screaming uncontrollably is our new little brother named Willi. This is a wondrous occasion for us all, especially Papa, who is overjoyed to have a son at last. We girls fuss over the baby and argue immediately over who will hold him and play with him. We lean forward in amazement trying to get a better view of the tiny fingers and toes of the new little being, his eyes tightly shut. Mama and Papa explain that we have become big sisters now and that Willi will need us to take care of him. We each nod our heads in acceptance of our new roles and consider this to be a serious responsibility.

Papa is proud of his only son and speaks glowingly about plans for him as he grows. He has so much to tell him, sharing with him the advice that he has learned, guiding him along his path. He will become a young Austrian, comfortable in his native land, able to take over the business or to pursue a profession of his choosing. With a large family such as ours, Papa puts great importance on provisions for our futures. He and Mama talk about the suitable marriages that will one day take place for me and for my sisters and a look of peaceful contentment settles over his face. He is satisfied and confident that everything will be as it should.

We are awed by the changes in the baby within his first year. Every day he seems to learn some new word and we marvel at his performance. We rediscover our commonplace surroundings, seen through his fresh eyes, everything done or observed for the very first time. Entranced, we watch as he reacts to his small world with the pure delight of innocence and magic. When I put my finger into his hand, he grasps it with all his might and doesn't want to let go.

Bath time is an adventure of slapping and splashing. We gather together, wide-eyed as the pudgy arms flap and splatter the water, and the baby's startled reactions make us giggle. His first tastes of food are met with gusto or adamant rejection and squishy grimaces. When we go outside, the miracles continue from the surprise of the first raindrop flicking on his eyelash to the touch of any unfamiliar object clutched in his round baby fist. His first gurgling laugh is greeted with applause from everyone. Crawling on all fours like a puppy, he surveys his home. Although only five years separate us, I feel grown up and protective of my little brother.

I am allowed to feed the bottle to the baby sometimes by holding him in my arms very carefully and letting him suck on the rubber nipple. The milk is tipped towards him and the liquid pours down his hungry throat. He gulps it so quickly that I'm afraid he will choke.

While he drinks he holds my finger firmly in his fist, not letting go, and if the rubber nipple slips out of his mouth he immediately starts howling for more.

"I want to feed him next," Stella says, pushing my arm. "It's my turn anyway."

"No," I shout, "it's my turn, you just did it last time."

"Stop fighting or Mama will be cross with you both," Erna admonishes us.

Papa does not interfere in our squabbles. He sinks back into his favourite chair, which hugs him like an old friend, and rustles his newspaper. A contented smile crinkles lines around his lips and eyes. Things have returned to normal, sound and secure: his wife is busy with the children and his household is at ease.

CHAPTER 2

CHANGES 1922

When Willi attempts his first few wobbly steps, we girls squeal with pleasure, then race through the house looking for Mama and Papa, who must come to see. As we burst into their room, giggling and chattering all at the same time, we sense a cold stillness that has never been before and we become suddenly quiet. We are stopped at the doorway, then shushed and hustled away by our nanny. Doctors have been visiting for several days, and we have become used to seeing them scurrying in and out of the house. But there is something different this day as we see them leave in a strange shuffle of muttered regret and shaking heads. We are asking questions anxiously, all at the same time, in an unintelligible swarm like buzzing bees. I can see Erna and Stella starting to cry. I can't comprehend what is wrong, so I return to the other room to play with Willi, who has tumbled to the floor from his last attempt at walking on his own. I struggle to pick him up, but there is no one else around to help and he begins to wail in frustration. Soon we are both crying and the nanny can't settle us down. We want Mama but she doesn't come.

Tears streaming, shoelaces untied, I wander through the house searching for Mama but find my sisters instead. "What has happened?" I ask them. "Why is everyone crying all at once? Where is Mama?"

"You can't see Mama now. Papa is gone, don't you know?" Stella answers through impatient tears. Stella always makes me feel foolish and tells me that I don't know anything.

"Where is he?" I ask in bewilderment.

Stella is eleven now and considers me to be nothing but a baby. I know she thinks that her sadness is more important than mine, and maybe she is right, but the sharp needle of hurt inside my chest is real and painful and I can't stop crying.

I am barely six years old when Papa dies and vanishes from our lives forever. His loss is a constant lump of sorrow that burrows deep within me. I cannot completely understand the void he has left nor overcome the feeling of pain, of abandonment. Unable to fully grasp what has happened, I am overwhelmed by the outpouring of grief around me, adults in fits of tears that have always been reserved for children, and Mama weak and desperately sad.

For seven days we sit *Shiva,* a time of remembrance for the departed. A thick candle in a glass, set on our bureau, flickers day and night. All the mirrors are covered with cloth. We, the mourners, sit on low stools, and each of us has a torn black ribbon pinned to our shirt. Relatives and neighbours, their faces contorted in pity, come to visit every day to console us but their words can't fill the cavernous emptiness.

I huddle with the baby in a corner and repeat nursery rhymes to him or sing little lullabies, faltering as I try to remember all the words. He is too young to be aware of the loss, and although I am expected to understand, confusion overlaps the sadness and I can't resolve it. No one can explain the situation to me as each person in the household is absorbed in her own private mourning. The usual buzz of children's voices is absent and even our constant arguments and bickering come to a standstill.

I don't want to believe that he is gone forever. I wait at the front door at the end of the day, or peer longingly from the window, expecting Papa to come home as usual, patting my head with his palm and asking me questions in his deep voice. I think that he might be playing a trick on us all and will suddenly appear again, a twinkle in his eye and shaking with rollicking laughter at a clever joke. I pretend that he is just late from work and that he will be home soon. For a while I stand at the window in the evening, staring out at the darkening street, despite my sisters' angry protests at my stupidity. Finally the truth is clear to me and reluctantly I know for certain that he never will come back again and I can wait no longer.

Often I find myself curled in his big chair, closed away from the rest of the family, dreaming of Papa and of our moments together. Trying desperately to hold on to the memories, for they are all that I have left of him, I look for signs that he is still around. Maybe he is whispering to me in the wind or winking at me in the bright sunlight pouring through soft white seedlings that flutter by the window. Sometimes I think I can hear him whistling to me in the bird's song in the branches or calling out to me in the raindrops thumping on the road. I keep these thoughts deep within and share them with no one so they can't fly away. I fear mostly that I will forget his face and his scent and that he will drift farther and farther away from me.

Our lives have changed as Mama has had to take over the running of the business as well as the household. She seems always to be tired, and we feel disconnected and alone. Still, Papa has left us with his most precious gift, our Austrian homeland that we cherish and his words of encouragement that give us all the strength to face our lives without him. Whenever we doubt ourselves, we remember his eyes, animated and kind, and the stories told as we used to crowd around his big chair.

"Children," Mama says one evening in her most serious tone, after we have finished dinner. "I have found something among your father's papers. He wrote this when he knew how ill he was. I have kept it with me for days now, wanting to read it to you, but couldn't. I want you to know how important you all were to him and that his thoughts even near the end were of you."

We all become silent as stone and look at her with scarcely a blink. Papa has sent us something, even though he is gone. We wait for her to carefully unfold the precious page of paper that she touches with solemn reverence and tenderness. She takes a deep breath and begins to read,

To My Dear Children,
Today you are children, nestled and safe
Warm beneath parents' wings.
But the time will come when we have gone,
Then, alone you will face many things,
When the nest is cold and the belching wind howls,
And danger lurks at the door,
Unguarded, unshielded from harm you will be,
Against the world, you four.
When one of this brood is mired in pain,
And suffering creases his brow,
Shoulder the burden, lighten his load,
Do all that your strength will allow.
Remember the poor, that is my wish,
Give charity without restraint.
There will always be those more humble than you,
Listen to the beggar's complaint.
Thus says your father, thus taught your mother
Through example and through deed,
Before you we set a path that is straight
And beg you our words to heed.
My legacy this will remain,
Words that may not suffice,
But all that I have, I give to you,
Your father's heartfelt advice.
Your father

Tears begin to form in our eyes, and we brush them away with the backs of our hands. We hug Mama, whose white linen handkerchief, edged in lace, is a damp wad clutched in her fist. Papa is with us still and will be forever. We each vow to learn the poem by heart and to cherish and keep it with us all of our lives.

Before long everyday happenings draw us up into a new reality. Our home is soon bustling again, full of daily routine and noisy confusion. We girls are off to school, Mama goes to handle the business affairs, and the baby is left behind with the nanny. Each of us becomes enmeshed in the multitude of things that perpetuate our ordinary lives, filled to the spilling edge with activities and obligations.

In the evening we are all together again at the dinner table. It is then that we are truly aware of our loss and of how much things have changed. At the head of the dining table, Papa's seat stands empty but draws all our thoughts towards it. The baby cries woefully in the background as we eat in unusual silence. Mama stares at the vacant spot and doesn't even notice the food before her. She can't hear us when we speak to her and soon we stop trying. We have lost half of Mama along with Papa. We spend many nights in tearful retreat in our rooms with lonely dreams.

We girls tend to our lessons and try to help with Willi, who is the only one unaware of the changes and all that we have lost. He will never know Papa, not even for the few precious years of my memory. Mama seems to have aged so much. Her carefree laughter and humming melodies are no longer heard. She works long hours in the business and struggles to manage the burden she must bear alone. When she comes home, she slumps into Papa's chair and hugs the big feathered cushion to her chest as if searching for his comfort to ease the load. We understand that the seat is now hers as she has become the head of the household, the one who must make all the decisions.

Summer is coming to an end, and I will be starting first grade in the fall. While the days are still warm and the sunshine bright, Erna, Stella, and I go to the park with our nanny every day. The grassy smells and happy sounds of children playing are a welcome change from our sad household. We skip on the lawns, tossing a ball to one another while the nanny sits on a nearby bench with Willi, asleep in his carriage. She takes out her knitting needles and ball of yarn to pass the time, looking up now and then to be sure we are not getting into any trouble.

There's never enough time at the park for all the games we find to play. We tumble down the green hills, letting the world spin and blur, rolling faster and faster until we reach the bottom, laughing and so dizzy that we stumble and weave, drunk with abandon. We race to the swings, then stretch and bend our knees, flinging the seats high above the playground, arching and straightening our backs with the movement. We feel like birds, wind blowing wildly through our clothes and swishing our hair into our eyes. The nanny is already calling us to come down but we pretend not to hear her and continue swinging forward and back in wild swooping loops.

Finally she comes right to the foot of the swings, her expression of annoyance clearly creasing her face in an unattractive way as she shouts loudly, "Come, all of you, time to go now. Your mama will soon be home and expecting you to be ready for dinner. We still have to get you cleaned up. You're a sight to see, covered in grass and dirt. The baby is awake and screaming, wanting to be fed. Come right this minute!"

We have been told to listen to our nanny and to show her proper respect. We know that Mama can no longer be with us all the time and that we need someone to care for us, but this one will leave just like all the others did before her and soon there will be another "fraulein" in the household folding our clothes and organizing our lives. They do their jobs in an efficient matter-of-fact way but offer no arms to hold us and have no kind word for our daily concerns. Some are nicer than others but we have learned not to count on anyone for too long as they will soon disappear. Mostly we have one another and no one else. We leave the playground reluctantly and head for home to wait anxiously for Mama's return.

CHAPTER 3

REMEMBRANCE 1923

The wind hurtles angrily across the cemetery in harsh gusts so I hold on more tightly to Mama's gloved hand. September is the time for *Rosh Hashanah*, the Jewish New Year, when all of us who have lost a parent must go to visit the graves. Stella tells me that we will have to do this every year, forever, because we have become "half-orphans." My woollen cap is tugged down firmly over my ears but the cold still bites and burns. Mama whispers some words that I can't understand as we all stand facing the rock before us that has some writing and a star carved into it. It is one of many that are lined up neatly, row after row.

I stare transfixed at the bunches of flowers sprouting from the earth where I am told that Papa is asleep, never to awaken. I imagine that he has grown the flowers especially for us, each small yellow and white bloom a tiny present from his resting place to remind us of him and to tell us that he has not forgotten. In my hand I am clutching a small smooth stone that I have found on the gravelly roadside as we walked to the grave. When Mama and the others go towards Papa's place, I go too and kneel to set my little stone next to theirs. Everyone is sobbing, bursting with tears. I think of Papa asleep below the flowers and whisper to him, "Good night, Papa. Don't be afraid of the dark."

On the High Holy Days of *Yom Kippur*, the Day of Atonement, I am taken along to the *Yiskor* service in the synagogue near our home. There we stand, Mama and we children, in silent prayers in memory of the departed. Those over thirteen must fast for twenty-four hours, no food or even water, to clear their thoughts for remembrance of all that they have and all that they have lost. I have been told I will be expected to do the same when I become thirteen, but I am seven and that seems so far away.

The temple building appears vast as I stare up at the high ceilings and brilliantly coloured cut-out shapes in the glass windows through which sunlight is filtering in ribbons of blue and green. Painted into the glass are pictures of things I can recognize, such as a menorah of candles like the one we have at home and the ram's horn *shoffar* like the one that was blown at Rosh Hashanah just a few days before to welcome the New Year. I think of the strange bellowing sound emitted as the trumpeting notes leapt from the twisted horn's open end and swept through the silent congregation. There are other pictures of trees and clouds, but none of people. Mama says that Jews don't pray to people, only to an invisible God that we keep in our mind. The only image in my mind is that of Papa's face.

People around us are reading from their black prayer books as the men chant aloud in their even rhythm, bobbing up and down quickly from the waist, repeating ancient Hebrew blessings, fully absorbed in meditation and religious fervour. They are tented from their heads down nearly to the floor in white silk prayer shawls, *tallisim*, fringed at the lower borders and banded with broad stripes of blue or black, and on their heads are small round caps, *yarmulkes*. Some of them have curled the fingers of their right hands at the knuckles, balled into loose fists to tap their chests lightly over and over again on the left side, over the heart.

"Why are they hitting their chests, Mama?" I ask.

"They are remembering their sins committed over the past year, asking God's forgiveness for any departures from a righteous path, symbolically doing penance for the wrongs, vowing to improve their ways in the year ahead, and beseeching the Almighty to inscribe them into the Book of Life for another year. It means, Nini, that we should try to do better next year and to become kinder to others."

I can't understand everything she has told me but I see that the people's faces are calm and held in deep concentration. They are begging for life despite things they have done that were wrong. We are all facing in the same direction, and at the front is a raised platform with the carved oak doors of the sacred ark, containing the Torah scrolls, written by hand, the most cherished symbol of the Jews. Even as a small child, I can sense the reverence given to these pages of scripture that tell the long arduous tale of our history. When the ark is opened, we all rise in respect. The Torah, wrapped in velvet covers and bright with silver adornments, is carried up and down the centre aisle for all to see. It is held high, in regal splendour, moving away from the ark and then back again in a procession. The heavy scrolls are lifted by the elders, then supported against their shoulders and carried slowly past the worshippers, who remain standing next to their wooden seats. As the Torah is moved by, men stretch forward into the aisle to touch the knotted fringes of their *tallisim* against the sacred scrolls and then to their lips to show their devotion.

"Can I say a prayer too, Mama?" I ask, tugging her sleeve.

She turns towards me, the trail of a tear marking her cheek, and looks at me in surprise, as if she has forgotten that I am here.

"Yes, Nini, say, '*Shema Yisrael, Adonai Elohanu, Adonai Ehud,*' which means 'Listen, all Israel, the Lord our God, the Lord is One'."

"But Mama, I don't understand what that has to do with Papa."

"It means that there is only one God for all of the Jewish people and that He is watching over us all, even Papa, although he is gone away and we can't see him any more. Our God will protect us forever. I know that it is hard for you to understand now, but when you grow up it will become easier. For now, repeat these words whenever you want to, in special memory of Papa, and then again when you hear other people saying them too because that is the one prayer that every Jew knows by heart."

On these High Holy Days the synagogue is a solemn refuge for our family, a sanctuary in which to hide from the personal sorrow and grief we have kept buried within. The assembly of figures wrapped in white join together as one voice, chanting the rhythmic melody of Hebrew words that blend in unison. In some way the strange words and songs work to soothe the blistering wounds of sadness and isolation that we all share. We allow ourselves some comfort and healing, and each of us begins to find her own inner tranquillity.

CHAPTER 4

VIENNA 1926

Over the next few years life moves along with its own momentum, seasons following one another with birthdays to punctuate the years flicking by. There is school to attend, music lessons, and in the winter, our favourite pastime of skiing. Not far from Vienna stand the softly rolling mountains which I love, Kobenzl, Kahlenberg, and Schneeberg. I think of them as stately giants, solid forms planted forever on the earth, faithful and enduring, their soaring peaks rising into the clouds. Whenever we go skiing I look up and think again of Papa floating somewhere between the sky and the snow. I feel the comfort and protection of his arms again whenever I gaze up where the blue and white meet, and I imagine that that is where Heaven begins.

A new normalcy has replaced the one that we knew before Papa died. Sundays are special because the stores are closed and Mama is home. This is also a day for family visits, and we are often invaded by a troupe of relatives. From the kitchen drifts the aromatic delicacy of apple strudel, cinnamon-laced and buttery, baking to golden crispness. Sweet and tart apricot dumplings bubble in the pot. The bitter delight of coffee brews on the stove amid the frenzied anticipation of visitors arriving for the afternoon feast. We children must prepare by dressing in our most uncomfortable clothes, polished shoes that pinch at the toes and high-necked dresses that are buttoned all the way up the back. We practise our greetings and must remember to address each one correctly by name so that no one will be offended.

These meetings are a daunting ordeal filled with rules and protocol that are not to be ignored. We are warned especially not to contradict any of our elders, for if we do there will be consequences too dire to contemplate. At even the slightest provocation, they react without hesitation with flurries of inflamed indignation. Like a barnyard full of chickens, feathers flying in all directions, flapping in outrage, they squawk and cluck their disapproval. Faces grow red and puffy as they scowl without mercy. Trying helplessly to repress our giggles, we poke and elbow one another, and soon are sputtering with exploding laughter despite ourselves. The elders will not endure this ridicule without rebuke.

One of the most unbearable transgressions is that of neglecting to offer immediate and appropriate greetings such as "A kiss on the hand, noble lady," a formal expression of respect that always makes us cringe in discomfort from its archaic oddity. If we are distracted momentarily or are forgetful, one of us might walk into the room without the proper salutation. Then the outrage is certain to begin. "Look how she enters the room like a cow, without even a 'moo' to us. What impertinence!" blurts one of the aunties.

"Such a fresh brat. Are there no manners left in this household?" agrees the next.

On these occasions, Mama is disappointed with our behaviour and insists that an apology be offered, and before long we find ourselves outside the parlour so as not to further upset the precarious civility that has been disturbed. After many such encounters, our manners become somewhat tamed and we commit fewer transgressions. Willi and I, as the youngest, still find ourselves ousted for our mistakes, but Erna and Stella are considered to be young ladies and are expected to behave better. Erna is now eighteen and engaged to be married, so this Sunday is to be a special celebration. We have all promised Mama that we will be especially good because Grandmother will be visiting as well as the uncles and aunties. Our hair combed neatly into place, hands and faces scrubbed till they glow, our unwilling bodies restrained and fastened securely into our Sunday clothes, we prepare to meet the onslaught at the door. We remember to ask each of them how they feel and to answer all their questions with polite responses, listening intently to their suggestions and advice, keeping any opinions that we might have locked carefully away in our private, secret thoughts.

They arrive precisely on time. It is considered rude and insufferable to be late. The traditional Austrian obsession for order and punctuality is obeyed. They enter in a flourish of rustling skirts, kissing each of us on both cheeks and talking incessantly with barely time to take a breath. Wafting through the melange of cooking aromas, there lingers the soft, fragrant scent of ladies' face powder, rouge, and cologne and men's aftershave and hair pomade. My proud, severe uncles and aunties demand their kisses and curtsies and above all, honour and respect.

The ritual is a revered tradition of civility and good manners to be carefully observed without fail. I watch in fascination as my relatives carry out the Viennese observance of four o'clock *jause*, akin to a high tea. Manicured jewelled fingers raise fragile porcelain cups to red lips. Chains of hammered gold swing from wrinkled necks. The aunts' greying hair is pulled back and up into neat twisted knots. Our uncles are attired in white starched shirts, suits with ties and vests buttoned over thickening waistlines. Pocket watches on chains are ready to be consulted when they have stayed long enough, and then there is a nod to their wives to indicate that visits are done. If we misbehave, they scowl disapprovingly at our mother. If we neglect to offer our polite greetings to each one formally, in turn, they will pout the whole time and forgiveness will not be forthcoming.

Sometimes they bring coveted Swiss milk chocolates, individually wrapped in coloured paper. We must be particularly obedient if we are to receive our share of these treats. We stand in military fashion, lined up for inspection, according to age. First is Erna, her long dark hair held back by a silken bow then falling in a thick mass on her back. Next is fifteen-year-old Stella, with freckles, light brown hair, and blue eyes like mine. Then me, the youngest of the girls, now aged ten, fidgeting from one foot to another, eager to receive my chocolate and escape. Tugging at my dress is Willi, a shy child, dressed in a white shirt and short pants, with wire-rimmed glasses, now five years old. Maids in white aprons, heeding Mama's commands, bustle in and out of our dining room where starched linens and monogrammed family silver are set. Mama holds her head high with pride and will not condone the pity of the relatives for her situation. She makes certain to impress them with her disciplined management of the servants and the efficient running of the household. Our manners are also a reflection on her abilities to cope with the onerous responsibilities that have been thrust upon her. She surveys her domain with the calm demeanour of a general reviewing the troops while, with apparent nonchalance, chatting in animated pleasure. Her smile reveals that she is pleased with the surroundings and the approving nods of the visitors. She hugs each of us in turn and whispers, "Papa would have been proud today. You have done well."

Mama glances casually around the room. Everything is as it should be, each item in its undisturbed place. She sighs softly in contentment, taking comfort from the place itself, the feeling of familiarity, the home where each of her children was born and where she can look forward to a tranquil old age. The walls are clothed in proper muted floral patterns, dusty-rose and celadon green. Throughout are hung the gilt-framed petit-point needlework that my sisters and I have laboured to produce. They depict appropriate pastoral scenes of the Austrian countryside in the eighteenth century. These are fabled figures, gentlemen in satin knickers with silk hose and buckled shoes, and ladies in voluminous gowns of taffeta and lace. As I stare at the framed hangings, I rub my fingers in recollection of the many needle pricks endured before my work was completed.

Respectable young ladies are required to become accomplished in such pursuits, as well as parlour-level conversational French and some form of musical skill. Our piano stands in a corner, keys yellowed and bruised from pounding by many young hands. My violin rests on top but I am an unruly child, unwilling to spend tedious hours practising.

Steaming tea is poured from an old burnished copper samovar, and orange flames dance in the fireplace. My grandmother, who is frail and thin, is warming herself, rubbing her cold, blue-veined hands together. Her wooden cane rests against the wall. As I watch her, I try to imagine ever being that old but it is an impossibility. She is hunched over, dressed in a long, high-necked black silk gown that falls in gentle folds, just grazing her black lace-up shoes. Her hearing is impaired and she is usually absorbed in her own thoughts, responding peculiarly to questions that are asked of her or ignoring them completely. The conversation continues with laughter and familiar stories being shared, but she is isolated and soon forgotten.

Hardwood floors gleam from hours of hand-waxing and buffing. They are covered with rugs, multi-patterned Orientals, dark garnet swirling through a background of ink-blue, with pale fringes at the borders. Windows are draped with weighty hangings of damask. Cut-crystal vases break the sunlight and toss it against the walls in a shimmering prism. The polished, lemon-oiled mahogany furniture is so heavy and solid that it appears rooted to the floor. There is a permanence and stability and certainty that things will remain unchanged forever.

Beside the rigid protocol, we must also be wary of the superstitions that guide and threaten us with every word or action. When the discussion turns to talk of anything bad, but most especially anything to do with the pogroms or sickness or death, we must never, never sneeze. This is an alarm to all evil spirits hovering in the vicinity to swoop down and bring a curse upon us. Fortunately there is an antidote to this as to many other such fears. If we are forgetful or unable to subdue our sneeze at the inopportune moment, one of the nimble adults rushes over and gives our ear a few hearty tugs. It is essential then to pay close attention to the conversations and to restrain our inappropriate sneezes even if we feel ready to explode. We learn the trick of pressing our tongues up tightly against the roof of our mouths to stifle an oncoming outburst.

Even our seating at the table is observed for infractions. Anyone within seven years of marrying age is not supposed to sit at the corner of the dining table for fear of dire consequences – that he or she may never marry, a dreaded fate. When any of us of the younger generation expresses our doubts of the possible connection of sitting at the edge of the table with our marriage prospects, we are advised that it is wiser not to tempt fate or to take any chances. One never knows what action taken in the universe could affect anything else. So calculations are quickly made and discussed; twenty plus seven would likely be considered too old to wait, or in some cases there might be a dispute – after all, fifteen and seven is twenty-two, maybe not too bad. And so it goes. As Stella is now in the questionable age category, she is very careful of where she finds her seat, but if she forgets and moves towards the corner there is a mad scramble and shouting by everyone present to redirect her in time to avoid disaster.

"Stella!" one of the aunties shouts. "Are you mad? Do you plan to be an old maid? Move away from the corner of the table or your fate will be sealed."

How, I wonder, will I ever learn all these rules? There seem to be new ones added to the list all the time. I'm not to leave keys on a table because it will start an argument. I have to walk out of the house with my right foot first or bad luck will befall me all that day. The superstitions are not questioned. We seem to walk a precarious line between safety and danger at every turn. That is just the way things are.

After a while, Mama signals to us to say our polite goodbyes and then we are allowed to go to our rooms or out to play. I am glad to be released from the formal restraints and rush to change my clothes and to hurry outside. The bristling tang of clean air renews my spirits as I inhale. Snow falls in feather flakes, huge, delicate and pure, and the air stings our faces until they are flushed pink. Our energy is boundless. Running breathlessly, arms outstretched, falling backwards into snow banks and letting the icy cold surround and enfold us, we laugh until we ache and hot tears of joy spill and freeze against our cheeks. Winter in Vienna is a child's paradise, houses and trees coated in soft white finery, dazzling in the sunlight. We love to skate and ski and race through our streets, dressed in thick, hand-knit sweaters in rainbow hues. Freedom is delicious and hungrily devoured. We expect always to have it in abundant supply and need not hoard it.

CHAPTER 5

GROWING UP 1931

At school we are told that primitive foreign lands exist beyond our own, where strange languages are spoken and people, with skin the colour of raisins, cocoa, or saffron, walk barefoot. We learn about climates where snow never falls. My daydreams pull me away to those steamy jungles where I am an adventurer, hacking through the thickly tangled tropical foliage. What ferocious beasts prowl in those forests? My imagination takes over and I don't hear anything more that the teacher is saying.

I wonder how such people could live and how odd and frightening they would look. In my meandering thoughts I encounter alien beings like the ones pictured in my school books and envision myself as an explorer prowling the surface of some uncharted planet. The exotic appearance of people wrapped in peculiar clothing and speaking an unknown tongue is a glorious fantasy, but in truth I don't expect ever to meet one of those strangers. Africa and Asia are blobs on the atlas, mysterious and dangerous, where elephants and tigers roam. Those places are dark and ominous, in a universe unknown and foreboding. In my real world, in Vienna, we feel secure and safe in a very predictable place where all the people are the same.

Hours spent in school are tedious and dull. My brain refuses to be confined to the musty classroom where the teacher's droning voice eases me into a stupor. My mind turns towards the mountains and freedom. The teachers have advised Mama that I am a poor student, unable to concentrate on my studies and lazy in my work habits.

"Karpel!" the teacher barks. "You are not listening again! Where is your mind this time?"

We are given lessons in English, a language whose strange sounds and words make no sense to me. The teacher's monotone voice drills the same words again and again, "I am ... you are ... he, she, or it is" – peculiar and unnecessary, I think, and what a waste of time when there are so many more exciting things to do. The clock on the wall ticks the minutes with maddening lethargy and the stuffy air in the room is making my head spin. When the bell clangs at last, I am first to rush from the prison and the teacher's icy stare.

Once I am freed again from the restrictions of school, the wind against my face restores me to life. In the school yard my friends are waiting to play and to tell of all their news. One day as we are walking home, chattering to one another, engrossed in our gossip and giggling till our sides are sore, we are startled by a loud, angry shout from behind, "Shut up, you filthy Jews!" One of our classmates calls out and begins a chant, *"Sau Juden, Sau Juden* [Jewish pigs]."

Without a moment's hesitation, I drop my books and hurl myself at the other girl, who is taller than I, but I disregard the difference in our sizes and dive at her in a rage of indignant fury. I grasp handfuls of her copper hair and rip at her clothing, knocking her to the ground. We tussle and twist, arms and legs poking at odd angles until I can force her beneath me, a knee on either side of her chest to pin her down. Her nails dig into my arm and tear a stinging gash under my elbow. As she squirms and screeches for help, I feel my fist come down hard on her fleshy nose, which begins to squirt sticky blood onto my hand and sleeve. She is crying grimy tears that dribble down her cheeks, all the while screaming for me to leave her alone. I get myself up and retrieve my schoolbooks, admonishing her to keep her stupid insults to herself unless she's looking for more trouble. Then I return to the others and continue on my way home.

My friends think I am a hero and slap me on the back in hearty congratulations for my courage. They agree that the anti-Semitic sentiment should be beaten out of her and any others who hold such thoughts. We will not permit the destructive sprouts of hatred to flourish in our cherished homeland. I expect Mama to be angry when she sees me coming in, my arm and knee scraped and bloodied, my school dress soiled, and my hair hanging in sweaty strings over my eyes. But her face is suddenly pale and grim when I start explaining what happened. She holds me tight and I feel her trembling. I tell her not to be frightened because I am strong and can take care of her.

The confidence of youth warms and protects me, brimming with promise for a future that holds infinite possibilities. My friends and I dream of adventures, plans for the lives we might have. Perhaps I will become a great and famous actress, my very secret ambition. I practise before my mirror, laughing and crying intermittently, sweeping my arms in grand gestures, then taking my deep and serious bows before the imagined cheering crowds. Even my sisters will have to applaud me then, and Mama will be proud.

On Saturdays we visit the Volksoper, where students purchase tickets at special prices for the matinees. I love the operettas and soon know every word of the songs by heart. The stories of love and coquetry are fascinating and beguiling, stirring my young imagination with thoughts of romance while the music fills me up, flowing through my veins, mixing and pounding through my blood.

Vienna glitters like jewels in a crown, and we take full advantage of its attractions. We meet at sidewalk cafés for Viennese coffee topped with billows of fresh sweet whipped cream and rich confections of pastries like Black Forest cake, the huge dark cherries suspended in layers of cream and chocolate. As we grow older, we attend fancy-dress balls and parties. Spinning endlessly, we waltz in elegant swirls to the melodies of Strauss throbbing around us. How proud we are to be Austrians, in the cultural centre of the world. We need nothing more and have no desire to travel beyond our borders. Where else, after all, would one find a palace to rival the opulent Baroque grandeur of Schönbrunn? Where would mountains, emerald-green in summer and icing-sugar white in winter, welcome as ours do? Where would food taste so good and everyone you meet be your friend?

In the springtime and throughout the fragrant summer, garden cafés are filled with explosions of newly blooming flowers and tender young leaves. People of all ages laugh boisterously, clinking tankards of beer or glasses of new-harvest wine. Music surrounds us. Young men in bright suspenders and lederhosen and Tyrolean hats with small thick brushes in the bands slap their thighs in merry time to the cowbells and fiddles. Women, their hair woven into shiny braids pinned in circles around their heads, are dressed in traditional dirndl skirts and white starched blouses with puffed sleeves tied with colourful ribbons. They spin round and round in a dizzying whirl. The dips and trills of mountain yodelling ripple in the air with their lilting melodies. The scents of cut lawns and fresh-baked pastries fill our nostrils and energize our spirits. The hillsides are dotted with bursts of wildflowers, so abundant that people pick bunches and tuck them into their hair or jacket lapels. There is camaraderie and goodwill towards all.

We stroll arm in arm along the shores of the Danube, its muddy water churning in lazy currents. From the bobbing boats that drift by, passengers are waving, smiling broadly and shouting greetings. Picnickers sprawl on the moist grassy banks, their delicacies laid out on crisp checkered cloths. A breeze blows gently, causing the leaves in the trees to flutter and boughs to creak. Children chase after rubber balls, and their laughter, like the chime of little silver bells, rings in the air.

Summer melts into autumn, a time of cool winds and falling leaves, sun-spangled colours floating in the air and rustling underfoot, earthy smells and change. But for me nothing compares to the Austrian winter months. I take my woollen sweaters out of their mothballs and lift my skis from their summer storage nook. All of us have skis and poles that are lined up in a neat row, each pair wrapped in an old bed sheet, then bound with twine. On the floor matching pairs of leather boots are set side by side, toes and heels aligned, neat and trim, not a thing out of place. We take very good care of our skis, and at the end of the always-too-short ski season we put them away grudgingly until the next year. My skis are my most cherished possession. I remember the day they were presented to me. The bright red painted wooden slats were for me alone, just my size and the best gift I ever received. Since Papa's death there had been a turn to a new kind of austerity and Mama had had to save the money for them bit by bit. For both Willi and me, as the youngest, financial restrictions have been the way of life that we've known for all of our childhood. We have been taught that nothing we have should be taken for granted. So when, the winter after I turn fifteen, I am given my very own pair of new wooden skis with poles and boots, all wrapped in smooth brown paper, I know that this is a special gift.

As the winter months unfold each year and the first snow falls, we greet the new season with eager anticipation. We know that the weekends will be a time for the exhilaration of the slopes. I have to work in the store for at least one day each weekend but I can go out to ski on the other. The first few crystalline flakes that swirl outside stir our excitement as we imagine the pleasure ahead. Staring up at the evening sky, Willi and I sit by the window, and full of boisterous energy we bicker about the possibility of a good ski day to follow.

"I think there will be lots of snow tonight," I tell him.

"No, you're wrong, Nini," he answers back. "There are just a few wet flurries and the ground is still dry and hard. Can't you see that this is not ski snow, just the kind that will melt by morning?"

"What do you know about it?" I answer indignantly.

"I know more than you," he says, shoving me. Of course I shove back and before long Mama is in the room trying to settle us down.

"There will be no ski outings for anyone if this keeps up." She gives us her sternest look until we become silent.

When a good week of packing snow has fallen and is just perfect, we test its texture by tossing snowballs at one another and at passing strangers, who shout in annoyance. Then we know that a day of skiing is ahead. We arrange for rendezvous with friends and wait impatiently for the day when we can head out to the mountains. There is typically a debate among my friends before we decide on our destination to Kahlenberg, Kobenzl, Der Rax, Hohe Tauren, or Schneeberg. We are so familiar with each of them that we can argue about their merits or shortcomings without hesitation. If ever there was an escape, a time when worries and responsibility might be left behind, it is on the rolling mountainsides near Vienna. On those days, when I feel the crunch of new snow beneath my skis and the clear air in my lungs, I am fully alive.

The night before one of our much anticipated outings, we go through the all-important preparation routine. Bursting with pent-up energy, we soon find ourselves squabbling over the necessities for the next day.

"I need the wax, Stella," I shout to my sister.

"Well, you can just wait your turn until I've finished," she says, taking the chunk of hardened paraffin wax from the shelf.

"You're always so selfish. I already have the iron heated and I'm going to take the first turn," I reply adamantly.

She plunks the wad of wax on the table and storms out in a huff. At twenty-one, Stella considers herself a young lady while Willi at eleven and I at sixteen are just lowly children. She will pout and act indignant and there will be arguments and disagreements, wearing Mama down and causing her to threaten to curtail our plans and put an end to it all, but she always relents and lets us go. Erna is twenty-four now and married, no longer a part of our frenzied day-to-day activities, but to our great pleasure her husband is a ski instructor and we have profited by it. He has taken us out for lessons and now we believe ourselves to be experts.

"I'm next," Willi calls from the other room and soon appears at the doorway. "I'm going, too, and my skis are just as dry as yours. My friends are serious racers, not silly girls. I have to treat my skis with more care to make them go faster."

"What a big man," I scoff. "But you can still wait till I'm done."

We tease one another relentlessly and argue about the smallest of things. Everything about the ski day is so vital to each of us. We take our turns setting one ski at a time on a table, rubbing the wax in a circular motion up and down the length of the wood, covering it with a piece of cloth and then pressing it with a hot iron backwards and forwards, warming the wax until it is softened and the wood becomes smooth. When we are certain that the finish is at its best and that it will offer a slippery glide on the snow, we head for our beds and a restless night.

We rise before dawn, dress quickly in the frozen darkness, and rush about, gathering our belongings. We prepare our lunches, stuffed with whatever goodies we can scavenge in the pantry and head off, lugging our cumbersome gear. We meet with friends at a designated spot, then crowd into a trolley car that will take us from the bustling city to one of the small rural villages only an hour away. We know each mountain well, which ones have the best runs, which have the best snack bars.

At the foot of each mountain there is a chalet with refreshments. If we've saved enough money for the day, we also have the treat of steaming cups of hot chocolate and a delicious cheese and sour cream strudel still warm from the oven. Then we begin the long trek on foot up to the top. Our boots are heavy with snow as we clump our way up the thickly blanketed incline. The muscles in our legs strain with each step but we jostle and joke and tumble along. The weight of the skis and poles plus the rucksacks full of sandwiches for lunch makes us perspire despite the winter's chill. My favourite sweater is a cherry red sleeveless one. My bare arms sting from the cold but I feel invincible and thrive in the frosty air. Halfway up on some of the bigger mountains, there's a rest area with tables and benches where we can stop for lunch. Finally, at the top, the stunning vista spreads beneath us. No matter how many times we see it, the view is always a dazzling surprise. We marvel at the sight of miniature rooftops capped in white and hunchbacked evergreen trees that stand bowed by their snow-laden branches.

All day long we ski the trails. My skis have become an extension of my body, extra appendages that obey my commands with ease, swerving side to side with the motion of my hips and the bend of my knees. The wind bites my cheeks and blows my hair. My breath floats in puffs of vapour and the hard-packed snow under my feet allows me to slip and hop with ease, gliding downwards without restriction, free, totally free.

CHAPTER 6

POLITICS 1934

For all of my memory we Austrians have lived in a Social Democratic state. Papa was a keen supporter of this party, and from my earliest understanding of the rules that govern us, I have also believed in its idealistic premise. It has been a source of enormous national pride and a cause that I have fiercely supported and defended. I have found a rallying cry, stirring the spirit of hope for all. This is the doctrine of egalitarianism, one people, none elevated too high above the rest, none too lowly. Each is allowed to live in his own way and is given the respect of his fellow Austrians, who now number seven and a half million, of which two million live here in Vienna. Of those, some two hundred thousand are Jewish. Our municipal programs and public works are impressive and are heralded throughout Europe as the epitome of civilized government.

Certainly there are detractors, foes of the ruling party who condemn the money spent on welfare projects. They want to cut pensions, public school grants, the health care that serves us all. I am enraged at these critics. My friends and I are unwavering supporters of the existing left-wing government. Freedom has come to us through this means and we defend it in marches and rallies. Mama is always worried when I participate in these outward expressions of my boisterous enthusiasm but my feelings are strong and won't be silenced.

In the newspapers we read mounting criticism of the welfare debt. Our country, they say, can no longer support those who are a burden to the coffers. When in 1929 foreign credit supporting this deficit was withdrawn, loud protests and angry debates broke out, both in the government itself and then out into the streets. In 1931 an attempt to create a Customs Union with Germany, our closest ally, was blocked by international intervention and failed. Austria was struggling to stay afloat in an atmosphere of political and financial peril.

In 1932 a Christian Socialist cabinet under Dr. Engelbert Dollfuss had attempted to bring order, but by 1933 a new faction has emerged in Germany and Austria, the National Socialists, an extreme fascist party with strong anti-Semitic overtones. Their numbers have increased to such an extent that they can no longer be ignored. Their leader is Adolf Hitler, an unlikely little man with a loud voice who thunderbolted from obscurity to notoriety by ranting in public places, gathering the disgruntled and outcast at first, and then engaging a wider following. Originally an Austrian, he espouses the unification of German-speaking countries.

We have read about him in the papers, without much concern at first but gradually becoming aware of his increasing importance. His book *Mein Kampf* is being distributed widely and turning many towards his incendiary ideas. In it he outlines in precise detail the road to German supremacy and world domination; he blames the ills of the world, as so many have done before him, on a Jewish conspiracy. Hitler's astounding rise to power in Germany presents an unparalleled threat to the stability of our government. In a desperate attempt to maintain his rapidly slipping grasp on the reins of power, Dollfuss dissolves Parliament and proclaims himself dictator.

One summer morning in July 1934, I read the front page of the newspaper with shock. "My God, Mama, Dollfuss has been killed!"

She too is stunned. I continue, "There will be riots in the streets. I'm sure my friends will be against this outrage."

Mama has turned pale. "Nini, I beg you to be careful. You just don't understand how dangerous this situation is."

"Don't worry, Mama," I answer, my heart pounding with anger and confidence. "I know what I'm doing."

Now that a Nazi coup has failed, and Dollfuss has been assassinated in the process, chaos and uncertainty have taken over. Everyone I encounter talks about the ongoing political turmoil. I still meet my friends in coffee houses and we march to express our opinions, but some are already siding with the frightening movement and I have noticed that many of my Jewish friends are not joining us any longer. They are afraid to be seen in the street or their parents have curtailed their activities.

Finally, though, we experience a lull in the increasingly volatile atmosphere when the Nazis are ousted and Kurt Schuschnigg, a supporter of Dollfuss, takes control. There is general relief and renewed optimism that we will return to a lawful society. With the help of the Italian government, Schuschnigg has restored order. At eighteen, I am a keen advocate of his policies. Once again, Jew and Gentile march arm in arm waving banners and scribbling slogans on buildings and sidewalks, declarations of freedom and righteousness. We shout in sweaty excitement, emboldened by our youthful spirit and determination to be heard.

We are modern young Austrians, with adventure flowing in our veins. Politics are thrilling and daring, and we fear nothing as we speak in agitated voices of our dedication to a strong Socialist regime. In the coffee houses where we gather, we brandish slim cigarettes in our fingers and laugh freely as we argue about politics. We are the future generation, prepared to take control when our turn arrives and to lead our country and the world to a better understanding of one another. We are not bound to the religious doctrine of our ancestors, holding us captive by the archaic rituals that we believe to be meaningless. We are determined that Christians and Jews will coexist in peace. To show my resolve, I wear a gold cross next to the Star of David dangling on my neck chain.

Flushed with enthusiasm I arrive at home full of excitement and find Mama absorbed in her needlepoint. She looks up at my ruddy face and the shiny medallions hanging around my neck.

"What ideas you have, Nini. So naïve, so young. I'm afraid that idealism like yours won't last long in this world," she says sadly. "Will the Jews not hate you for wearing the cross and the Christians despise you for being a Jew?"

"Mama, your old ways are gone. This is a new world."

Although Mama is distressed by my careless bravado, I won't change my mind. She tries to warn me that things are not as they seem. "Nini, you have always been obstinate and strong-willed, but this time you are too close to the centre of the fire. You believe that we are all equal and that your Jewish heritage will be disregarded, but I have seen much more than you have and I am worried. This is a dangerous time to be a Jew, even more so than usual. War is all around us, bringing the walls that protect us in closer and closer. I am afraid for you young people. You don't know what terrible things might happen in these times."

"Mama, your generation was born in fear, but we are free," I respond indignantly. "This isn't one of those uncivilized villages in Poland where primitive superstitions and ignorance confined you. You don't understand the new wave of political power that's about to emerge. This, after all, is our Vienna! Hitler's a buffoon. Once reason is established again, he'll be thrown into jail where he and his mad ideas can rot !"

Mama doesn't respond to my outburst. She has too many other worries to deal with. She soon puts aside her concern about a rebellious young woman.

Although I remain tenacious in my resolve, the events that are unfolding every day are beginning to prove Mama right. Our precious freedoms are being eroded bit by bit. Oppression is burgeoning within our city as the new government starts to impose restrictions. Seeds of a fascist regime are being planted, and we are witnessing its spread. Soon even my friends and I must admit that our resistance is insufficient to resist the inevitable direction of events. Even within our favourite cafés, support for the Nazis is more prevalent. Jews are selected at random and ridiculed or forced to leave after being brutally attacked. We are hardly equipped to fight the bullies who feel empowered by their growing numbers. The police seem to ignore the violations and refuse to intervene. Slowly and hardly perceivably, a malevolent undercurrent is gripping our city.

Elections and plebiscites are no longer allowed, and our voices are drowned. Our zeal has been quashed. The only activists still fervent are the omnipresent gangs of hoodlums, harassing citizens, shouting angry epithets of hatred in public places, appearing more and more often to disrupt and disturb. Splinter groups are vying for control of the Parliament. Our youth groups no longer rally in the streets shouting slogans openly. We begin to stay inside more often after dark as the politically motivated exchanges become increasingly aggressive and usually result in violence.

Political uncertainty is not unusual in Vienna. We are aware of the various conflicts and shifts in power, but for us as Jews there are only two outcomes to change in government: worse or much worse. The older generation finds it prudent to recede into silence and to hope for the tide to change again to a more tolerant atmosphere. It has always been the way of European Jews to accept the most dire of consequences with a shrug and philosophical resignation, hoping simply to outlast the anti-Semitic sentiment of ever-present fringe groups. Now, even my contemporaries are following the lead of the elders. We reason that this is a passing phase, difficult to be sure, but hardly cause for undue alarm.

Family gatherings have only one topic of conversation these days. The events that surround us and fill the papers with frightening propaganda have focused our thoughts in one direction. Mama and the relatives are talking heatedly about the current trend to more open slander against our people.

"You see," one of the aunties says, and the other relatives agree, nodding their heads over Sunday coffee, "hard times are always followed by better times. It is just a matter of patience and keeping a low profile, not causing a stir or drawing unnecessary attention to ourselves. Every Jew must be vigilant of his actions because the errors of any one of us are sure to bring the worst consequences to the rest. In Poland we had to mind ourselves in everything we did or a pogrom would surely erupt. We must keep silent, and things will return to normal. Vienna will remain strong, and our homes will endure in safety despite the crazy rantings of that madman in Germany."

"This time may be different," Mama says. She is leaning forward in her chair, eager to emphasize the need for a more careful approach within our community. "There is too much support for this fanatic and it is not just local. It is happening in Germany right now. Just look at the newspapers – you'll see that thousands rallied in the streets of Nuremberg to show their solidarity with the Nazis. And don't forget about that plebiscite – ninety percent approve Hitler's policies!" It is clear that Mama has trouble controlling her irritation with the sit-and-wait attitude of the uncles and aunties. The uncles and aunties aren't alone. Others in Vienna, too, still hope for things to improve and try to convince themselves that we will outlive the current upheaval and return to normalcy. But Mama sees a different, much more frightening future. She tries again to persuade them of the dangers on our horizon.

The uncles begin fidgeting, getting ready to break up the conversation that has grown too serious. They are offended by this outspoken young widow. Mama ignores the clearing of throats and scratching of heads. She means to be heard this time.

"We know that Poland is a fertile soil for hatred too. Even the United States! I read about a pro-Nazi rally in New York when thousands turned out to show their animosity towards us."

My aunts exchange sideways glances, apparently unmoved by Mama's concerns. One of them decides to put her in her place. "Johanna is always nervous. Listen, my dear, you have to have confidence that things will get better. Besides, you can't possibly imagine leaving Vienna, can you? Where would you go with all your family and no man to support you? Don't be ridiculous. Everything will be fine again. We only need patience."

I have gathered courage from Mama's words and decide that I am old enough to voice my own ideas. Besides I am annoyed with the way the relatives dismiss Mama and cause her face to flush in frustrated anger.

"We can hardly be patient now. We should do something," I say to everyone's obvious surprise. "They blame us for everything!" I add as the relatives whisper their amazement at my outburst.

"How senseless these accusations are!" I continue, raising my voice. "They talk about an international Jewish conspiracy to control wealth and government. If we had any power or influence at all, would we have been victims of persecution throughout history? Would we be hounded and driven from one country to another as penniless refugees, struggling over and over again for some recognition of our worth and acceptance of our existence? Would we be objects of ridicule, riddled with self-doubt for our beliefs, trying to melt into the background, shivering in fear? Unless 'Jewish conspiracy' means the endless struggle to be allowed to live as others live, then it is truly the most insane concept ever conceived!" I know my face is crimson for I can feel the blood rush to my cheeks.

If the relatives had no patience for Mama, they certainly have very little regard for anything I might add. "Nini, don't be a child," my auntie snaps. "This is not a time for reason. When anti-Semitism starts to spread as it is doing now, stay clear of the enemy and wait for a quiet time to return. Rational arguments are lost on those driven only by fear and hatred. There is no way of fighting this menace. We have heard about Hitler's doctrine of national pride for Germans and hatred for all others, first and foremost us Jews. Our leaders condemn his words but cast them aside as vicious nonsense. Once again we have been chosen as scapegoats for malcontents. Here is just one more of these, loudly vocal to be sure but likely to disappear in good time."

The relatives begin to rise from their chairs. They say their farewells and for now anyway the matter is closed. The long-ago respect for our elders, drilled into us over the years, prevents me from arguing further.

I am quiet but I sense a new kind of tension. My parents' generation dealt with hostility directed towards them in two ways, denial and silent acquiescence. My generation has tried for peaceful coexistence. I wonder whether any of these methods will succeed this time. I realize only that the machinery of hatred is churning with increasing and more overt momentum daily and that we Jews are in the path of destruction.

CHAPTER 7

POLDI 1936

The uneasy political atmosphere in Vienna is a cloud that settles upon us, then lifts once more. Whenever there is a burst of anti-Semitic sentiment in the papers or when a violent upset of government takes place, we sink back into our gloom, but whenever there is a time of quiet, we hope that things have returned to normal and we go about our day-to-day lives without concern. Maybe, we think, the worst is over.

In the end, what are we but Viennese? For me, there is no other way of life and this, I believe, will always be my homeland, so there is no choice but to live every day to the limit and to revel in all that a youthful spirit can attain.

Stella, like Erna, is now married. Walter is quite a lot older than she, but offers a kind of fatherly protection that she craves. His straight black hair is sleeked back and parted neatly on the side. He likes to play the piano when he comes to visit and then to tease me and Willi. We find him a comical sort but soon get used to his antics and accept him as one of the family. Mama sighs with relief as one by one her older daughters are settled away with husbands and new lives of their own. I tell her not to expect me to get married soon. There are so many things yet to do and to see and my life is too full and wonderful to pin myself down to marriage. Young men come to call on me and I have a whirlwind of activities to occupy myself. To be young and carefree in Vienna is a delicious daily delight, and my hunger for its bounty is never satiated. I help Mama in the store, but also choose fabrics for my own use and spend my extra time going to the dressmaker to be fitted for new clothes for all the parties and occasions that fill my head with frothy dreams.

Early in the mornings I walk to work at our store on Klosterneuburger Strasse, peering into shop windows along the way. On sunny days I stroll nonchalantly, waving to the friendly old man at the watch repair shop as he looks up over his spectacles from his work. His door is open to let the fresh breeze in as he sits bent over at his bench. The hat shop window is one of my favourites. I like to stop and take in the latest display, narrow brims with swooping feathers in the fall, bright flowers and trailing ribbons on wide brims in summer.

There is a bakery where the smell of fresh loaves or sugary cakes fills the air and then the barber shop, its white and red swirling pole spinning round and round. Men seated in the black swivelling chairs with foot rests, their faces covered in white shaving cream, make me smile. The butcher shop is always busy. Ladies stand in line to argue about the rising cost of meat and examine each cut with care before it can be weighed, then wrapped in brown paper and white twine. The butcher sees me walk by and shouts a greeting.

Streetcars clatter by and cars honk horns. There is an ice factory where huge blocks of ice are produced and delivered daily by horse-drawn carriages to restaurants and grocery stores and to those homes that have ice boxes. We don't have one and need to purchase fresh food every other day or so but it is hardly a problem with the abundance that is available. The milkman arrives at our door early each morning in his wagon with old horse that nods its head up and down as if to say hello.

I unlock the door to our store and go in. The display cases are covered in white sheets each night to keep out the dust and have to be uncovered in the morning. I turn on the lights and get myself situated behind the counter to welcome customers as they come in. Our store sells many types of dry goods. Rows of fabric are stacked on shelves, wrapped tightly around bolts; all types of clothing are displayed on mannequins and racks. One day, when I'm working there with Mama, a handsome young salesman comes to the counter with a sample case of gloves and stockings. He's wearing a fashionably fitted double-breasted suit, starched white shirt, and wide silk tie. He's bronze-tanned with black wavy hair, beaming with a contagious smile that lights his shining brown eyes. Before long he is telling us about his travels, for he has only recently arrived in Vienna. In fluent German he describes his journey from his native Poland, holding us spellbound with wonderful stories about the places he has been and the sights he has seen. From his suit pocket he takes a slim silver case and offers me one of his cigarettes. When his lighter ignites the narrow cigarette I'm holding delicately between my index and middle finger, I feel very sophisticated and mature, like Claudette Colbert in the movies.

Day after day he returns to talk, and I'm glad to see him when he comes through the door. His name is Leopold, but his nickname is Poldi, which suits him better. He and his older brother, Adolf, who is called Dolu, left Lemberg, a city in Poland, when they were about to be conscripted into the army. As Jews, his family had already experienced the anti-Semitic turbulence of the Cossacks destroying property and lives in vicious purges. I am fascinated to learn that he has experienced the unbelievable stories described by my relatives. His ambition had been to become an engineer but the universities refused entry to Jews. This year, 1936, has been especially cruel to the Jews of Poland and so Poldi's parents insisted that their sons flee to some safer haven, such as Vienna. I ask him about the circumstances that drove him and Dolu from their home.

"Things were growing more precarious each day. You must understand the nature of the Polish government and the general mood of the population. Pogroms have been common for years. The cardinal of the Polish Catholic Church spoke against us just this past February. He made it clear that conversion to Christianity would be acceptable for us, nothing less."

"And if you refused?"

"Refused?" Poldi looks at me with amazement. "You have no idea to what extent the violence of hatred can grow. Beatings and murder, of course, but the sheer brutality of it, the boiling madness cannot be explained. No, there was no way to refuse. We had to leave. "

He talks in animated detail, conjuring vivid word pictures, drawing me into his mind and sweeping me along on the journey he has travelled. Having never ventured beyond the Austrian boundaries, I'm enraptured and soon lost in his images and feel that I, too, have seen all the marvels he has experienced.

Poldi has told me that his parents hold faithfully to Orthodox Jewry, observing laws of *Kashruth*, cooking the traditional foods of the Eastern European Jews, foods that are foreign to us. I sympathize with his stories of persecution and dislocation, but I am adamant that this could never happen here. "In Vienna, Jews and Gentiles share life without conflict. We eat the same foods as other Austrians. It is our differences that brought suffering to our people before but now we are the same as the rest so it would be foolish to worry about persecution where there is no cause. The current waves of anti-Semitism in Vienna are only due to the temporary state of the government. Jews always suffer in unstable times, but we're sure it will pass as it has before and allow us to return to the normal life we've known." I pause, then add, "I will admit that my mother seems particularly concerned this time."

Poldi recounts his memories of home, his eyes revealing pangs of nostalgia. He describes his mother preparing the Sabbath dinner by making her own *challah* bread, kneading the dough and braiding it into shiny loaves to be baked brown in their wood-burning stove. She used to make her special gefilte fish, using a plump whole carp that was stuffed with a mixture of chopped whitefish and carp with her special ingredient, sweet almonds, ground finely and blended into the filling. Candles were lit and blessed in the ancient way, her head covered with a lace shawl, circling her hands three times around the glowing flames.

She closed her eyes and whispered the prayer for peace, but at night, when the house was still, she went to bed with a butcher knife tucked safely under her pillow in case the Cossacks attacked while they were asleep.

I tremble when he tells this story and my eyes fill with tears for the pain they all have endured. He must bring his parents to Vienna, I insist, where they will live in peace and freedom. He is already working on this plan and hopes to bring them soon although he is concerned for their well-being. They will be displaced, with no landed status, strangers to a foreign place and new language. I know that Papa used to help Jewish refugees from Poland settle in Vienna. Were he alive today, I know he would have urged me to do all that I could to help Poldi reunite with his family.

CHAPTER 8

PASSOVER STORY 1937

Over the past few months Poldi and I have spent nearly every day together, going on long walks by the Danube, sharing coffee and pastries at coffee houses and talking endlessly about our future lives despite the unrest that surrounds us. We go to the centre of Vienna to Stefansplatz, the main square of the city. We stare up at the soaring spires of the Gothic edifice of St. Stefan's Cathedral, where I point out the huge bells and explain that they are rung in loudly clanging peals to call worshippers to prayer on Sunday mornings. Strolling hand in hand, I take Poldi to my favourite spots and show him the wares that are sold in the stores – all manner of goods from handcrocheted shawls to music boxes with charming lilting tunes that play when the lids are opened.

High above the square the ornate gilded Anker Clock, perched atop the Anker Bank, marks each hour. At noon twelve figures representing key personalities in the history of Austria from Emperor Marcus Aurelius to Joseph Haydn move in an elegant procession across the face as the bells chime. I have made sure to take Poldi at lunchtime to watch his expression of delight at the sight of the moving statues above us.

We talk about our plans and concerns in the face of unsettled political conditions throughout Europe, but are full of excitement as we take in the wondrous sights of the city. I take personal pride in my descriptions of the famous landmarks and am glad to see Poldi's interest in the history and culture. He tells me that he is eagerly anticipating the arrival of his parents in Vienna and asks me to promise that I will give them this same tour.

When they do come and get settled into their new home, I am invited to spend one of the Passover *seders* with the Kosiners. Although I have met his family briefly before, this is the first time I have been included at a *seder*. It is especially significant to me because our family has lost touch with religious traditions. Mama and Papa were secular, modern and assimilated, considering themselves Austrians first, Jews second, a sentiment that is currently popular in Vienna and the way that I have felt myself. Few Jewish traditions were practised in our home. But now that we are being singled out and condemned more and more often, I wonder what it all means and am grateful to be included so I can understand the past as it relates to the present.

Poldi's family keeps a Kosher home and retains all the observances. When Papa died even minor attempts at preserving the rituals evaporated in our home, so this is my first real view of such religious practice. Poldi's mother is the essence of traditional Jewish motherhood, warm and kind, opening her heart to me as though I were her own. Her rough hands are callused from years of toil. Hardship and worry have driven grooves into her forehead, but her eyes remain tender and bright. Her hair is grey, pulled back from her face and pinned up simply. A few strands always manage to pull loose around her temples. She is wearing a gold double-sided locket watch, suspended on a long chain wound twice around her neck. Opening it with care, she checks the black numerals imprinted on the creamy face. This is one of the few treasures she has preserved from home, a reminder always of the days allowed to each of us, the time so fleeting.

She notices my observation of her absent-minded motion and explains, "My mother, may she rest in peace, gave me this watch on her death bed. When the Cossacks ransacked our home, I hid it, wrapped in newspapers, buried in the cold ashes of our stove. I have kept it safe from thieves and scoundrels for all this time and wear it close to my heart. I often rub its surface for comfort whenever I'm worried or agitated. It gives me a sense of reassurance somehow. I have my watch," she says smiling, "and Papa has his books."

Volumes and volumes of books fill the shelves all around their home. In Polish, Russian, German, Hebrew, and Yiddish, they are lined up row after row. Poldi shares his father's passion for study and reading and cherishes these papers, worn from constant thumbing, bound in tattered leather, but revered as if they were written on leaves of pure gold.

We sit around the table, set with white linen and old candlesticks of hammered silver that have been salvaged from their home in Poland. "Wandering Jews," I think, words that take on meaning only when you see the agony of people driven by bigotry and barbarism from their native place and tossed like pieces of broken driftwood on any shore that will take them.

"I wonder if you realize, Nini," Poldi's father says to me, "how remarkable it is for us to sit here together in this place without fear. Passover, 'Pesach,' coincides with Easter, you know."

"Yes, of course," I answer. "I was often invited to the homes of non-Jewish friends to share an Easter dinner with them and even to receive an Easter chocolate."

"In Poland, it was different," he replies sadly. "Easter was the time for the most vicious pogroms. Christ died at Easter, you see."

"So?" I reply without comprehension.

"So, what better time to punish the non-believers, the scapegoats, the Jews? For us and our neighbours, Passover *seders* were observed with one eye at the front door, not to welcome the spirit of Elijah, the prophet, as is the custom, but to watch for Cossacks ramming their way in. Daughters would run to hiding places to protect themselves from the most violent rape, anything of value was concealed from looting and still, every Easter there would be Jewish blood shed."

"You would not believe," Poldi says, "the vile lies we heard frequently in the schoolyard. Once a gang of thugs beat us blue, all the while screaming that Christian blood was used to make our matzoh."

Poldi's mother adds, obviously agitated remembering the times that her children had been harmed because of their faith, "The ignorant bastards never understood that our religion forbids us from consuming any blood. Even a tiny dot of red within an egg yolk is enough reason to discard it, and eggs were precious to us. There were many times that we had to do without rather than to taste blood on our tongues."

"Hatred, you see," says Dolu, Poldi's elder brother, "hatred is blind and dumb. There is no explanation for it."

"All right, children," their mother says. "Dinner will soon be ready and you still have to read the Passover story. For tonight, forget about the past. Be thankful that we are together and safe. We have a new life here in Vienna, a better life."

At the dining table, we follow the religious tradition of the ancient Israelites and recount the story of the Exodus from Egypt in times long past. I look again at Poldi, who is talking with his father and brother. Soon they are deeply involved in the tale, conjuring images shrouded in the past, recollected in this way, once a year so that it will not be forgotten. We read from the *Hagaddah*, the description of the ten plagues that God created to force the Egyptians to allow the Jews to escape from slavery. Matzoh is piled on a plate in the centre of the table, and as we break the crisp unleavened bread, burnt black at the edges, we recite Hebrew chants and blessings, led by Poldi's father. We are reminded of those who died so long ago and are told to consider the saga as though we, ourselves, had made that journey. We dip our green parsley leaves into salt water, in memory of tears that were shed.

It is written that an enemy will arise in every generation to try to destroy us, and in each of our hearts, we ask, "Why?" Page after page the Passover story unfolds, recounting the journey of the Jews who escaped bondage in haste, fleeing towards a new land. Many of the old people were to perish along the way, leaving the young to build a new stronger nation. That was the way prescribed by God.

Although this tale is repeated year after year by observant Jews, and I myself have heard it many times throughout my life, never before has it hit me with such foreboding and gloom. This story always seemed to me an exaggerated myth, but this time I can easily imagine the sad displaced mass of people trudging away from their homes, clutching bundles of cherished belongings. At the *seder*, it is customary to dip one's small fingertip into a glass of sweet, dark wine and to spill one drop for every plague onto a saucer set for that purpose next to the dinner plate. We recite the plagues in unison, one by one, a drop of wine spilled for each. The first three, the original tests to Pharaoh begging him to free the Israelites, are named together and three drops of wine stain the plates: "Blood, Fire and Pillars of Smoke." Then we recite the ten plagues, one after the next: "Blood, frogs, vermin, wild beasts, pestilence, boils, hail, locusts, darkness, and the slaying of the first born."

As the blood-red drops stain the white china, we fall into a hush and each of us stares silently at the little pools of liquid in a way we have not done in years past. As the Hebrew words are spoken, I can visualize each of the plagues vividly before me, the blazing pillars of fire scorching the sky, the terror of vermin rampant in the streets, the sudden darkness, the pestilence, and finally the skeletal fingers of the Angel of Death cloaked in a black shroud, floating over all the homes in search of the doomed first-born children. The miracle, we are reminded, is that only by the grace of God did the evil pass over the Jewish homes and spare those who were meant to perish.

The Egyptian Pharaoh, we read, was so obsessed with the very existence of these people that he sent his armies to follow them. Even after he had released them from bondage, ragged and poor as beggars, each living breath from their lungs caused such an inflamed madness in him that he commanded his forces to pursue and destroy them. The mighty chased the weak until they reached the edge of a threatening sea that stretched ahead to the horizon. Their only salvation lay on the other side of that watery expanse. A shiver of dread ripples down my spine. Again the hand of the Lord allowed them to escape as the sea parted before them, then closed once more to drown the soldiers.

Through the flames of destruction that threatened to swallow them, through disease that swelled around them, and the torment of their enemies, the ancient Jews, my people, my ancestors, penniless and destitute, were driven on by willpower and faith. They wandered with faltering hope for many desperate years in search of a place of belonging and stability. The ancient Israelites, so it is written, suffered for forty years in the desert, a hostile place that they could not call home until they reached Canaan, the promised land of freedom.

A story, I think, like a fairytale in a child's book, that's the story of Passover. Are there really miracles? As I begin to clear away the dishes into the kitchen at the end of the dinner, I am quiet and absorbed in my thoughts.

Poldi's mother can see my emotion and worry. Tears mist her eyes as she wipes her hands in her apron, then cups my face between them. I can smell cooking aromas on her body as she leans towards me and starts to speak. "We cannot know what the future holds for any of us, Nini. In my life there have been many changes and sorrow. A Jew's life has always been a bitter one. But I do know that Poldi has a good heart and loves you very much and that you will be good for one another and strong together. You are young and you have a future to build. Be brave and you will both survive, no matter what obstacles lie before you."

I try to shake off my sombre mood and to listen to her words of wisdom and encouragement. The political unrest in all of Europe is fermenting, my family's worries are not far from my thoughts and the fears that Mama expressed are all melded this evening with the warnings of the Passover story. Will our generation suffer as previous ones have done? I want to have a carefree life, the life here in Vienna that I hold dear. Tonight it is difficult for me to think of anything but the prediction of doom.

"Nini," Poldi's mother says, interrupting my flow of thoughts. "You are right to worry. Things have been bad for us before, and now Vienna looks like it is becoming another Lemberg with ruffians pushing us around and laws that restrict our freedom. But, my child, it does no good to wallow in fear. Live for the present, this single moment when things are fine, when loved ones are together and we can feel the touch of love. Tomorrow will come soon enough."

We hug one another with new love and understanding. These people are like family to me now as I have been taken to their hearts. Their strength supports me and renews my hope. The men are laughing, their faces flushed by the warmth of the wine, the good meal and tales of the "Old Country," told again and again, recounting the experiences of home, better times, before they became outcasts and refugees.

They are sitting in comfortable chairs, leaning as is the Passover tradition, to demonstrate the fact that we all are free, no longer the slaves of ancient times in bondage as in Egypt. Here we are at ease in the security and comfort of our own homes, with no taskmaster to control our words and actions. The three men reminisce about the days of a simpler life now gone, to be retrieved only in fragments of memory. "Remember, Papa?" Poldi begins. "Remember the time in *Cheder*, Hebrew school, when we played that trick?"

"Listen, Nini," his father calls out to me, "listen to this story. Bluma, come in here. Poldi has a story to tell." They recall the day long past in their home town, so far away, when Poldi was a child, and as he tells his tale, I am captivated again.

"Always getting himself into trouble, my little brother, isn't that true, Poldi?" Dolu says smiling broadly, adjusting his glasses on the bridge of his nose. Behind his smile is an air of condescension. "You see, Poldi was always full of mischief and daring, not a keen student like me."

"Let him go on with the story, Dolu. It is a good one." Their father gently interrupts his older son's speech and arrogant bluster. Dolu's face is flushed and he falls silent.

"It was in Jewish school," Poldi begins, "a stuffy hot day in Lemberg, Poland, and we boys were trapped for endless sweat-soaked hours, studying thick books of Hebrew script, filling thousands of musty yellowed pages. The rabbi-teacher had fallen asleep, slumped over his worm-eaten desk. Then looking slyly at one another, an idea came to us for some wonderful fun, made more delicious by possible consequences."

We watch his eyes twinkle with the delight of reminiscence. "Go, on," I say, "what happened then?"

"So we arose from our seats, whispering and trying to control our laughter. One by one we crept, trying not to step too heavily on the creaking floor boards, ever closer to the old man's chair where he snored. His grey straggled beard spread across his folded arms and spilled over on to the surface of the desk. We each were made to touch the strands in fearful delight to show solidarity. Then with a pot of glue and a thick brush the beard was affixed to the surface."

Rollicking with teary laughter, we all hold our sides with glee. Even Dolu reluctantly explodes in laughter as he listens to the description. Everyone is mesmerized by Poldi's stories. He is a gifted raconteur, able to draw his listeners into his mind's eye so that we feel the moment as he felt it.

"What a story!" his father exclaims. "Tell what happened next."

Poldi takes a sip of wine, then speaks again, the mounting tone of his voice underlining and building the tension of the description.

"How he raged when we woke him, bellowing our names, cursing our lives, pulling his sticky hair painfully from the desk and then in storming fury chasing us around the room, his face red as a ripe tomato, waving his cane in frantic circles over his head. Each one that was caught suffered the blow of his hard cane on his back or the pull of his bony fingers on his ears, but how we laughed and it was all worth the agony for the fleeting sweet seconds of joy."

When the tale is told, Poldi's father taps him good-naturedly on the back and we all laugh again till tears moisten our eyes. Just for those moments, life is innocent and pure. Happiness is suspended in mid-air like a hummingbird and time stops. The talking continues until the candles' glow has disappeared and the wax has melted away to a trail of pungent smoke that swirls up from each candlestick in a puffy grey spiral.

CHAPTER 9

LETTERS FROM ITALY 1938

Conditions in Vienna are worsening daily. Poldi has told me that he and his brother are planning to leave in search of a safe haven. They will travel to Milan, where they have family and where they can escape from the fear that many Jews are facing daily. With the aid of their Italian relatives, Poldi and Dolu hope to find work. Here they have no opportunities. Even those employed worry from day to day that their livelihoods will be jeopardized.

Our farewell is a sad one. My attachment to Poldi has become increasingly strong and I share the pain of his departure with his parents, who are staying behind here in Vienna. They hug their sons in an emotional leave-taking, and we are all in tears as the two young men board the steps into the train and wave goodbye. Poldi and Dolu, throwing kisses, are both craning their necks as they peer out at us through the train windows. I return my own to them as the train starts to move away. I look forward to receiving the letters Poldi has promised to write but know that my days without him will be lonely. We remain at the station platform, Mama and I with the Kosiners, and watch the lumbering motion of the linked cars as they grow smaller in the distance and finally disappear.

Arm in arm, we leave the station, all trying to comfort one another, especially their mother, who is obviously heartbroken. She fears she will never see her children again. Our attempts to convince her otherwise diminish as we pass uniformed Nazi soldiers who scowl and mock us even in our private sorrow.

53

Within several weeks letters start arriving from Italy. I store each of them in a cardboard box, but they are becoming frayed at the edges from the many times I've removed them. Some are so stained with my tears that the writing is smudged into blotches and word fragments. I love to touch his words with my fingers and trace the deep sweeps of his script, then close my eyes and think of our hands together once more. I begin reading his words, picturing his face.

"Dear Nini,

"One day, you must visit Italy. Every city has a personality of its own. Florence is the heart of art and culture, the very spot where the Renaissance began. Everywhere you walk there are paintings and sculptures attesting to the human thirst for beauty and the creative genius of which humans are capable. Rome is a wonder to behold. I love it best at dawn, before the streets fill with crowds. When the sun rises, a ruby red wash descends over the bleached pillars and the tiered steps of the Coliseum. Just then, you can truly imagine ancient Roman chariots racing, as they once did in that exact spot, their wheels clattering against the bumpy cobbled streets, fine Arabian horses galloping ahead as cracking whips cut the air.

"You would be amazed to see the grand marble sculptures, looking down from their pedestals, standing everywhere on the streets, huge Roman gods, chiselled and frozen forever in their smooth perfection. Italian food is like nothing that you know. It captures the spice of life, juicy ripe tomatoes and fresh handmade pasta, fragrant with garlic and herbs, pungent cheeses with crusty bread and always bottles and bottles of dark red wine. The risottos are creamy and smooth concoctions of rice and other ingredients blended together.

"Italians speak with their hands, as well as their mouths, waving and articulating, slashing the air with emphasis to fully express the feelings that are too great to be explained by words alone. Fingers are cupped and motioned up and down to underline and reinforce every thought. Everything seems amplified and magnified beyond what the rest of Europe knows. I feel such affinity for the people and to the country and am studying the language with a passion. You would laugh if you saw all the books I have and the way I repeat the phrases and intonations each night alone in my room.

"I am now in Milan, which is the epitome of Continental style and glamour. My family here is in the fur trade and this is where I am working. My uncle is instructing me in the fine points of the business, the many variations in the pelts, how to differentiate one animal's skins from another even when they have been dyed to resemble something of higher value. There is much money to be made in this as Italian ladies of substantial wealth and position spend wild fortunes on the garments made for them. In fact, Milan is a fashion centre for furs known throughout Europe for the finest styling and quality.

"I have found this to be a fascinating field which my uncle has encouraged me to pursue. He says that I have a good eye for detail and that he can teach me to become an expert easily. Mostly I am hoping for some security here, which has not been mine for any part of my life but I am afraid that the political atmosphere is precarious and uncertain. Unfortunately we Jews must live by our wits, trying always to be one step ahead of our enemies and never to sleep very soundly.

"I have met a fellow here named Leon Druck. He is a good-hearted and jolly young man who is going through an apprenticeship just as I am in the fur trade. You would like him, I know. We spend lots of time together taking in the sights of Milan and talking about our futures, hoping that as Jews there will be something better ahead.

"I know that you have visited my parents in Vienna, for which I am grateful. They are so lost in that city, having never really adapted to the culture and are always considered as outsiders. Now, with the political unrest and hostility of the Nazis spreading like a plague throughout Europe, I fear more than ever for their lives. Send them love from Dolu and me and tell them that they are in our thoughts.

"Please write to me as I miss you and our talks together.

"Yours faithfully,

"Poldi."

Reading his words, I feel a mixture of joy and sadness. I can imagine his dark eyes gleaming as he describes the rich splendour of Italy's many virtues, a country where he would feel at home. At the same time I know that the fingers of oppression are long and I fear for his safety.

I have tried to keep in contact with his parents as much as possible as they are struggling terribly. Mama goes with me to take them food and to help them endure the difficulties they have encountered, first as displaced persons, and now as parents worrying about their absent and beloved sons. I read Poldi's letters to them and see the tears fill their eyes. His father holds a white handkerchief to his eyes and turns away from us, not wanting us to see his pain. I hand the pages to his mother and feel her sadness as she holds the sheets of paper in her hand, running her fingers tenderly over the words as if trying to connect with her son's touch. We know she is thinking that they might never see each other again. Tears glistening in her eyes, she turns to me and says, "In my heart, Nini, I believe that you and my son are *beshert*. Do you know that word?"

"No, what does it mean?"

"It means that you are destined to be together and that somehow in this mad world, no matter how wretched and terrible it may seem, no matter how great the distances that separate you, you will find one another and unite for a lifetime."

I stare at her, absorbing the words and wondering if they are true.

"But," she continues, "I'm afraid that Papa and I will not live to see your union."

"Don't say such a thing!" I cry in fright. "You will be with us. We need you!"

She shakes her head in sad denial and says, "I have feelings, intuitions that have proven to be right before. I don't know what will happen exactly but if I am right, please be good to each other and hold tight to your love.

There may be a time when you have nothing else. And if his papa and I never see Poldi again, tell him how much we love him and Dolu too."

We embrace, crying again. The next letter I receive from Milan carries a much more sinister message, one that I cannot share with Mama or with Poldi's parents. It fills me with such fear that I decide to keep it to myself.

"Dear Nini,

"Mussolini's Fascists in their black shirts are already marching through the streets with heavy steps, waving red flags, determined to rule the world. This is a time of military might and spreading violence. The often repeated chant here is *'Credere, Ubbidire, Combatere!'* meaning 'Believe, Obey, Fight.' For Jews there are no safe places for very long. Our bags must always be packed by the door, ready to set out again. At first, we were tolerated in Italy but Mussolini is wavering and will join the forces that are likely to be victorious in this war. He wants power at any cost and will gladly unite with whoever is strong enough to guarantee his ambition. His ties to Hitler are strengthening and it seems that he will pull Italy in that direction. Hitler's obsessive hatred of the Jews is an essential part of the plan. The goal is clear enough, world domination and, at the same time, the complete annihilation of our people. Only this will satisfy him and any nation that finds itself allied to Germany will have to agree to the same terms.

"My safety in Italy was always fragile but it has become necessary for me to conceal my true identity from the authorities. They are starting to harass Jews and to take many away without explanation. I have had to join the Fascist Party to preserve myself and to survive. By blending into the general population, as a native Italian, one of the patriotic masses, I can hide in the crowds, while out in the open. I suppose that with my dark features and tanned skin, it is not so difficult to be taken for a native, especially now that my fluency with the language is sufficient for me to pass as one of them.

"As long as I am accepted as a loyal supporter of 'Il Duce' I will be all right, but this is only a temporary solution. I know that it is essential to find a way out before I am discovered as a Polish Jew and made to suffer for it.

"Of course, conversion to Christianity has always been an option and I know a number of Jews, even some of my relatives who have remained in Italy, having chosen to accept the Roman Catholic religion. But for me that can never be a possibility. The Jewish spirit of my upbringing has dug deeply into my flesh, permeated my bones to the marrow and allowed me no alternative. I believe that the more that we are downtrodden and pushed into unwilling submission by others, the stronger our resolve must be to exist no matter the consequences – and I am fully aware how grave they might be. It is a simple truth that our faith arouses suspicion and hatred. This has always been the way and it may be so forever.

"I won't tell you that I am not afraid but fear cannot be allowed to rule us. We have to use our wits to overcome the evil and to prevail. I do miss you, Nini. When there is a quiet moment, I remember your ice-blue eyes and smile and think of the time when we will be together again. I cherish the letters that I have from you and reread them many times. Give my love to your family and of course to Mama and Papa who are always in my thoughts. Tell them that Dolu and I are safe and that we think of them all the time. If only I could find some way to get them to safety.

"As always, yours faithfully,

"Poldi."

I agree with his words and admire his bravery, but I wonder whether I would have the courage to cling to my faith in the face of such adversity. I think of the tribulations he and his family have already faced, amazing tales that started in the small towns of Poland where Jews could not live in peace, then into Italy, where civilization has flourished only to be dominated by savagery. When they talked of these experiences, I was always shocked and frightened that places so close to Vienna were withholding liberty and that violence was an accepted part of life there.

Yet even here our ability to live our normal lives is becoming more and more tenuous. Although waves of anti-Semitic sentiment have been expressed more and more freely recently, I still want to believe that democracy will triumph. In Vienna, there are Jewish doctors, composers, scientists, and lawyers – the foundation of a settled community – but the laws have begun to change here too. Jobs and schooling have been restricted and more and more opportunities for us are being blocked. Willi can no longer attend school and Walter has lost the property that he had inherited from his late parents, as it was confiscated by the Nazis. Fritz tries to work at odd jobs when he can beg them but there is hardly enough money to buy the necessary groceries.

I have written a reply to Poldi's last letter which I hope will arrive safely in his hands. I try to word it carefully to send my feelings to him and to offer some encouragement to remind him that our situation is grave and that we are waiting for some help from outside. The news from Italy suggests that their situation is not as terrible as ours, but how can we compare the degrees of treachery?

"My dear Poldi,

"It has been so long since we have been together but circumstances these days are not what they were, even worse than when you left. I miss you so much and whenever I receive word from you I feel that I can breathe more easily again, at least for a while.

"My mother and your parents are well and send love. We see them nearly every day and try to help them whenever possible. All of the family is struggling but we are still together and alive. What more can we say these days? I'm afraid that Vienna is growing more dangerous by the minute and we must try to find some way out. Of course in the end it will be a matter of money and finding some place that will take us in.

"My heart longs to be with you again. Don't forget me.

"All my love, Yours,

"Nini"

CHAPTER 10

ANSCHLUSS 1938

Nearly a year has passed since my first Passover dinner with the
Kosiner family. It will soon be time for another Easter and
Passover season but this spring holds more dread than promise and we are not making plans for a *seder*. My family and Poldi's have
come together often for meals and discussions and Mama has told me
how much she likes them, but there is more to think about these days
than pleasant conversation and holidays.

The political situation has worsened, and everyone in Vienna is talking about the unrest and threat of war. The Rome-Berlin Axis has been
announced and newspapers show photos of Hitler and Mussolini smiling broadly, strolling at ease, surrounded by their bodyguards and soldiers. This means that Italy has withdrawn its support of Chancellor
Kurt von Schuschnigg in his stand against Germany, and now Austria
remains vulnerable and alone. More than all the political propaganda
and rhetoric, treaties, and negotiations, it is Hitler's obsession with the
Jews that haunts us. The daily routine of life has become distorted by
the political turmoil churning almost palpably in the air.

On March 11, 1938, Germany announces the Anschluss, the annexa-
tion of Austria. We sit spellbound by our radio as Schuschnigg's tremu-
lous voice announces our capitulation. "God save Austria," he says with
the desperation of defeat. When we hear his words we know that all is
lost. Schuschnigg is immediately overthrown and Hitler's forces march
triumphantly into Vienna. There are enormous banners bearing the

Fuhrer's face everywhere we go. The majority of Austrian citizens greet the news with jubilation and take their patriotic ardour into the streets, wasting no time in slandering their Jewish neighbours and engaging in wild rioting, vicious name-calling, and the brutal destruction of property. With horrible consequences to the Jewish population, the anti-Semitic fervour in Austria has been magnified even beyond the hatred that has spread its menacing terror in Germany. Every pretence of tolerance and egalitarian respect is disappearing without explanation.

When exactly did the nightmare begin? When did this insanity first seep into our settled and secure world? When did my lifetime friends become enemies and the good-natured red-faced butcher and cheerful delivery boy change into SS monsters?

Like a tower of playing cards that is falling apart, our world is collapsing. Day after day we experience more devastating losses of freedom, and our lives are at increased risk. In the first week after the Anschluss, Jews are dismissed from their posts in theatres, community centres, and public libraries. On March 15 it is announced that all Jewish state officials have been fired from their positions, and two days later Jewish judges are removed. On the twenty-second, lawyers in all Austrian courts are required to wear swastikas. Any cases involving Jewish defendants are no longer brought to trial and all are immediately convicted simply because they are Jews. On March 26, Jews are fired from universities and colleges, then schools, markets, and slaughterhouses. Kosher ritual slaughter of meat is forbidden. On March 31, Jewish lawyers are prohibited from practising their profession. The swift, sudden, and irrevocable impact of these laws comes as a devastating blow. Freedom is being withdrawn on every front. The weak and elderly are forced to scrub the pavements with toothbrushes, bent down, made to erase Schuschnigg slogans. Jews are dragged through the streets, made to perform inane gymnastic tricks; heads are shaved; and wherever we go, we are jeered and scoffed at by the gathering crowds. We shake our heads in disbelief. How has this happened?

March folds into April and all the Viennese springtimes I have loved have become a distant watercolour, the pastel patches of sunlight and shadow replaced now by dark shades, heavy strokes of hatred and bloodshed. We move like sleepwalkers going about our daily chores, keeping the store open despite the smears on our windows and the threats from passers-by. I cherish the letters I receive periodically from Poldi and re-read the tattered ones that I take often from their little box. When I write to him, I have nothing but distress to share. Comfort is not easy to find. We are only Jews now, nothing more; our identities as Austrians have evaporated.

Daily disturbances surround us – a neighbour attacked, a friend's husband taken away for interrogation and never returned to his home, properties looted without police intervention or means of retribution. The dangers move closer and closer like a menacing fog.

Each new day seems to bring some more bizarre catastrophe. On the morning of April 23 we are awakened once more by the sounds that are beginning to become routine, the sound of screaming citizens being forced down the street in some new horrific plan of degradation and destruction. We peer cautiously out our window and watch the agony below. People are being dragged along by soldiers, rounded up this Saturday, the holy day for Jews, and taken to the Prater Amusement Park. We dare not follow the mob so we wait inside to learn of the fate that befell them.

Fritz has come to see us, to bring us a bit of food. It is too dangerous to leave our flat for any purpose and we are struggling to make do with our last supplies.

"What happened this morning, Fritz?" I ask, taking the bread and cheese from him. "There was some commotion in the streets again and we saw the Nazis storming about. "

"I was passing by the Prater earlier today and noticed a crowd gathered, " he answers, his head down, a look of disgust on his face. "There were Jewish people, rounded up and forced to cower on hands and knees like dogs or cattle." He pauses.

"And then what happened?"

"Then? Well, then they were made to eat the grass. Those helpless souls, old men, young girls, women, all of them, forced to chew and swallow it, only to be beaten if they refused. A crowd was cheering the Nazis, slandering the victims. There was no pity even as they began to vomit up the foul green stuff that had been forced down their throats. There were a few who collapsed of heart attacks and even several who, I was told, later died from the ordeal."

Chaos surrounds us. In the streets motor vehicles are tooting horns, making a mad attempt at escape. Those with means and some foresight have arranged for a way out. The traffic is a hectic tangle as people try to leave the city. We know of some who have received exit visas and are able to flee; even a few of our relatives are leaving, abandoning all possessions as they race out of Austria to other destinations – to South America or anywhere that will offer sanctuary. But we are stranded. We and our widowed mother have no plan in place, no connections abroad to welcome us.

Our only option is to keep on with our lives, trying to survive day to day, continuing to earn whatever bit of money we can just to provide food. Each night we lie in bed thanking God that we have lived through another twenty-four hours. Even though we are one step ahead of starvation, I try to put some food aside for Poldi's parents, and he and his brother manage to send them a little money from Milan.

April rain has soaked the streets and the sun is beginning to slip out of the clouds. I am dusting shelves in the store when Erna bursts in, her long dark hair matted with sweat. Her arm is bruised and her sleeve is torn. The usual blush on her cheeks has vanished and her eyes are wild with fear. She storms through the door and rushes towards me and Mama behind the counter, where we stand in petrified disbelief. She is shivering, and when she touches my hand I feel that she is as cold as ice.

"My God, Erna, what has happened to you?" Mama asks, as she hurries towards her eldest child.

In a trembling voice, Erna tells us what happened as she was on her way to work. "Oh Mama, the Nazi soldiers forced me to scrub the sidewalks, and one of them struck me when I couldn't understand what they wanted of me. I couldn't believe that they expected me to get down on the street, down at their boots, down on the ground, down, down, down, where dogs howled in my face." Tears smear her pale cheeks; in her distraught state, she wipes the palms of her hands on her skirt, over and over, oblivious to what she's doing. Her crazed appearance terrifies us.

We enfold her in our arms and try to comfort her but she can't stop shaking as she relives the agony.

In the streets of Vienna these displays of humiliation and treachery continue. Many families have begun to depart for unknown lands. Everywhere we go people talk about leaving, trying to decide whether it might still be possible to stay and hope for peace.

When we make our usual visit to the cemetery to visit the graves of Papa and Grandmother, who has died in the past year, we are horrified to find the whole area has been vandalized and much of it destroyed. Flower beds have been trampled, headstones overturned. The loathed markings of the swastika emblem are smeared over everything.

I pick up the dislodged headstones for Papa and for Grandmother and try to set the flowers upright again but it is not safe to linger long in the Jewish cemetery. We are apprehensive of the Nazis, who seem to be squirming up from the very ground everywhere like maggots, increasing in number daily, spreading their contaminating hatred. We touch the markers gently and with heavy-hearted sadness leave our small stones behind.

Nazi troops are stomping through the streets of Vienna. These are the "Brownshirts," in their flapping trench-coats, with blood-red armbands bearing the brazen swastika emblems that strike deadly fear into our limbs. Day by day, fragments of our lives are wrenched away. Suddenly we are not welcome in the homes of our closest non-Jewish friends. Stunned, I look at myself in the mirror: I have not changed. I look at them: they have not changed. Yet everything is different, and I have suddenly been abandoned by those I counted as friends.

Whispers in the beginning, then loud name-calling follow us home in the streets. The authorities condone and encourage the persecution. Jewish children are not allowed to attend classes, and Jewish teachers are dismissed. We are forbidden to go to the theatres, to restaurants, and to the shops. Workers in offices and factories are fired. In the newspapers there are evil caricatures of the ugly Jew, ridiculed and despised, reduced to the level of rodents or insects.

By Nazi decree all Jewish citizens are made to present themselves at the nearest government office where they must provide complete details regarding all possessions. Mama, sombre-faced like the rest, stands in line with hundreds of others for hours in the damp cold. Under supervision of the armed SS soldiers, she dutifully signs her name and date of birth to the papers outlining everything that may be of interest to the occupying troops and Nazi government. All bank accounts, domestic and foreign, all property holdings and furnishings, jewellery, artwork, gold, all are to be carefully entered into the record books.

When she returns home, weary lines of defeat are etched into her face. She doesn't want to talk to us. No words can express the sorrow and helplessness that encumbers her like a constant leaden weight. The strength of her spirit and resolve have been trodden to dust by the Nazis' heavy boots.

One late April morning, Mama is sipping her coffee and reading the newspaper. Across the table, I watch as she sets the cup down with a trembling hand. In the newspaper there is a piece from the Nazi propaganda paper, the *Volkischer Beobachter* (People's Spectator). She reads it aloud, her voice quivering with emotion, pausing now and then to catch her breath so she can continue.

"By the year 1942 the Jewish element in Vienna will have to have been wiped out and made to disappear. No shop, no business will be permitted by that time to be under Jewish management, no Jew may find anywhere any opportunity to earn a living and with the exception of those streets where the old Jews and Jewesses are using up their money, the export of which is prohibited, while they wait for death, nothing of it may show itself in the city. No one who knows Viennese opinion regarding the Jewish question will be surprised that the four years in which the economic death sentence on the Jews is to be executed seems much too long a time to them. They are puzzled by all the fuss, by the pedantic attention to the maintenance and protection of Jewish property; after all it is very simple: 'The Jew must go – and his cash must remain.' "

Mama rises abruptly from her seat, leaving us sitting, open-mouthed, at the table. Her fear and the words she has read send ripples of dread through us.

"I am going to the bank – now!" she declares, pulling on her coat and hat. By the time we move from the table, she is already outside. We run to the window to see her dash around the corner, her coat flapping in the wind, and soon out of sight.

Willi and I wait in worried anticipation for what seems hours. When we hear her opening the front door, we rush to greet her. She had left in such a state and hurry that we knew something dreadful was about to happen, and because she was racing for the bank, we feared our money was somehow in jeopardy. She staggers unsteadily into the room and slumps into the nearest chair, without removing her coat. She holds her head in her hands and begins to cry, her body heaving and shaking, unable to speak. We run to bring her a drink of water. Terrified, we plead with her to stop and to tell us what has happened but she can hardly breathe.

When exhaustion overcomes her at last, she is silent. Looking up at our horrified faces she reveals, her voice weak, cracking from the rivers of tears she has shed, that all Jewish bank accounts have been frozen, confiscated by the Nazis. We have nothing.

If the earth had opened before me and swallowed all of Vienna into itself, I could better have understood what was happening. How could everything Papa had worked for so diligently be taken from us so easily?

"But Mama, what has happened to all the money that Papa had and all the money from the business?" I ask perplexed.

"Oh, Nini, what can I say? There is no one to ask and no one to fight," Mama answers in weary resignation.

"But the money?" Willi repeats, as confused as I.

"All the money we had is now in the hands of the Germans – their laws govern us. They have stolen it just like common thieves and will not give it back. We are Jews and we have no rights, not to claim our own possessions, not to work, not to live in peace."

She stares blankly into space, unable to cry any more. We look at one another, our faces ashen. For the first time we realize that Mama is emotionally destroyed and cannot save us and that we will have to find a way out ourselves.

Of course, we are not alone. Nearly every day for weeks, Mama has received word of relatives who have been stripped of all their belongings and taken away. We no longer have contact with any of the aunties, but we know the Nazis have confiscated their businesses and homes. Jewish neighbours and friends, people we have known all our lives, are disappearing, taken by soldiers from their homes to be interrogated, then never to be seen again. Gentile neighbours shun us as though we were diseased. Shop windows are smeared with yellow stars and the word *"Juden"*, or they are smashed and looted. Businesses are confiscated, means of survival are removed, and the government and police have become the enemy. Law and order is replaced by corruption and indiscriminate bloodshed. Convicted murderers are being released en masse from the prisons, given Nazi uniforms and the most brutal and cruel are given senior status. Terror runs amok.

At night, I lie awake, trying to think of an answer to the dilemma. Mama and Papa taught us never to give up but they could not have foreseen this apocalyptic crisis. We seem to be trapped and our time is growing short. It is clear that things will not suddenly return to normal. I struggle with my thoughts until dawn's light begins to flood into my room and still I have found no plan for rescue. But I am determined to try, to speak to everyone we know who might help, to beg Poldi in my letters to work on our behalf. I clench my fists and shake away the tears in my eyes. I am not ready to give in.

My brother, Willi, is sixteen when he is arrested on the street by Nazi soldiers in broad daylight. One of his friends has come running into our apartment with the news that Willi, like so many other young Jewish men, has been taken away by the SS.

"We were just going to meet for a coffee and then, in front of us we saw them approach and before we knew it he was taken, one of them grabbing him by each arm," he tells us.

"Where?" I ask in frantic disbelief. "Where is he?"

"They took him in a car and I think they went to Nazi headquarters but I don't know. We couldn't follow him, you understand. It would have done no good, they would only have taken us too."

I spend no time talking to him. There is no use accusing him of cowardice. In the end he is probably right, but Willi is my only brother. I will not let him down even though my own life is at risk.

If I don't rescue him, he will be sent away to be imprisoned somewhere or killed. In outrage and horror, I rush up the steps into Nazi headquarters to find him. The headquarters are in the old Metropole Hotel, which was previously owned by a Jew but was confiscated from him "for the good of the Reich." Now the Nazi flag flies from his building.

"Karpel." I give our name to a Gestapo officer seated at a desk. "My brother, Willi, has been brought here."

"Yes, you are his sister – we will want to question you too." My arms are numb, my mouth goes dry, and my palms are damp and cold as I follow him. I wonder if my knees will buckle beneath me. I remember that Mama will soon be home from the store and will be worried. I didn't leave a note for her but then, what could I have said?

He leads me to another room and opens the heavy door. Inside, the lighting is dim but I can see Willi seated on the edge of a wooden chair, the harsh overhead light reflecting off his glasses. Perspiration has moistened his forehead but when I reach for his hand, it is as cold as mine.

For hours, we are interrogated by members of the SS, hard men with scars etched into their faces, who stare at us with empty eyes, unable to see the human beings before them. In barking commands and unanswerable questions, they accuse us of undermining the government of Austria, of political subterfuge, of the crime of our own birth and mere existence, of Jewish conspiracy, and of any other madness that strikes them. We cannot answer these senseless accusations and remain silent throughout the questioning. The men exchange some words, then one of them takes us down the hall to another room and orders us to remain there. The door shuts with the heaviness of anger.

Finally, we are left alone, standing in the small dark room with no windows, no chairs. The air is stagnant and dank. We whisper to one another, terror in every word. We may not see the light again or may live only to be shipped away to somewhere unknown, never to return home.

The door opens. We shield our eyes and try to adjust to the white light. We see three uniformed Gestapo officers positioning themselves around the room.

"You," he blurts, looking at me, his fist smashing the little table before him, "you have been plotting against the Reich, forging visas for Jews to escape their just punishment. You are a traitor and traitors must die!"

"No, that's not true."

"You have been seen with others who are traitors, meeting, scheming, working like rats in the night, the way Jews do, to gnaw their way into the German stronghold. We will destroy you all before your plans can succeed."

"Where is your father?" another demands.

"He is dead," I answer quietly.

"When did he die? How did he die? We believe that he may be in hiding, committing crimes against the state."

We shudder in horror at this accusation.

"No, sir, we remember that the doctors said he was dead."

"Yeah, Jewish doctors who signed the death certificate. We know that you people all lie and conspire together only for the money."

"We were very young but we know. We haven't seen him since 1922. That has been fifteen years already. We went to the funeral and saw the wooden casket lowered into the ground. We visit his grave."

"Who holds deed to your property then? Is it this young man?"

"No, our mother holds the deed. She will tell you herself that our father worked very hard for the sake of the business. Everyone knows that."

"Quiet! Jews only steal from others. We are here to take back the possessions that rightfully belong to the Austrian people."

"We are Austrian too," Willi says, trembling, barely audible.

"Jews are not anything. They have no right to walk on the same earth or inhale the same air as true Austrians. Tell your mother that the SS will be at her door in the morning. She will sign all the documents without resistance or there will be a more severe penalty than you may imagine."

They turn and storm out of the room, slamming the door behind them as they leave us shivering in the dark again. Another hour passes before we are finally allowed to leave, without explanation. Hand in hand, white as chalk and shaking, we emerge from Gestapo headquarters. I breathe deeply to fill my lungs with clean air and to expel the hot nausea that has overcome me. Our nerves are taut as wire, at the very limit of endurance. My legs will not support me, and I collapse on the bottom step in a heap of quivering exhaustion. Willi is terrified and shaking. His glasses teeter on the tip of his nose as, pulling on my hand, he begs me to stand up. "We have to go, Nini. They could change their minds any moment and call us back inside. If we are taken again, we will not get out. Please, get up. We can make it home. I'll help you. Come on."

Leaning on one another for support, we make our way through the streets, where every shadow presents a new menace, every passing soldier stomping by, a source of renewed terror. Eventually we are able to stumble back home but the pervasive poison enters with us.

Mama is in the parlour, having coffee with her friend and neighbour, Frau Kaufmann, who is also a widow but with no children. Their chatter stops suddenly when they see Willi and me, arm in arm, staggering into the room. We sink into the closest chairs as if we had no bones and were just floppy cloth dolls.

The two women rush to us in alarm, peppering us with questions about where we have been and what has happened to us. Still in shock, we are too dazed even to respond. After we manage to swallow some hot coffee we tell them fragments of the story. Mama puts her hands to her face in dismay, then suggests that Frau Kaufmann should leave saying that we are obviously tired after our ordeal in Nazi headquarters. Standing in the doorway, Frau Kaufmann looks back to us and shakes her head dismally. "How can we endure this life? What merciful God could allow this treachery to exist? Maybe it would be better to die now than continue to suffer like this." She closes the door sadly behind her.

We tell Mama that the Nazis questioned us about Papa and demanded to know who was in control of the family business. That was why they had taken Willi for interrogation. We explain that the Gestapo will come to our home in the morning to see her. If she signs away all deeds and rights of our properties to the Reich without resistance, they may allow us to stay in Vienna until we can arrange to emigrate. We know we have no options in the matter and that we will be lucky just to preserve our lives.

CHAPTER 11

THE DEVIL'S WARRIOR 1938

Early the next morning the heavy boots of Gestapo soldiers thump on the steps as they enter our home. They present the documents of confiscation to Mama. Her hand is trembling and her face is ghostly pale but she signs the papers without a word and without a tear. Standing as straight as I can beside her chair, my hand clenched tightly on the frame, I try to remain as brave as Mama, who will not cower before the uniformed men. Towering over us, tall and unflinching, one staring vacantly and disinterestedly into space, the other two sneering their haughty disdain, they have come to plunder all of Papa's hard work, the dreams of his lifetime and all that he had believed in and treasured. I know that her heart is pounding with fear like mine, and with anger at the corruption and injustice.

When they shut the door behind them, we remain suspended in silent agony. The full impact of the act hits us with a blunt thud. At first we cannot move or speak, cannot fully comprehend what has happened. We focus on Mama's face and search for the courage she has always shown, courage that will allow us to endure this latest travesty. But she has changed. She no longer seems the figure of resolve that could surmount the most severe obstacles placed before her. She appears suddenly shrunken, her shoulders hunched in defeat, dry-eyed, gazing into space, her mind trapped in shock. We fear she has given up or that she is suffering a nervous breakdown.

I smooth the wisps of grey hair back from her forehead, then kneel beside her, at her feet. Holding her hand in mine, I try to speak to her as gently as possible, although my own emotions are rattling in my chest and threatening to overwhelm me. With tears clouding my vision I beg her to listen. "Mama, we will be all right. You know at least that we are all still together and safe. We have not been taken away like so many others. We will find a way to leave Vienna and to build a new life. Please, Mama, we need you to be strong."

She turns towards us. The pride that was so important to her, the sanctity of her household, the safety of her family had been eroded. She reminds me of a stray animal, searching for a way home. When Papa died we feared she would fall apart and never conquer the pain, but she was able to carry on. Throughout the hardships of widowhood with four dependent children she carried on, but now, what has she left to keep her from giving up?

All day she sits by the window, hardly speaking, not able to eat or function in any way. Willi and I are worried about her but go about our own activities. I still go to open the store and Willi heads off to see Fritz and Erna. The circumstances of our existence are more oppressive than ever.

That evening when we return home there are only a few words exchanged among the three of us. After our simple dinner, just bread and some stew reheated from the night before, Willi and I are surprised to see Mama reach for the needlepoint in the basket by her chair.

"Nini, perhaps you could make some hot tea for us all and then we can go to bed. Tomorrow I will search for some solution to this mess," she says in a matter-of-fact tone.

Willi and I head out to the kitchen to make the tea.

"Do you think that Mama has gone mad?" he asks as we wait for the water to boil.

"No, probably not. I've seen this before." I take cups and saucers from the cupboard. "She sets her mind on something familiar and comforting and then she can go on. No matter how awful the circumstances, she is determined to persevere. We will have to do the same."

I have tried to comfort Willi but only believe part of what I have said. Mama's forced composure, I think, will not be enough this time. We will need more than that, a real plan of escape, a destination and means of leaving this horror behind.

All the family is caught up in the whirlwind. Whenever I see Stella and Walter or Erna and Fritz and their little girl, Lily, we talk about rumours, news of places that might take Jews in – countries that don't demand visas or vast sums of money to open their doors. But until now there is nothing definite, no place to go.

The next day I am alone in the store, trying to attend to business. Somehow, life goes on – people still need the things that we sell, yards of cloth to be made into clothing, linens, hats and gloves, stockings. But I am worried that the shelves are growing sparse, wondering how long we will manage with what we have as we are unable to purchase more from manufacturers who will no longer do business with us.

Suddenly, as I am waiting on a customer, an SS officer enters. He is dressed in a black uniform, precise in its detail, terrifying in its cold perfection, from his peaked cap and white gloves pulled tightly on his hands to the sheen of his high black leather boots. A gun hangs at his hip and a scarlet swastika armband encircles his upper arm. He has come to claim the business. Without it we will starve to death. He holds the documents that Mama has signed under duress as he marches into the store. He has the pompous air of a conquering hero and the calm arrogance that the uniform has provided.

In dismay I observe our customers raise their arms in a stiff Nazi salute and utter "Heil Hitler" to the officer at the register. Some of them are familiar, some are even known to me by name. The same people who would have greeted me with a friendly smile and a "Good day, young Fraulein Karpel," now divert their eyes or stare at me in revulsion as if I have become too ugly and repulsive to even acknowledge.

I am anchored to my spot, quivering and choking back the tears that are always ready to fall. My skin prickles with goosebumps. Can I think of any course of action that could save us now? As the soldier walks towards the counter behind which I am standing, I search my mind for some salvation. Papa's face flashes in my thoughts. What would he do? If only he were here, he could help me somehow. I force myself to look directly into the face of the Nazi officer. He is not much older than I. My only hope might be to soften his heart.

Papa's words, hidden away safely in the darkest crevice of my mind, return to me: "If you need him, cut the murderer from the gallows to save yourself."

I obediently show this man, who is my declared enemy and possible executioner, all the contents of the store, the bookkeeping, and everything he requires to run it. He has been given orders to take control of the daily operations and to take all the money to the Nazi coffers. People bustle in and out and move about whispering, their heads flicking back in nervous concern, returning again and again to the man in black, who observes every detail with an unwavering gaze and silent control.

All day we are together. I speak to him as if he might be just another human being. "This is a difficult time for everyone, isn't it?" I ask with all the courage I can muster.

At first he seems startled with the question. After all, he is in control of the situation and has been given the power over life and death. Nevertheless, a ridge between his eyebrows indicates that he is considering the question carefully. He responds with a degree of kindness that was too much to hope for. "When we were told to remove property from people we have known all our lives, we wondered at first if it was right. When violence became common practice, we wondered if it was right. But now the reasons are clear. We want a strong Austria and our Fuhrer has the solution and so, we are prepared to follow him no matter the direction. Our faith is solid now and even when there are doubts, we must push them aside."

"You are a thoughtful man," I say, trying my best to control my anger and frustration, all the time thinking that any excuse for the evil that is happening is wrong, hating his doctrine and his Fuhrer with every fibre within me. "I'm so worried, though, about my poor mother and how we can exist without this business."

"You must try to leave Austria for now," he replies. "The war is only a temporary situation. We are confident that once the Reich has been established, the strength of a united Austro-Germany will be prosperous and magnificent again. Then you and I, Fraulein, could become very good friends."

"Yes, of course." I smile as confidently as I can. If ever I wanted to prove my acting ability, this was the time. How could he dream of such a friendship? How could he imagine that I might see him without the constant reminder of the cruelty I have witnessed? I look straight into his eyes, which are filled with the promise of youth and the fervour of national pride, ignited by his leader's fanatic rhetoric. He can't see the devastation, only a vision of glory.

I have shaken hands with the Devil's warrior for the sake of our survival. In my thoughts Papa's voice whispers his encouragement and promises to guide us to a safe haven. The plan is successful. I have been able to break open a tiny crack in this man's hardened shell, armour created by continual brainwashing and reinforced bigotry. The human being within the uniform has been forced to see me as another living creature, battling to survive through the insanity of war. The Gestapo officer violates his orders by allowing me to take something from the till at the end of the day and every day thereafter so we will be able to eat and to survive. This is a small miracle in a time of desperation and very little hope.

CHAPTER 12

MEANS OF ESCAPE 1938

S ummer in Vienna is perfumed with the scent of roses that bloom in mad profusion, aglow with the magical twinkle lights of fireflies blinking in the night. It is young girls in large-brimmed straw hats, ribbons streaming and floral dresses that billow and flutter in warm breezes blowing off the Danube. In open-air concerts, violins are playing the music of our great composers, Mozart, Schubert, and Strauss. The sweeping melodies are so well known that everyone hums along. Sidewalk vendors are cooking bratwurst sausages that crackle and splutter as they are roasted. The aroma is too tempting to resist and there is no shortage of customers standing in line waiting for a hot thick wiener, which will be dipped generously into a glass jar of spicy mustard before the first crunchy bite can be taken with eager pleasure. There are heart-stopping rides on the enormous Viennese Ferris wheel, the Reisenrad, at the Prater Amusement Park, turning into the sky and down again to the earth, and the delightful sensation of laughing out of control about nothing at all. This is the Vienna I have known since my birth, a place that has always been my personal treasure. Every crack and crevice on the pavement is as familiar as the crisscrossing lines of my own palm. The smells and sounds are intertwined with my own heartbeats.

Ever since I can recall our family has spent the hot months of July and August in Kobenzl, at our hillside home, a rustic cottage where urban restraints are abandoned. As children we used to count the days to our holidays and as soon as school was over we chattered endlessly about going away. We assembled our things and prepared to trek up the trail to the chalet. Year after year this was our ritual; our backpacks stuffed with clothing, playthings and little books, we made our way, waving to those we knew as we passed. Along the way there were other cottages large and small, wooden structures with sprouting vegetable patches and brightly coloured flowerbeds growing in splashy abundance up to the stone steps. Away from the city we spent our most carefree times, no schoolwork, no chores, just sleeping late, playing, swimming in the huge public pool, developing ravenous appetites for the hearty suppers we devoured. We fetched drinking water from our well, pumping the handle with mad vigour, waiting impatiently for the cool liquid to gush from the spout and fill our cups, then gulping it with pleasure as it dribbled down our chins. At night we would lie on our backs in the moist grass and trace the patterns of stars strewn across the pitch sky as frogs croaked their gruff serenade.

But the summer of '38 is no longer a place like that for me. In May I had my twenty-second birthday, a birthday with no celebration, no parties, no candles on a cake. The Nazis have confiscated the summer home at Kobenzl and now even the escape to our favoured retreat has been denied. We are Jews, and the gaiety of Vienna is no longer available to us. The treachery that has befallen our city forces us to hide from anything of joy or beauty. Even a casual stroll is a danger that we dare not attempt. We leave only for the most crucial of necessities and then hurry back like frightened rodents to seek shelter again in the hot, darkened rooms, curtains pulled to hide from the eyes of our enemies, who are lurking everywhere. Jewish women have been pulled out of their homes and forced to get on hands and knees to scrub the pavement with their lace-trimmed lingerie and fur coats. Crowds jeer. On June 10 we read in the paper that the main synagogue in Munich had been burned to the ground the day before. Daily, atrocities are committed against us and there is no end in sight .

President Roosevelt has called for an international conference to take place in July in Evian, France. We hold our breaths at this news, hoping to see an awakening of basic humanitarian values. But when the much-awaited meeting takes place and the "Jewish Situation," as it is called, comes up, the matter is resolved in the most catastrophic way for us. There is to be no easing of immigration laws, no global responsibility taken or remedy offered for the Jews of Germany. We are left to fend for ourselves. "Ever since Evian," people are beginning to say in sombre acceptance, "our fate was sealed."

The news from Evian has hit Viennese Jewry with such a blow that there is panic everywhere we go. The Germans have taken the results of the conference as a green light for continued persecution. Violent arrests increase and bloody beatings are commonplace. The elderly and infirm are most frequently victimized. There is a mad rush to every foreign consulate in the city. The staunchest Austrians who had waited patiently for better times to return are finally convinced to flee. But is it too late? My family is blocked in Vienna and, just like the others, we are trying to find a way out, but the possible destinations grow fewer each day. One by one, ports of refuge are being closed.

In a magnanimous gesture, the British cabinet has agreed to accept 10,000 unaccompanied Jewish children from Germany, Austria, and Czechoslovakia in an action called the Kindertransport. We have read of it with dismay. To separate children from parents and settle them in Christian foster homes is a sin, but because this seems the best the world can do, our community offers humble appreciation.

The United States has issued its own announcement. Its quota for Jews is filled for the next three years with even more stringent conditions that eliminate most who would seek asylum. Some of those who have applied have been advised with apparent ignorance or apathy by the American authorities that they should wait, but the desperation many feel is evident in the rising suicide count.

We have saved whatever we could for as long as we were able to work in the store, but the young German officer whom I had convinced to help us has been removed from the position and now we have been permanently ousted. The Nazis have seen to it that we cannot return. The small amount of money remaining, hidden away in a secret spot under a loose floor board, must be used sparingly just to stave off starvation.

In our quest for options, one word is beginning to recur: "Shanghai." We hear it whispered behind cupped hands when we pass haggard neighbours on the streets. News travels in a human telegraph line from one to the next. "Shanghai," they say, the strange word pronounced with an Austrian accent, odd, exotic, remote, spoken with fear and hope, the only possibility. A new kind of excitement comes from the slim prospect of rescue. Those we meet brim with guarded enthusiasm, their dull eyes and malnourished faces suddenly brighter. They are eager to share their news and we are desperate to find details of this place. "There are no visas or police certificates required, and no passport inspection in Shanghai," we are told. The Chinese are not requiring proof of financial independence either, something that other countries have demanded. Such an assurance is beyond most everyone we know, as all our bank accounts have been frozen and assets confiscated. "Shanghai," our friends say with some trepidation, "could be our salvation."

Since I first heard of the possibility of the escape to Shanghai and then that my sisters were already making plans to go there, I have been obsessed with the idea that Mama, Willi, and I (and Poldi's parents, of course, as they have become my responsibility) should go to China too. What would Papa have done, I ask myself. I have decided I must search for someone who could help.

Early one morning in mid-July I dress with care to appear most grown-up and serious, in a navy blue skirt and suit jacket with a matching hat neatly set on my head. I run red lipstick over my lips, purse them together, then summon all my courage and head out to join the crowds of others in the daily vain attempt to find a country that will let us in. If it is to be China, how would we manage to get there? The day is hot and hazy, the people frantic and distraught as I force my way through the streets. Everywhere are the gruff German soldiers, who pull Jewish people out of their homes at random for the usual bouts of torture. The noonday sun is glaring down on me and perspiration is dripping into my eyes. I wipe my face and neck with a handkerchief that is already damp.

After several futile hours, my clothes crumpled and my hat squashed down on my ruined hairdo, I stop, worn and dejected. Overcome by the heat and exhaustion I lean against a building and look up at the sign: "Berger, Attorney at Law."

I climb the steps as if drawn in by a magnet. At the front desk I say, "Please, I have to see Herr Berger, the lawyer."

"Do you have an appointment, Fraulein?" the secretary asks, looking me up and down to assess my situation and station in life. She is stern and proper, and as she takes her black-rimmed glasses off she stares at me in disapproval.

"No, but this is an urgent matter, you see, urgent." I can feel the effects of the heat and fatigue beginning to overcome me.

Just then the office door opens and a man comes out to hand her some papers.

"Please," I say to him, "I have to see a lawyer."

He turns towards me, obviously surprised by my direct approach and dishevelled appearance.

"She has no appointment, Herr Berger," the secretary says stiffly.

"For God's sake, can't you see that she is ready to drop right here on the floor?" He guides me by the elbow, moving me past her desk and scowling face, into his office. He takes me to a comfortable chair and gives me a glass of cool water. I gulp it down and begin speaking immediately.

"We need your help or we will all die here," I say at once. "We are Jews, you see, of course you do, and yet you let me in. I don't know why but maybe there is still someone in Vienna who will do something for us. I am at my wit's end, you see. I don't know what to do, and then there's Mama and my brother and the others, my God, all of us and we don't know how to get to China and we don't have enough money and...."

Seeing me so upset, my words rambling on and on, Herr Berger finally interrupts and tries to get me to slow down. I breathe deeply and attempt to control my quivering hands and trembling voice.

"Just take your time," he says with a smile and great courtesy that is uncommon in the current environment. He is a fastidiously attired gentleman in his early forties. I notice the knife-sharp creases in his trouser legs and the high-gloss polish on his shoes.

"Thank you, Herr Berger," I answer, holding my handbag tightly on my knees. I decide the best approach is the direct one. "You know what is going on here in Vienna. I have come to ask for your help."

I can hear my voice cracking, and despite my resolve to be brave I am afraid I will fall apart at any moment.

"What can I do, Fraulein?" he asks, shutting the door to give us privacy. "As you know, there are informants everywhere these days. The Nazis have corrupted the most loyal secretary and the most honest clerk. Words have wings, I'm afraid."

"We can't go to our store any more and we have no income," I tell him, putting my pride aside. "We fear for our lives every day. I don't know what to do, but we have been told about Shanghai, we think we could get in there." My voice falters, and I choke back the tears. "I don't know how to go about it. Can you do anything for us?"

"Here, drink a little more water and try to calm down a bit," he says kindly, pouring water from a crystal pitcher, then going back to his big leather chair.

He begins to write on a notepad. "I will need as many details as you can provide. How many people are involved?" he asks, looking up over his eyeglasses.

"Well, there is Mama and Willi, that's my brother, and me. My sisters already have passage arranged through their husbands' families. And there are the Kosiners, a couple, parents of a dear friend of mine who is in Italy. Yes, five all together. That will cost a fortune of money, I'm sure, to secure train and boat passage. We'll never be able to afford that." I start to shake again.

"All right, all right, Fraulein, please, have some trust in me." He continues to ask for details and writes everything down.

Finally, he puts his pen down and removes his glasses. "I am ashamed of my people. Whatever has happened to the integrity of the Austrians?" he asks with a sigh. "Well, there may be a few of us left willing to risk something to help a fellow human being. I want you to stop worrying now. Leave this matter in my hands. I still have something to say in this country despite this new rule of terror."

"I had nowhere else to turn, Herr Berger," I say, wanting to explain my appearance here. "Certainly I would not want you to jeopardize your own safety. Can you be sure that it will be all right, that the Gestapo will not blame you for anything?"

"That is not something you should be concerned about. I have lived my life with a deep regard for fairness and I'm sworn to serve justice. Now that justice is nothing but a hollow word, I will adhere to my own justice."

Despite my resolution to keep my emotions in check, tears well in my eyes. Just when I had believed that there remained not one courageous and righteous person in all of Vienna, this man has offered to risk his own life for ours.

"Fraulein," he says, "I know how hopeless this seems but I will see what I can do and will get word to you within a day or two." Getting up from his chair he adds, "Don't worry about the money for now," and pats me on the shoulder. "I will advance any necessary funds and you can pay me back one day, after the war perhaps, when we can return to a normal life again."

"I don't know how to thank you, Herr Berger." I pump his hand up and down vigorously.

When I finally get home, I tell Mama and Willi what I have done. They are incredulous that I would have had the nerve to approach a stranger, someone like Herr Berger, a Gentile, influential and probably connected to the Nazis, and they are shocked further that he agreed not only to help but to use his own money for our sakes. They agree it would be wonderful if he is successful, but they are still sceptical about his promises.

But Herr Berger *has* kept his word, and in two days he himself comes to our door. Sending a messenger is too risky. He sits down with Mama, Willi, and me in our front room and tells us what he has arranged. He has purchased all five tickets. We only have to get our emigration documents approved and we should be able to get out.

I am so overjoyed that I jump up and hug him. His face reddens at my emotional outburst but he smiles and shakes hands with Mama and Willi, who both thank him profusely.

That same evening I hurry to the Kosiners' apartment to tell them of the wonderful news. They are overwhelmed with gratitude but are still concerned. They are Polish citizens and have not been able to obtain exit visas till now, but I tell them they must pick up their tickets at the shipping office in person and then we will somehow arrange the necessary documents – "freedom papers" they are called among the Viennese Jews. I have emphasized how much I trust Herr Berger, that I'm sure he will get everything arranged, and that before long we will all be together again, reunited in Shanghai, and that Poldi and Dolu will be with us too.

CHAPTER 13

KRISTALLNACHT NOVEMBER 1938

Things have grown worse since the Anschluss. All summer we have suffered more and more abuses and loss of liberties. I am with Willi, Stella, Fritz, and Walter at a coffee house one evening. Erna is in her own home with her baby, and Mama has stayed behind, alone in our flat. The night air is chilled as we huddle together in silence with just a few candles lit so we can see one another in the shadows. We are all nervously puffing cigarettes and swallowing cups of hot dark coffee, sweetened with lumps of sugar. We stare forlornly out the shop's windows, which have been smeared with anti-Semitic slogans.

A few other patrons are seated at the café's small tables. Only the owner is serving as he has no more employees. Non-Jews are not allowed to work for Jews, and anyway business hardly warrants waitresses here these days. Everyone is discussing the latest story buzzing around in Vienna. Walter shows us the frightening headline in the newspaper crumpled in his hand: "Jew Kills German Aide in Paris." A young Jewish man, only seventeen years of age, named Herschel Grynszpan, has murdered the German chargé d'affaires when the young man's parents were sent to Poland.

"At least he killed the Nazi bastard, one less to torment us," Walter comments bitterly, scanning the report. "But I wonder what repercussions this will have on the rest of us."

Willi replies in an agitated voice, clutching a cigarette tightly between his permanently yellowed fingers and inhaling the nicotine like a drowning man gasping for air. "He must have been mad to try such a thing. Not only did he ensure his own death but we will all suffer for his act."

"What more can they do?" I ask in frustration. "They have stolen all our belongings, they are driving us out of our homes and making us hide like rats, trapped in cellars."

We are all hushed for a moment, thinking about this latest event and considering what it might mean. Then Stella, nervously stirring her coffee, her face drawn and pale, says, "We have to concentrate only on leaving this place, nothing more. Our tickets are dated for January, a month ahead of yours. Nini and Willi will follow with Mama. With God's help we may all meet in Shanghai."

Teary eyed, we clasp hands around the table as we look at one another, wondering if we truly will see our family again once we've left Vienna.

Suddenly the door flies open amid screams of horrific distress. Mama's old friend, Frau Kaufmann, has come running down the street, shrieking out of control and cannot be subdued. She cries, "The *shul* has been torched! My God, we are finished!"

She continues screaming but we try to calm her to find out what she knows.

"Sit down, Frau Kaufmann, slowly, tell us what has happened." I lead her to a chair by the window.

From where we stand, we can see the flames. Paralyzed by the sight before us, we watch as thick smoke rises in black clumps to the sky. In the distance, we are able to make out the stained glass windows of our temple, so familiar to us all, pierced by thrown rocks, raining to the ground in an avalanche of coloured shards.

Behind us, Frau Kaufmann rants in wild confusion. "It is a plague, a catastrophe. They... they are everywhere. They are destroying our place, our holy place. I can't bear it any longer. Our only bit of peace, the only sanctuary from the endless hatred, ruined. They are killing us all, one by one, one by one, one by one."

Captivated by her story and distressed by her wild-eyed hysteria, we listen in amazement as she continues her account in a tumbling barrage of words.

"The sacred Torah scrolls have been violated, do you understand? They have been ripped from the ark, desecrated by muddy boots and all the time the brutes were laughing and cursing profanities. Old bearded men in white fringed prayer shawls with black yarmulkes on their heads have been beaten and left for dead, their blood pooling around them until the floor was a sticky, slippery mess. They cried and begged for mercy, for pity, but there was none. No one could answer their pleas," she sobs uncontrollably as the other customers, now jolted from their quiet conversations, are trying to look out from their positions by the window.

"Don't you see," she continues, "they have murdered God, Himself, and only Satan remains. This has become Hell on Earth. It is the very end, can't you see? Listen to me, listen to me, I was there. Listen to me, I saw it with my own eyes. Listen to me!"

There are moans and frenzied activity as everyone becomes fully aware of what is taking place outside and that Frau Kaufmann's rambling tales are factual. The others hurriedly pull on coats and hats and within a few minutes they have all scurried out the door. We are the only ones still inside and the owner is preparing to close, taking the money from the till, dashing about in his kitchen to turn off ovens and lights. We will be forced to go soon but first we want to do what we can for the poor woman.

"Please, Frau Kaufmann," Walter implores, "calm down. Come, we'll try to get you home."

"We are doomed!" she continues to screech in escalating octaves. "We are doomed!" Her whole body is shuddering and she seems to have gone into shock. We try in vain to settle her down but succumbing to hysteria, she pushes by us and runs blindly out to the street, into the path of the oncoming mob. We watch in horror as she is trampled and kicked in the stomach and head by several uniformed Hitler Youths, who shout obscenities and violent curses as the poor woman rolls on the ground, bleeding. Before our shocked eyes, they continue to beat her senseless until she has become a bloody bundle, limp and silent.

We hear shouting outside and the sound of glass smashing as store windows are reduced to heaps of shiny splinters. After quick farewells and promises to meet later, we disperse. Fritz is agitated with worry about his wife and child, and as he rushes out the door, we call, "God be with you."

The others have disappeared into the night, each to a safe shelter from the turmoil engulfing us. I remain with Willi outside the café, where we try to decide what to do and where to go.

But we are disoriented, still in shock from witnessing Frau Kaufmann's murder and numbed by the frenzy of those rushing past us. Finally our paralysis of fear dissolves when Willi suddenly asks, "What about Mama?" and then we are even more terrified as we think of her alone at home. We can hear shouting as rowdy crowds crash their way through the glass-strewn streets. "Down with the Jews," we hear, and others call out, "Death to the Jews."

Pressing against the shadows of the houses we have known all our lives, we make our way home. Willi, clutching my hand, tells me to have courage. My throat is raw from the thick smoke hanging in the cold night air and the sheer panic I feel. Fear is so overwhelming that there is room for nothing else. We move forward like the blind. We are not aware of where our feet are going or what thoughts propel us forward.

On a wild rampage of bloodlust, Nazi soldiers, followed by crowds of eager Viennese citizens, shove through the streets, looting the shops and scorching their way along a path of random violence. In my mind I see Mama lying on the floor like Frau Kaufmann, tortured, bloodied. Maybe they have taken her away. We rush through the black streets, showers of broken glass crashing around us as the destruction continues. We are coughing and gasping from the dense smoke, clouds of soot, and odour of burnt timber.

At last we arrive home and begin to call frantically, "Mama, where are you? Mama, are you all right? Mama, please answer, please, please."

Still there is no sound as we creep cautiously through the dark, hollow rooms, terror strangling our throats. We are sleepwalkers, gliding through a nightmare of unspeakable horror, every step drawing us closer to an awakening that we dare not confront.

Then we hear a weak voice from behind a door and we hurry towards it. "Nini, Willi, oh, my God in heaven, you've come back. I thought this was the end and that I would never see you again."

We find Mama shivering in a darkened room, a small candle, its dwindling wick still lit, resting on the table next to her chair. She is sitting near a window from where she can see, peering from behind the pulled drapes, that Vienna is ablaze. The leaping scarlet flames create a dance of light and shadow on the wall and on her face. A silver needle shines in her quivering hand. There, alone in the dark, she has been sewing pockets into the hem of her dress to conceal her pieces of jewellery. Next to her on the table is a hot poker, pulled from the last shimmering embers of the fire, that she was planning to use as a weapon. She knows that this night is the final blow, that we must flee or die in the attempt. I run to her and fold my arms around her neck. Together we cry until we are exhausted.

Willi is kneeling at her feet, his head on her lap, his body shaking, tears in his eyes.

"Mama," he says, "will we really die tonight?"

"Shhh, my child. We are still together. There is still hope. We can't give up as long as there is breath."

Then she remembers where we have been and asks, "What about the others, are they all right?"

"The family is fine, as far as we know. We were together at the café and everyone was all right then. We will try to contact Stella and Erna tomorrow. With God's help they will all be safe. But," I say at last, after a long pause, "they have killed Frau Kaufmann."

Mama stares at me in stunned disbelief, then replies simply, "*Alevah Sholem* – she should rest in peace. Children, we have to get away or we will be next."

She has no tears left to shed for her dear friend and her response seems strangely detached, but Mama has a family to think of, to preserve and protect. We have seen this strength before when Papa died. In the face of great adversity she has been able to concentrate on one goal, the preservation of her brood. Her eyes are fixed ahead, dry now, and her expression of resolve provides some courage to us.

Willi and I exchange surprised glances at one another. Mama's reaction to Frau Kaufmann's death is not what we had expected. Once again she has had to dig deeply into her diminishing well of bravery to find the will to carry on. We try to recoup our own fractured strength from hers.

"There will be many things to do tomorrow," she says picking up her needlework from a basket on the floor, her fingers starting to stitch up and down.

In the morning papers, the heading describes the preceding night, naming it "Kristallnacht," a pretty name for the most dire catastrophe to befall us. They have named it the night of crystal, but for us it was the night of broken glass and broken hearts.

Dawn, as always, awakens the citizens of Vienna with its golden radiance, but on the day following Kristallnacht it also illuminates the destruction of the previous night, revealing the full extent of hatred's fury. Looking down from our window, we see the ugliness spread out before us, no longer concealed in the previous night's shadows but clear and sunlit in a harsh new reality. The persecution, however, has not ceased, but is only starting anew. Brazen Nazis have devised new forms of torment. To our horror, we see old Jewish people on hands and knees, bent and terrified, cowering at the boots of the SS officers who, with horsewhips in their hands and pistols at their sides, are standing above them, convulsed in fits of laughter. Defenceless, the victims hold small wooden scrub brushes in their reddened fingers. The soapy water, mixing with blood, turns sickly pink as bits of glass become embedded in the flesh. Tears mingle with sweat, as they are forced to clean the streets of the city, trying in vain to wipe away the sins of their oppressors.

Kristallnacht has become a clear demarcation point. Nothing after that date is as it was before. Every moment now is more harrowing, as just navigating through the streets is hazardous. As much as possible we don't leave our homes, but the isolation is difficult to bear. One evening, I go to visit Stella. She's just made some coffee and hands me a cup absent-mindedly, her hand shaking so that it rattles the saucer. Her eyes dart from me to the door, over and over. "Nini, I don't know what has happened to Walter," she finally confesses. "He should have returned from our shop hours ago."

"I'm sure he'll be back soon. Time always seems to drag when you're waiting." I try to sound confident, but wonder whether something sinister has happened. Stella relies on her husband to make the important decisions in their life. His fatherly role reassures her and fills some void within her. Without him she would be directionless and desperately alone. The idea of that possibility comes to us both at once. It's mirrored in her bright blue eyes, wide with terror, wet with tears, as her fingers are twisting in nervous tension.

The clock ticks loudly as if to announce the passing of each minute, and the clicking noise speaks like a voice, proclaiming disaster. Where has he gone? What is he doing? Has he been taken? Is he alive?

When he finally arrives, we are both dumbfounded by the state he's in as he stumbles through the door. He is blood-soaked, bruised nearly beyond recognition, his left eye puffed closed so that he cannot see. His head tilts sideways as if to compensate for the impaired vision. He is hardly able to walk. He staggers, weaves, leaves a trail of red splatters on the floor behind him, and finally collapses into a chair. He hugs his ribcage, embracing his sore, battered sides. When he lifts his stained shirt, we choke back our nausea at the sight of his raw flesh.

Stella is immobile at first, staring at the transformed man before her.

Her voice choked dry, she looks in horrified disbelief at the pulpy face and gaping wounds.

"We have to clean him up and find a doctor," I say at last, realizing that I must assume the position now of a rational voice.

"No," Walter says weakly, "there is no doctor to find. They're all busy trying to protect themselves and to flee. Just do whatever you can. Patch me up and I'll be all right. At least I escaped. They stopped short of killing me this time, but we are outrunning death by millimetres. The Nazi gangs are out of control."

In shock we press our hands over our mouths as we listen grim-faced. He tells of the brutish beating and memory lapse when he apparently fell unconscious. Holding his hand against the inflamed wound on his side, he pants for air. We sponge him and wipe away the dried blood, bandaging the tender wound. He is moaning and Stella is crying uncontrollably.

"Here, take some coffee." I offer him a sip of the hot liquid, but his lip is cut and the heat burns the open gash.

"Ah!" he cries, feeling the aching sore. Through swollen lips he says, "Nini, you have to go home. The streets are unsafe and it will soon be dark. Go back to Mama and try to stay inside."

I decide reluctantly to leave them behind. What else can I do? I scuttle through the streets, which are no longer neat and orderly as they used to be. An ugly squalor has befallen the city. The veneer of civility has been lifted and suddenly I am fully aware of the metamorphosis. My beautiful Vienna has been stripped of all its finery and lies before me, its belly split open like a ravaged carcass in the sun, festering, stinking, and decaying.

CHAPTER 14

FAREWELL JANUARY 1939

I n Milan, Poldi has been working in an underground resistance movement in an attempt to rescue Jews trapped in Italy. He has begun to forge exit visas, a risky business, trying to help those who need a way out. He was not able to write about this to me but I have heard about it from his parents who have been in contact with Italian relatives. I have just written to him about our latest turn of events, about my meeting with Herr Berger, and the results which are the best that we could have hoped for, that all of us will get out safely.

By January of 1939 we have managed to get tickets on a train that will leave Vienna next month for Trieste, then our passage is booked on the next ship from Italy to Shanghai. We still need the permission of the Viennese government to allow us to leave but with this proof of our exit route there is a greater chance that we will be successful.

Mama has tucked the documents from Herr Berger carefully into her purse. In them he has guaranteed our travel arrangements and confirmed train and ships' passage. Willi and I set off with her for the Emigration Office. An endless line of people is queued day and night, waiting to be seen. As we await our turn, the faces of those leaving the office make our skins crawl in fear. They are bruised from beatings, trembling fingers touching red splotches on their swollen cheeks or wiping trickles of blood from a cut lip. They look shaken from the ordeal they have endured, yet the fortunate ones who have procured exit visas wear weak smiles of triumph and several nod to us as a sign of encouragement. We have no choice but to wait and pray that we can somehow get the documents that will allow our escape.

Inside the building we watch as those ahead of us approach the desk, heads bowed in dread. We have witnessed the uniformed men, tall and muscular, standing, legs astride, suddenly strike women, old men, whomever they choose, for questions they have dared to ask or been unable to answer. We flinch every time, as if the blow had hit each of us.

We must face Eichmann like everyone else, trembling as our name is called.

"Karpel!" The bark is like a warden announcing the name of the next to be executed.

Mama steps forward, holding the papers shakily, and presents them to be read by the first man, to the left of Eichmann.

"Shanghai," he says, chuckling in disgust. "A good place to send you Jews to die. There will be a slow death for you all. Go to the stinking hole of yellow-skinned mongrels. At least you won't be here to spread your contagion."

We are choking back the fear rising in our throats, afraid that Mama will respond in indignant outrage and that she will be beaten for it. She has always been outspoken and would not have suffered this kind of insult before, but she says nothing. Her head is lowered in meek silence as the brutish words are hurled like darts.

Shuffling timidly, we move before Eichmann and are confronted by a man of icy demeanour, his jagged features carved into his face of stone. He shows no sign of emotion as he methodically examines the papers we have presented to him. He meticulously scans them, searching for details that will give him a reason to deny exit. His steel-grey eyes reveal the contempt he has for us. As I observe his actions, a shiver of nervous terror tingles down the length of my spine and prickles the skin on my arms. We don't dare to speak, hardly even to breathe. He waves his hand to dismiss us and we move along towards the next desk. Finally the officer seated to his right stamps our papers with several loud thuds.

Each of us is required to sign one more affidavit, that we renounce forever our rights as Austrians and that we will never return to this country. We are then released and find our way out into the street again, the
passage to freedom clutched in Mama's quivering fingers.

We hurry home through streets already dark and then upstairs to our
apartment. Not until the door is latched and we find ourselves seated,
with hot tea soothing our parched throats, can we feel our limbs again.
Mama is seated in Papa's chair as usual, her teacup held in both hands
to steady it and warm herself. She is the first to speak, saying aloud the
thoughts that are in our minds: "I thought I might collapse at first from
fear, standing before those Nazis. Then the anger rose like boiling blood
when that beast insulted us, but you see, I said nothing. What could I
say, after all? They have all the power over life and death now. They have
stolen more than our money and property. They have taken away our
humanity."

We try to regain some composure, following Mama's lead, but Willi
is still incensed. "They are just trying to undermine us, to destroy whatever they have still not taken away. How can we preserve dignity when
we are so degraded?" Willi suddenly appears old although he is just seventeen. He sips some tea, then sets the cup down. A cigarette as always
is held in his fingers and the remnants of others already smoked down
to twisted curls fill an ashtray. The smell of nicotine drifts in the musty
air of the room

"Vienna is no longer our home," Mama says with finality. "We have
become outsiders here. Tomorrow we will begin to pack our belongings
and maybe, I can hardly hope for it, maybe we will get away with our
lives. We have been spared until now – we've been lucky. The only thing
to do is to look ahead to the future and try to forget this place."

Mama's determination is fierce, and we gather whatever strength we
can muster from her lead. Taking more gulps of the warm tea, filled
with sugar and milk, a luxury we can scarcely afford but necessary now
to revive us, I can feel the terror melting away. My words crack like dry

twigs as I speak. "I was so frightened in that office I felt myself growing faint too. My knees were wobbly as jelly and every time that Nazi spoke, I thought I would drop to the ground."

Willi, holding his teacup shakily in his hand, drawing heavily on the cigarette, his eyes watery with restrained tears behind the steamed lenses of his glasses, adds, "My heart was beating like drums every time the papers were stamped and all the time I was praying to just let us out, let us be free."

Willi and I are both smoking now, the room filling with the filmy grey puffs of our exhaled breath. Willi squishes the butt of his cigarette in an ashtray and immediately reaches for another. His cheeks are hollowed as he draws the soothing nicotine deeply into himself. I drink the smoke as well, forcing it into my lungs and waiting for its sedating effect.

We can hardly sleep that night, but the next morning, we begin the task of packing our belongings for departure. We can take only the most important and precious things. They will be loaded into trunks and valises and sent ahead by courier to await us in a holding warehouse in Shanghai. We pay for the service and hope that we will see our things again. The men from the transport company load our trunks into a truck waiting outside which will take them to the train station, but before the cases are locked they have to be inspected by the SS. We will not know what has been approved or confiscated until the day we may arrive in Shanghai to retrieve them once more.

We separate those things that are too cumbersome to carry; they will go into the huge trunks. We fill suitcases with things that will be taken aboard ship for the month-long journey to the Far East. If we'd been told to pack for a voyage to the moon, I might be more settled in my thoughts, but China, what could that possibly be like? Sitting cross-legged on the floor next to the empty steamer trunk, I wonder which few bits of my life could be stowed into that case and how much more I must leave behind. I examine the twelve square pieces of petit point, each hand-stitched over many tedious months with a swirling floral motif, each petal shaded and contoured with bits of vibrantly coloured thread. They are meant to be seat covers for dining room chairs in my home when I marry. I roll each one carefully into tissue paper and place it into my suitcase. Another of these pieces of needlework, a larger one to be used as a wall hanging, portrays a typical Austrian pastoral theme. It too is rolled and packed in the same way.

There is my wedding dowry, consisting of linens, in cream and pale blue, monogrammed by hand, sheets, pillowcases, duvet covers with little buttons covered in matching fabric. I place them inside a large trunk. Pieces of silverware, enough for a complete dinner set, and crystal goblets, are individually wrapped in tissue. Plans made since the very day of my birth, now overturned, my future life, which had seemed so clearly defined by the things in this chest, are now of no more relevance than last winter's melted snow. I touch each piece tenderly. Where, I wonder, will these things come to surface once again, what voyage will they have to endure before a real life can begin?

I begin to fold my sweaters, running my fingers over the thick stitches and embossed patterns, and then the other pieces of clothing, tailored by hand, that remind me of days and evenings of a happier time. I place each inside the trunk with care. There are shoes of every style and shade, things that were so important to me as a young woman. Finally, into the packed trunks of memories, I place my skis, ski boots, and poles, my most treasured belongings. Then I go to tell Mama I am ready.

When Mama comes into my room to check my progress, she is dismayed to see that I have packed my skis.

"You must leave those behind, Nini. They're heavy and bothersome and will only cause trouble."

Although I see the sad pleading look in Mama's eyes, I begin to storm uncontrollably in the only show of defiance I have allowed myself. Although my words pour out in angry frustration, they are not really directed at her. All the energy and emotion of my thumping heart spill out for the most trivial of reasons.

"These skis are a part of me!" I shout through hysterical tears, with all the dramatic flourish I can muster. "What more do they want to take from me than every single thing I care about? Wherever we go in this wretched world, I swear I will find the snow again one day and will feel the wind in my face. That is my right as much as the air I breathe! I will not go without them!"

Mama knows how stubborn I can be. She shakes her head in exasperation and walks out of the room.

CHAPTER 15

PURGE IN ITALY JANUARY 1939

have recently sent a letter to Poldi outlining our plans, explaining that I have secured train tickets for his parents and for Mama, Willi, and me to Trieste and also ship's passage to Shanghai and that we only have to get our exit visas approved. Despite the insufferable conditions here, we are in generally good spirits having finally found somewhere to go. I write to Poldi again, pressing him to do all he can to get out of Italy and make his way to China.

I am relieved to receive a letter from him. I tear it open in eager anticipation and sit back in the silent corner of my room to fully immerse myself into his foreign world. I begin to conjure an image of black-haired Italians and glorious, floral landscapes as I read.

"My dear Nini,

"I can only pray that this letter will find you safe. I know what is happening in Vienna as the Nazi scourge washes over the continent. Will we ever awaken from this endless nightmare? I am desperately worried about you and your family and of course my own parents. I am so glad and thankful that you have managed to arrange passage for all of you to get to Shanghai. Dolu and I will do what we can to join you there as soon as possible. For now, however, we are planning to meet you in Trieste when you arrive and to see you all off from there.

"Things are changing here too. As Mussolini has discovered, he is unable to prevail without German support, and he will have to acquiesce to their demands if he is to keep control. Hitler has made it clear that with conquest comes power, the power to recreate the world with himself as supreme ruler and within that new world there can be no Jew. Our eradication is a necessity. The rhetoric becomes more inflamed with every speech he makes. We have heard radio broadcasts from Berlin, his voice blaring with such vigour and resounding hatred we wonder how he can be stopped. And we have seen the reaction in the streets of Milan. Anti-Semitism is more apparent now and we are more aware than ever of the danger.

"I don't really want to worry you as I know that you and your family are struggling with your own terror, but you should know what is happening here."

I read the words voraciously, rushing through the sentences that seem to grow more tense as the letter progresses. It is almost as though he is here speaking to me, the anxiety of his situation growing more and more severe.

"Whatever we Jews have been able to do before to appease our enemies, whether that was conversion to Christianity, intermarriage, or simple concealment of our religious heritage, is no longer enough to protect us. There are new laws that are designed for 'racial cleansing' and Mussolini has declared the Italians a part of the Aryan race to which Jews do not belong. The Pope has done nothing to help us, not even a single word of condemnation. It would have helped, especially here, but we have no one to support us. We stand alone against the world, as always, in meek fear and impotent surrender, but I refuse to give up. If there is anywhere left to run, and as long as there is breath, we have to keep going. I hope that you agree. We are rushing about in a mad flurry trying to get exit documents. We are using every lire to get out."

My eyes scan over the words as I try to grasp the impact of the horrible events taking place in Italy just as they are here in Austria. Then I reread everything again to be certain that he has made the necessary arrangements to get out in time. Minutes are vital these days as governments change with alarming speed all around the world – what will happen if the port of Shanghai is suddenly sealed against us?

"With God's help we will try to escape and make our way to Shanghai just as you are planning to do. Shanghai, China, Nini, just think of it. It seems to me that we are being exiled from humanity, from all the civilized world. Still, with the insanity that has overtaken the entire globe, I suppose we should be thankful that any place, no matter how wicked or far, is willing to accept us. I have to choke back the tears as I write this letter, knowing what we are experiencing here, knowing that what is going on in Vienna is so much worse. Look up at the sky tonight, Nini, look up at the stars and I will be looking at the same blackness, filled with the same faraway torches of light. I believe that we will be together again, somehow. I hope that you believe it too."

At the beginning of January, Stella and Walter set off on the train to Italy after an emotional outpouring of hugs, promises, and tears. Erna, Fritz, and Lily are booked to follow soon. When there is a knock on our door just two days before their scheduled departure, we are alarmed to see the three of them on the step outside, looking terrified.

"We will never get out, never!" Erna cries, coming in and hugging Mama.

"What is going on?" I ask, ushering in Fritz who is holding Lily in his arms.

As they remove their winter overcoats, they begin to tell us what has happened. Fritz turns nervously towards the door or window every few minutes, fidgeting and uneasy. Erna is still distraught so Fritz explains.

"I ran into a fellow I knew at work, not a Jew, so he still has a job there. He told me that the Gestapo came by looking for me. I am on their list and they plan to pick me up and send me to a camp."

"But you already have the tickets and papers, don't you? What do they want?"

"I don't know. I'm on their list, that's all. If they come for me tonight, they will take me away. The tickets are for tomorrow but I won't be allowed to leave if they get me."

"But if you stay here, they will find you," Willi says.

"I know. If not for Erna and the baby, I wouldn't have come. I wouldn't have endangered the rest of you this way. This thing was unexpected and has pushed us into a blind corner. So close to leaving and now it's all up in the air again. We didn't know where else to turn." He looks frantic as he runs his fingers through his hair. "Maybe it would be best for them to stay and I will take my chances with the Gestapo."

At that, Erna's cries grow even more intense and she rushes to Fritz and wraps her arms around him. "We stay together," she sobs. "I'm not leaving you."

Putting on my coat, I tell them, "I am going over to Herr Berger's office. Wait here for me and stay hidden in the room at the back. I'll only be gone a little while."

Reluctantly, I go to ask Herr Berger for his help again. In an unbelievable expression of generosity and concern, he suggests that my sister and her family come to his office and hide there overnight until the next morning when they can board the train and get out of the country.

That evening when all the office staff have left the building, I arrive once more with Erna, Fritz, and Lily. They have no luggage, nothing but the clothes they are wearing. Their household items have already been shipped ahead to the warehouse in Shanghai but they have no belongings with them and cannot return to their apartment to pick up anything else. Feeling like fugitives, we wait for Herr Berger to let us in. He leads us through the dark halls to his office where we listen carefully as he explains what must be done. The three of them are to sleep in his office and the next day at sunrise, before anyone is at work, they are to take a taxi that he has already ordered to take them to the train station. I hold Lily in my arms so tightly that she complains I'm hurting her. I hug Erna and Fritz. We know we might never see each other again, but we still say, *"Auf Wiedersehen"* and hope that we will reunite across the ocean, in China.

CHAPTER 16

FATAL MISCALCULATION
FEBRUARY 1939

Things are in order for the first time in a long while. We have our tickets and the bags are packed. Our trunks have already been approved and sent on ahead, and soon I will see Poldi again in Italy. My sisters are on their way to Shanghai. I am as relaxed as the current situation can allow.

There is a ring at the door one cold afternoon at the beginning of February. When I answer I am shocked to see Herr Berger standing there, his overcoat speckled with bits of newly fallen snow.

"Please, come in. You look upset. Is everything all right?"

My heart is throbbing so hard that I can hardly breathe. Could the Nazis have changed their minds and revoked our passage? What could have happened that would drive Herr Berger to come to the home of Jews in the daylight, endangering himself in this way? Neighbours are looking as they pass, pointing at the strange sight of a well-dressed Austrian standing in the doorway of a Jewish family.

He comes into the entranceway and closes the door behind him. "Here is the story, Fraulein," he begins, taking a deep breath. "Your friend's parents have decided to return the tickets that I was able to get for them. I had a call from someone whom I trust in the office. They had a call from Herr Kosiner that he was planning to give the tickets back. He enquired about their value, how much he could get for them and he is on his way to get the refund."

"No, no," I say in disbelief, "that can't be right. Are you sure? What is there to do now?"

"I have a taxi waiting outside. I think we should get to the ticket office immediately and maybe it will not be too late to stop him."

I pull on my coat and hat and follow Herr Berger out into the street, nearly falling on the snow-covered steps in my hurry.

We insist that the cab driver rush to the shipping company. Engrossed in worry I am silent as we speed through the city. I can scarcely believe this latest development in the continuing trial of nerves and patience. As we approach the curb, I see Herr Kosiner walking towards us. He is leaving the shipping office, and when he sees me jump out of the taxi he waves. He is smiling broadly, surprised and pleased that I have come.

"What has happened, Herr Kosiner? What have you done?"

"Why, Nini, it's wonderful," he answers. "You won't believe how much money they gave me for these tickets."

"But, no, you can't have returned them for a refund. Don't you know how valuable they are?" I am shaking with frustration and dread.

"Nini, you don't understand," he says, "they had an expiry date, and we still don't have our exit visas confirmed. We would have lost the money within a few days. This way, I have it all so I can repay Herr Berger here, and then when we get the visas we can purchase new tickets."

"No, my God, no." Suddenly I notice several Gestapo soldiers heading our way.

"Fraulein Karpel," Herr Berger says, taking me by the arm. He apparently has seen them as well. "It's not safe for you to remain on the street here. Please, Herr Kosiner, I have a taxi. We must go. Kindly come with us and we will take you home."

"Yes, of course, Herr Berger, only please explain to Nini that I did the right thing."

After we have got into the cab again, Herr Kosiner takes his wallet from his inside jacket pocket and hands Herr Berger a roll of bills. With a satisfied grin he says, "You see, I can repay you now. This must have been the right thing to do."

Herr Berger takes the money, shaking his head. "It would have been better, sir, I'm sorry to say, if you had exchanged them for another departure date. It was so difficult to get passage confirmed on any vessel for Shanghai. I don't know how I can manage to do it again. As for the exit documents, I am processing them despite Nazi interference and will have them done in a day or so."

Herr Kosiner hangs his head. He meant to ease the situation but instead he's complicated it in a possibly irreparable way.

"Please, Herr Berger, please, I beg you to try again." I turn to him in desperation.

This day has become one of the most sorrowful yet. Within just a week, we are planning to leave Vienna and now Poldi's parents will not be able to join us. Every day I go to Herr Berger's office and plead with him for news. Every day I return home dejected and miserable. When I see the Kosiners I have to tell them that there are no tickets to be had. Every vessel to leave for Shanghai is fully booked and despite Herr Berger's best efforts we have no way to get them out.

At home we are prepared for our imminent departure, and Mama asks me constantly what will happen to the Kosiners. Then one day, just a few days before we are to leave for Shanghai, I am home alone. Mama and Willi have gone out just for an hour to get some food. There is a knock at the door. One of the Kosiners' neighbours that we know very well is on the doorstep. My heart sinks.

"They have been taken away, Fraulein," the young woman blurts out as soon as I open the door. She is shivering from the cold and distress as I show her in. "The Nazis, miss, the Gestapo. They had no papers, you see, nothing to prove that they were going to leave and the orders are in effect. Any Jew still remaining here with no evidence of immediate departure, well, you know, they are all being hauled away."

Despite my distress, I remember to thank her – she is Gentile and even this visit to us was a danger that she did not have to take. "Helga, thank you for coming – you are brave." But I need to know about the Kosiners. "Do you know where they have been taken?" I ask, trying to think clearly, my hands shaking so badly when I reach for her hands that we are both trembling together.

"Some camp called Dachau, one of those Nazi work camps where they have already sent so many. Maybe you can get them out, miss," she suggests weakly.

"I don't know, Helga, I don't know." I can scarcely think.

When she leaves, I collapse into Papa's big chair. I am distraught and my mind seems paralyzed. For ten minutes or more I sit there, frozen. What to do? What to do?

Finally I call a taxi. Ordinarily I would not squander money on a cab when I could walk or take a streetcar, but this is a disaster. Jews with no designated departure arrangements are being taken away each day, dragged out in full view of the general population.

I head over to Herr Berger's office. When he sees me, he knows the situation is dire. As soon as I walk in, my legs buckle beneath me and I lose consciousness. When I am revived, I see Herr Berger standing above me, obviously very worried.

"What, my dear, what has happened?"

"The Kosiners have been taken away. To Dachau. We can't leave now, you understand? We can't leave now." I start sobbing and can't catch my breath.

Herr Berger insists that I take a drink of cognac and I force it down.

"Now listen to me, Nini," he says, using my name for the first time. "You and your mother and brother will be leaving as planned in three days. You will get out of Vienna. You cannot stay or all of you will be arrested. Do you understand me?"

I nod my head.

"I will do everything possible to get the Kosiners back from the camp, everything that influence and money can do. I will get them out, I promise you. I will get them out," he says, determination in his eyes, his lips tightened in anger and frustration.

I go home once more, dreading having to tell Mama and Willi what has happened today.

CHAPTER 17

DEPARTURE 1939

We are prisoners of time. Each anxious day is spent in meaningless routine, eating whatever is at hand, tidying rooms that we will soon leave, peering out the curtained windows at the streets below to see if there is anything sinister happening. We have little patience to do our needlepoint. We have received no newspapers. No friends come to call and now the days of family visits are past. The radio bristles with static and sometimes the broadcast is clear enough for us to understand the hammering words of Hitler's incitement or the strains of some Viennese waltz but even in that there is no longer pleasure. The "Aryan" Austrians, as the Nazis now call themselves, are outside, still walking about carefree. They salute the Nazi soldiers, and some raise arms casually in patriotic greeting. "Heil Hitler," they say. Their children, well fed and grinning, are cherished angels to be petted and spoiled while Jewish children huddle out of the sunlight with nothing but hunger and despair.

With anxious anticipation we count the days to the date on our train tickets. Now it is here and the moment is bittersweet. Willi and I watch Mama closing the door of our home for the last time. She hesitates for a minute, wondering whether there is any purpose in locking the door as she usually does. Nothing has sense any more, not even the simple act of closing and locking one's door. For a person who has lived her life by convention and regulation, she is caught in a fog of disorientation. She seems uncertain about what to do next and remains stopped and immobile. Her eyes are focused on the number fifty-six on the door, the address that has represented safety for all of her married life. This was her home, the place where she gave birth to each of her children, where her husband died, and where, finally, the Nazis violated her sanctuary and stole her life.

I take her gently by the arm as if we were just going out for a stroll. "Come along, Mama, it's a fine day for a trip," I say, although the sky is heavy with dark, furling clouds and the damp air is holding back the rain just as we are holding our tears, unwilling to let the first drops fall in fear of the storms that will follow.

A taxi takes us to the train. Driving through the streets of Vienna we stare silently out the windows, each absorbed in our own memories as landmarks and favourite haunts flit by. At the station we walk together, Willi standing on one side, and I on the other, our arms linked to Mama, anchored to her for strength, we to her and she to us.

Our train will take us from Vienna to the port at Trieste where we are to board a ship for the long journey to the Far East. I am hoping to see Poldi at the station, but dreading his reaction when he realizes that his parents are not with us. His and Dolu's documents are not yet settled so they cannot join us, but they will come to see us off at the ship.

Clasping our precious documents tightly, we await inspection before we are allowed to board. We remain in line, bundled in our woollen coats, frightened, cold, and desolate. Our exhaled breath hangs suspended in the air. This is the only chance we will have to escape with our lives. We have witnessed a plague of death and have been spared.

Others who did not wait for the Nazis to slaughter them chose another route. From those around us, huddled together in the grey mist, we hear the whispered names of friends, neighbours, loved ones who had turned the gas on in their homes to take their own lives, to end the struggle they could no longer endure. They breathed their last as they stood by their windows, hand in hand, watching the temples burn and the streets of Vienna become a furnace of smoke and scorching flame. Some question if those were the wiser.

We wait in line for hours in the wet cold. Steam rises in thick clumps from the trains chugging and lurching into the station, their metallic fumes engulfing us. The uniformed men standing guard treat us with coarse brutality. Bit by bit we have been degraded and dehumanized. This is the systematic destruction of the minds, bodies, and finally the souls of a proud and courageous people. Nazi soldiers shout commands and demand our documents which are stamped, one by one. Every bag is searched to be sure we are not taking anything of value from the country; we must show papers that prove all taxes have been paid in full.

We are treated with revulsion and disrespect, a source of ridicule for the bored soldiers who think nothing of what they are doing to us. These men have the power to decide what we can take with us and what must be left behind. In the end, we are allowed one suitcase each besides the possessions that we shipped ahead and which we hope to see when we reach China. We have nothing but the clothes we can pack in our valises and things we can carry – more clothing, some toiletries, and other necessities but nothing of much value. The rest is confiscated. We are each given three English pounds, the only currency we have, then we're allowed, at last, to board the train that will take us across the Austro-Italian border and then to Trieste.

As the train pulls away from Vienna and I see the snowy hills of my youth receding behind us, it is too much to bear. The joy of my childhood, the sense of belonging that was always so important to me, has been taken away forever. I will not be able to visit Papa's grave again. Even this tiny morsel of his memory has been wrenched from me. How dismal the future appears and how suddenly old and tired I feel.

I think of my sisters and their husbands, who have gone ahead. Will we ever see them again, I wonder. And Poldi's parents, the source of such pain, have been left behind, alone and frightened, taken to a camp where they will be mistreated, of that I am sure. Once again, a wave of sorrow and guilt washes over me.

The train rocks and swerves from side to side as it snakes along the curving tracks that are taking us farther and farther from Vienna. Mama is asleep in her seat, her head slumped on her chest, her handbag resting on her lap.

At the border, military officials demand to see our passports, in which we have been listed as displaced persons. Each little book is stamped with the huge letter "J" for Jew, branding us wherever we will go, ensuring that it will be difficult to blend into another culture. We are marked and vilified, categorized as pariahs.

CHAPTER 18

THE VOYAGE 1939

The train slows to a halt at the vast station in Trieste. My face brightens at the sight of Poldi, who is waiting patiently for our arrival. From my seat by the window I am first to see him standing there. I wave madly and finally catch his eye. Our meeting is a mixture of emotions, joy and sadness at once, knowing we will soon be parted again.

"Thank God, Nini, thank God you're here," he says hugging me tightly first, then Mama and Willi. Dolu is brimming too, glad that we are here, but then he looks around and asks, "Where are our parents?"

Poldi looks at me and before I can say a thing he seems to know what has happened. His eyes fill with tears and his face shows all his wrenching pain. "Tell me, Nini," he says, "what happened?"

I explain what has happened and we all try to comfort them but they are devastated and inconsolable. We have to keep moving along with the crowd that is pushing ahead towards the dock, but this is not the departure that I had anticipated for so long, one of hope and joy. Now we are swamped in sadness again.

I try my best to ease their worries although the outcome of the loss of the precious tickets is so hard to explain. Dolu begins to rail against Herr Berger, blaming him for the outcome, but I stop him. "Herr Berger has vowed to do everything possible to get them out of the camp and book them on a ship to Shanghai. I'm going to write him as soon as we arrive – I'm sure he'll succeed. Don't give up hope."

Poldi and Dolu help us with our things as we move with the others hurrying from the train to the ship. We trudge through the high-ceilinged building, a troupe of vagabonds, our possessions on our backs or in our valises and bags. After all, we each have something of particular personal value, and although I have sent my skis on ahead there are many others who are labouring with musical instruments of various kinds, ladies dressed in fur coats and hats who are obviously hot and uncomfortable, teetering on high-heeled shoes and struggling with bulky bundles. Others are carrying crying babies or clutching the little hands of irritable toddlers. Down a stairway we go, a few hundred of us of varying ages but a common language and purpose.

We are most concerned about Mama. She is short of breath as we try to keep up with the rest of the crowd. When we emerge from the building and the sea air blows through our hair, we take deep breaths. We have come this far at least, and an escape seems possible. All the terror we experienced is behind us as we look out at the blue water.

Poldi has his arm around my shoulder hugging me close to him as we stare out at the sea, both of us seeming so insignificant against its immensity. We will not say a final good bye, but rather *Auf Wiedersehen* – "until we meet again." We vow to each other that we will be together once more and that somehow on the other side of the world we will re-unite and face the future. We embrace, unwilling to let go, clinging to one another with utter desperation. A shiver of emotion slips from one trembling body to the other. He promises to meet us in Shanghai as soon as he is able to get everything approved for his departure, and he will write as soon as I notify him of our location. He shakes hands with Willi, then they hug and he hugs Mama too. We are all teary-eyed.

Poldi lifts my hand to his lips and I feel a tear fall onto my fingers. He gently kisses my hands, leans to press his lips against my forehead and then mouth, trying to sustain a brave smile although his eyes are glistening. My own tears have no such restraint and pour freely down my cheeks until my collar is damp. I know these may be our last moments together.

"With all my heart, Nini, I pray we will survive to meet again in Shanghai. I will be thinking of you every minute until I can see your face and hold your hand again."

It seems more than I can bear. "I don't know if I'm strong enough to endure this hardship, Poldi. I haven't travelled like you – Vienna is the only home I've had. China's so far away – how can I live in such a place?"

Poldi comforts me. "You are strong, the strongest woman I have ever met. You can do anything you set your mind to. Be brave and watch over your mother and brother. And, Nini, have faith and wait for me. I will find you."

I nod my head in acceptance but can say nothing more.

A massive white ship, called the *Conte Biancamano* from the renowned Lloyd Triestino fleet of luxury liners, is anchored, awaiting us in the harbour. The name of that ship, our vessel to salvation, is quickly imprinted on our minds. This, we are aware, is the only chance we have to flee. Looking out to the horizon, we face our future somewhere on the other side of the turbulent waters.

It's time to leave. The loud horns of the ship blare their warning call, summoning us to board and we must go. Our luggage is taken aboard first. Contained inside are the salvaged bits of our lives. We have become just like the refugees we had seen so often trudging into Vienna. Willi and I hold onto Mama, her head down, her eyes focused on the steps ahead. Each of us is linked to an arm, clinging tightly to steady her as she makes her way onto the ship. She is concentrating on the task of setting one foot ahead of the other, grasping us for balance. Wobbly and struggling to catch her breath, she is exhausted from the strenuous journey. We are concerned about her increasing physical and mental frailty. At the age of fifty-eight she appears so much older, years added by the traumas that have befallen her since Papa's death and the devastation of the Nazi scourge. We fear that being uprooted so brutally may be more than she can endure. We tighten our grip on her arms when we sense her weakening and try to fortify and restore her courage for what is yet to come.

We crane our necks and lean forward against the railing, waving to Poldi and Dolu, who are standing below. Poldi's arm swings widely back and forth to be sure I can see him, but the smile on his face is forced. The ship's throbbing engine and loud farewell blasts signal our departure, and soon the port shrinks away in the distance.

We settle in small clean cabins and soon find that the food is good. After the ordeal that we experienced in Europe, it is the most peace and normalcy we have had for some time. Still this is hardly a holiday. We are stateless refugees aboard a ship to a strange land. The journey, a month-long stretch of over seven thousand miles, will take us from Trieste to Alexandria, through the Suez Canal, then to Bombay and Hong Kong and finally to Shanghai.

In a kind of surrealistic dream, we float upon the endless ocean on a fantasy ship where music plays and waiters in tuxedos serve the meals. The dining room is panelled in richly grained wood, heavy and smooth. Crystal chandeliers sparkle, and the handsome Italian ship's stewards in their gold-braided white uniforms smile white-toothed grins. They greet the regular passengers with a flourish of deep bows and cheery broken English while we lower-class outcasts are shuffled away in careless disregard.

The non-Jewish families keep their distance from us, offering no words of encouragement or hand of friendship. Our station in life has been determined by the Nazi decrees. The "J" stamped on all our documents might as well have been branded onto our skin for all the world to see.

We are glad to find other passengers from Austria and become closest with those who speak the same language. The current topic of conversation is money – and the urgent need to accumulate it. Those of us who were able to conceal anything of value, at great risk, are making good use of the time on board to find buyers and convert whatever few assets we have into American dollars or British pounds. Aware that the pittance we were given when we left Austria will not be enough to preserve us from starvation, we approach the wealthy passengers and endure their disdain. They are aware of their position of superiority and ours of desperation and know that they will be able to accumulate rare valuables for bargain prices. We sell anything we can manage to dispose of, from the coats on our backs to a few pieces of family jewellery sewn into our garments. The Germans intended that we would have nothing on which to live, that death would be our certain destiny. It is only desperate ingenuity and a string of tiny miracles that can save us.

"Mama, look, I have some money, American dollars." I show her a few dirty papers in my hand. "I sold my coat to a lady on the upper deck."

"Good, Nini," she says, examining the meagre compensation. "I suppose woollen coats will be of no use in Shanghai and even the most basic food is sure to cost us more than those bastards allowed us."

We gather together in groups reminiscing about the "Old Vienna" and comparing our experiences through the Nazi occupation. Some tell incredible stories of what we can expect to find in Shanghai. We listen to the tales in entranced horror.

"It is a port without laws," one of the passengers begins, "where criminals are allowed to run free and butcher people without cause or fear of punishment. You must strap your money and valuables to your body or you will be robbed at knife-point."

Others agree and there is an abundance of advice, all of it terrifying. "You must never trust one of them as they are all thieves. The Chinese are fearsome savages who will kill you for the sport and then steal everything you possess. If they don't murder you, you'll soon die from the food they cook. They eat anything that crawls on the earth and live in filth."

"And you know," another adds, "all kinds of diseases are rampant. At least we have our own doctors with us or we would all perish within a week in that wilderness."

Our eyes widen in trepidation. "However will we manage to live in such a place?" we ask.

"That's one thing about us Jews," another fellow interrupts, a mocking smile curving up the corners of his mouth. "Although not one of us has ever set foot in China, nor in fact has ever met a single Chinese person, we are all experts on the country and the entire race! Everyone has an opinion. We know everything there is to know, no questions asked."

We laugh in a spurt of unexpected amusement at the truth of his words. Despite the turmoil of our lives, we can still find some humour in the moment which allows our spirits and brittle tensions to ease. The lightened mood has supplied a temporary break from the memory of what has driven us from our homes and why we are here.

A young woman about my age is seated next to me on the long wooden slatted benches that are fastened to the side of the ship. She turns to me after the discussion we have overheard, obviously shaken about the fears and warnings of life in Shanghai.

"I'm so frightened of that place and, you see, I am alone. How will I ever survive?" she asks.

"What can we do? We will have to face whatever awaits us," I reply.

Perhaps fearing she was rude, she introduces herself. "My name is Herta Weinstein," she says, her hand extended.

"I am Nini Karpel." I take her hand in mine.

During the voyage she and I meet many times to talk about the lives left behind. She tells me she was brought up in a good family with prospects for a secure and happy life, engaged to be married to a young man, a lawyer, who was arrested by the Nazis and taken away, never to be seen again. She is still distraught about the experience, her eyes moistening each time she speaks about her sorrow and the uncertainty of her future. Her mother had died years before, and her father passed away from a long illness only weeks before they were to leave Vienna.

After the Nazis confiscated all their possessions, she struggled to save enough to book passage on this ship. She has nothing but the clothes on her back. Her fingernails, I have noticed as she wrings her fingers anxiously, are bitten down in nervous tension. Her pallid, narrow face is framed by wispy blond curls, giving her a fragile and vulnerable look. Her lips are parched dry. We share our thoughts and worries and promise one another to keep in touch in Shanghai. At mealtimes, she is seated at our table as she is alone and I have asked Mama to allow her to join us. Although the food on board is wonderful and beautifully served, Herta picks at whatever is placed before her, immersed in her own lonely thoughts and unable to swallow more than a few morsels at a time.

After we pass through the Suez Canal and sail down the Red Sea, weeks pass and we see nothing but sea spreading before us. Staring out to the horizon so far ahead, I think of the home left behind in Vienna, the slavish discipline and concern with customs, with order and civility, manners and respect. I remember my relatives, so preoccupied with perfect details, confident that the Austrian homeland would always protect us. I wonder what has become of them. We fear they have been killed by the Germans, but no one wants to believe it. Mama hopes she will see her family members again, or at least that they are still alive.

Most of the refugees expect that Shanghai will be a temporary stopover, just until passage to a civilized place can be arranged. We discuss events in Europe, getting our news daily from reports on the radio. There are conflicting opinions about what the future holds, but underlying all the talk about European affairs, we have our own specific concerns. How, we all wonder, will the outcome affect the Jews? No country has made much effort to help or protect us or to offer sanctuary.

The ship slices through the shimmering blue-green water and foamy white peaks. The wind lashes a salty spray against our faces. We are delighted with the romping dolphins that emerge from the depths and arch in curves, splashing, playing in carefree abandon and allowing us to dream that there may yet be a better life even for us. I think of Poldi's last goodbye. I miss his smile and encouraging words, his stories and his hand on mine. Half a world will separate us soon, and I wonder with a piercing sting of melancholy regret if we will ever meet again.

We are aware of the weather growing warmer, and we can see and feel the effects of the changing climate. The water, reflecting the sun's glowing power, is coated in a layer of molten silver. There is a feeling of suspended reality, a zone of dreams, disconnected from the confines of earthbound mortals, somewhere apart from reality. When the sun sets on the huge expanse of the Pacific, the sky and water turn flaming red, and we watch fascinated as the scorching orb disappears slowly into the darkening sea.

The ship glides forward through the night and I find myself lulled into a sound sleep. The possible fulfilment of wishes for peace and security allows me to surrender my weary body and disturbed mind to a silent rest. Like an infant being rocked in its cradle, I doze undisturbed. There may yet be a safe haven ahead.

CHAPTER 19

SHANGHAI 1939

From the vast Pacific our ship glides into the China Sea, then enters the broad mouth of the Yangtze River. The river extends over three thousand miles, its muddy currents winding through the heart of China. We stare agape, pointing and gasping at the sights before us, exhilarated, frightened, sensing the tingle of discovery and entrapment at once. The ship can only move ahead, being swallowed as though it were entering into the mouth of a giant beast. We dare not look back to where we have been, knowing there is no way of return.

Miles out from the shoreline, we crowd together at the railing of the ship's deck, our necks craning forward, jostling one another for a better view of our new destination. Before the image is clear, our senses are already attacked by the foul odour of garbage and raw sewage. Everyone is moaning, holding hands over mouths and noses to keep out the offensive smell. The cooling breeze of the ocean behind us has dissipated and we begin to feel the oppressive heat hovering like a heavy blanket in the air. Though we are still far from the Whang Po Wharf, the water is no longer the clear azure of the open ocean, but has turned to a murky stew, littered with debris. The huge Chinese population cannot be confined to the land mass and spills over into the sea. Strange houseboats, called sampans, their sails rounded as they fill with the wind, dot the sloshing mucky water. They are loaded with women and children, baked brown from the sun, clothed scantily in rags. Fussing babies howl for mother's milk. The odours of rancid cooking oil and dead fish accost us as the ship drifts closer to the dock. Men are standing on the pier, openly urinating into the stinking water, laughing boisterously. Are they congratulating themselves for the clever greeting they have provided for this new boatload of unwanted foreigners?

As the huddle of European refugees piles down the gangway onto the shore, everyone is visibly ill from the powerful sights and smells. In our heavy woollen suits and overcoats, some still in furs and stylish hats, we all seem suddenly so incongruous and inappropriate. Debarking from the ship and setting foot for the first time on the wharf, I am filled with overwhelming nausea. Heavy, sickly odours attack my nostrils. Thick hordes of people swarm the pier and coalesce into one throbbing dark mass, a monster with hundreds of wriggling arms and legs that surrounds and threatens to devour us whole. Staring at my white skin and round blue eyes, the filthy, ragged strangers laugh and cajole in their unintelligible language. I cringe as they stretch bony fingers to point and tug at my foreign clothing. We have chosen life over death and now find ourselves in a place that we hardly believed existed, the distant underbelly of the globe, a mysterious blob on the map, China.

I think of my beautiful things packed away in my dowry trunk and all the other belongings we left behind or were taken by the Nazis. Then I look around at these peculiar people bending to spit disgusting gobs on the sidewalk, the stench from the river rising as the heat of the day chokes like a cord around our necks. Standing on rotting wooden planks, I retch into the rank water and wonder if we have fled the peril in Europe only to perish in a hell never imagined.

Herta waves to me as she steps onto one of the many rickety buses, jammed in among a crowd of other dazed people, to be taken to one of the charity homes – *Heime* – that have been established to await the sudden influx of impoverished refugees. We have been told on ship about these places, which have been established by Jewish relief agencies, but they are the least desirable places, reserved for those with no resources or connections. As she has no money and no family, Herta is one of hundreds who are shuttled away to the buildings that have been converted to vast crowded dormitories to shelter the most destitute of us all. I see her grim face staring back at me and I wonder for a moment what will become of her as the bus rumbles out of sight. But then, huddling with Mama and Willi, my thoughts return quickly to our own situation. We remain standing together, our eyes flicking over the mob of strange faces, hoping for a better reception for ourselves, eager to reunite with our family who have already arrived here and will surely be trying to find us and make contact. We dare to dream of an improved life but are aware we have little reason to expect much. Mama's face is contorted with a mixture of anxiety, worry, and discomfort. We are all unnerved yet feel some faint satisfaction that we have outrun the Nazi horde.

Lined up on the dock to meet us are a number of Christian missionaries – a row of pale women, their hair pulled back severely from their faces, wiping their perspiring foreheads with white handkerchiefs and smiling weakly as they approach. Heavy chains hang from their necks, each with a large gold cross securely weighted on their chests. We are weaving like drunkards as we feel the first solid ground beneath our feet after so long at sea, and stumble unsteadily towards them. With mingled dread and relief, we accept their welcome, because there is no other.

We feel like lost children, uncertain of what to do next, waiting for someone to take us by the hand and lead us to a safe home. Unquestioning, we go with them. We and our stack of baggage are loaded haphazardly into open trucks, then we climb aboard, many of the elderly struggling for a space. We are crushed together, standing like cattle, rocking with the movement of the vehicle, holding onto one another's hands for support and encouragement, not knowing where we will be taken, simply hoping it will be to some refuge where we can stay in peace.

Our first impression of the city engages all our senses. We look in dismay at the dark masses of people, the sidewalks thick with pedestrians. Individuals break from the herd and go running in varying directions with determination and purpose. There is a powerful mixture of odours from bodies pressed too closely together and the peculiar aromas coming from the food being cooked in steaming pots out in the open. Our expectations of a bizarre world are exceeded at every turn as our vehicle rumbles through the streets, and as we are being jostled about we observe all manner of wares being loudly hawked – tiny bright-feathered birds twittering in bamboo cages, frogs croaking in others, eels writhing in barrels and live carp sloshing in tubs. Our stomachs bob up and down and many of us are sick along the way, fainting, vomiting, overcome by it all, and still the truck does not stop until we reach our destination.

We arrive at an old church being used to house those like us, considered transient refugees. As we enter, our shoes click against the wooden plank floor and the sound echoes within the vaulted ceilings of the hallway. There is a smell of damp timber and old books. We are settled in a small room, exhausted from the journey. Still in our travel clothes, we drop onto the cots that we have been assigned, thankful to be on solid ground. We are fatigued but unable to truly accept the reality of our escape. Besides our meagre possessions, we have brought something with us from home: the constant sense of apprehension that still haunts us.

I examine the surroundings, so strange, so foreign. At least clean sheets and solid walls separate us from the strange and hostile city outside. Huge wooden crosses are mounted everywhere around us. In the sparsely furnished rooms, the crucifixes are all the more startling. We gaze up at the carvings of an emaciated figure of Christ, every rib visible beneath the skin, arms outstretched, nails driven through the palms and feet from where blood drips for eternity. The representation of tortured agony only reminds us of the death and pain we have fled, and we are repelled by it. We feel our alienation here all the more because of our non-Christianity, our tangible Jewishness.

Our belongings arrive a day or so after our arrival but of the four trunks that we had in Vienna, only one has reached us. When Willi manages to pry the lock open, I am relieved to see that it is the one containing my skis. Mama and Willi are disappointed, though, that most of what they had packed has not come, and after considerable efforts to locate the missing baggage we accept that the rest is gone and will never be retrieved.

We live with the sisters at first and work for our food and shelter but must endure their daily efforts at conversion. We have seen them pack care baskets for Jewish hospitals but everything is wrapped in pages of the gospel and none is complete without a pamphlet with a cross on the cover. Having survived the ordeal of Hitler's attempt to purge our faith, we are not tempted to abandon it here.

As soon as possible we make inquiries about our family members, asking the sisters to check their rosters of recent arrivals, and within a few days we are elated to learn that they did pass through this same place and were then relocated. Finally we are able to make contact with our family when one of the sisters mentions that Erna is working at a nearby convent, a position that was arranged for her. When, at last, the whole family comes through the doors, tears of suppressed anxiety flood down our cheeks. We hold onto each other for long minutes and Mama, her body heaving with emotion, clutches each one to her.

"Where have you been all this time, tell us," Mama says. "And how is my little granddaughter?" she asks, swinging Lily up in her arms and hugging the giggling bundle of spindly legs and arms, freckled just like Fritz.

"What a time we've had, Mama," Erna replies. "We were first put in a refugee *Heim*, that's what they call the Jewish shelters, but they are anything but a home."

"That's for sure," Fritz adds. "But we applied for an apartment and because of Lily we were given some preference and we have a small place in French Town – well, that's what we all call the French Concession. Shanghai is divided up into sections but a lot of the refugees end up there."

"We have an apartment now too," Stella says. "Walter managed to sell a lot of the things that we brought from Vienna – some watches and a camera that he had packed away that the Nazis didn't take. I had fur coats, too, that arrived in our trunks. We sold them and with the money we have a large enough place that we have been able to rent part of it and get an income."

"Good for you, Stella," Mama says proudly with a smile.

Erna turns to me. "You know, Nini, I have a job teaching needlepoint at the convent. Do you want me to put in a word for you?"

"I don't know. Maybe I can find something else." I think I would be unhappy in the convent and not nearly as good as Erna at the needlepoint.

"All right, Nini, but the nuns have been good to us. I think you could consider coming to work there – and you will need the money soon," Erna answers.

I recognize the truth in her practical approach. Reluctantly, I reply, "Well, I suppose you're right. I'll work there for a while but you know I don't trust them."

Something about the way Erna and Fritz have exchanged a knowing look and turned to one another alarms me. "What is it? Did something happen?"

They tell us that missionaries are especially drawn to Lily, only three years of age. Some Jewish children have been surrendered to the Church for "safekeeping," and their offers to preserve her from hunger or death are a real temptation. Erna and Fritz are terrified for her safety. "Nini, please understand," Erna pleads, "we are so frightened that she will die too if we are taken away. At least the sisters will protect her life. You are so sure but we are not. They have promised to guard her if only we give them the right."

"It may be the only thing to do," Fritz says, desperation in his voice, "the only way to spare her."

"Now?" I ask, my voice shaking in anger. "Now, when we have reached a safe shore, you will give your baby to them?"

Holding the pieces of the family together is becoming more and more the driving passion of my life, just as it has been to Mama, and I am outraged by their suggestions. I know my sisters consider me high strung and given to dramatic outbursts, but the thought of losing a child in this way is unbearable. I don't want to hear any explanations or excuses. I can see nothing but the travesty about to be committed and become incensed at the idea of giving Lily away. I rant uncontrollably at the parents, who stare at me in sorrowful desperation. "No!" I scream. "No! Don't you understand? If you sign away her life to them, you will never get her back. They will make sure of it. Every Jewish soul, especially a young child 'saved' is a celebration for their cause. You will not give her away!"

Finally they accept my argument and, nodding their heads in agreement, doubt and fear filling their eyes, they promise they will keep her no matter the consequences. I sigh in relief as I look at the child playing contentedly with her rag doll. If the past is destroyed, I think, we can at least hope for the future, a new generation of this family.

When we were travelling to this alien place, above all else we had hoped, and truly expected, that we would find peace here. We were prepared for a strange culture, poverty, and struggle, but were unaware that we would also be plunged into the midst of a fierce war. We soon discover that we have been tossed into a battle zone, the centre of a brutal conflict that began in 1937. Japanese forces have been stationed here for the last two years, waging a bloody attempt to conquer and annex China. The hatred between the two peoples is almost tangible. Japanese soldiers in full military attire, heavily armed with rifles equipped with dagger-sharp bayonets, march through the streets. Sporadic gunfire is heard everywhere, and the havoc of war surrounds us again. Rape, pillage, and murder are common daily activities in this battle zone, and the civilian toll of misery lies, as always, in the wake of the skirmishes.

We are awakened one morning by the sound of shouting voices and ear-piercing screams. Willi and I, still in our sleepwear, join other befuddled refugees and a number of the sisters who run into the courtyard to see about the commotion. There we discover a gruesome display before us. On the gate's spiked rails are mounted about a dozen severed heads of Chinese who were captured through the night by their Japanese enemies, decapitated and impaled like slaughtered deer as a warning. No one could mistake the message that this sight was meant to impart, a graphic show to all that Japan is prepared to murder every Chinese, if need be, to bring the country to surrender and gain the control they are determined to secure over this country.

I stand very close to Willi, our arms hanging leaden at our sides. Then we cover our eyes with our hands and turn our faces away in revulsion and horror. With the grotesque image still fresh in our minds, we rush back into the Missionary Home. The children have been hustled inside by the sisters and Mama is still in her room. We are haunted by the grisly sight of the severed heads, dried blood caked around the vacant eyes and open mouths, expressions of anguish and terror frozen beyond death. We are shuddering in shock and nausea and try to blot out the sight we have just witnessed, a vision of such cruelty that I cannot wipe it from my mind.

The bloody conflicts between the Japanese and their Chinese "cousins" rage day and night with many more such exhibitions of savagery on both sides. Hatred burns all around us here just as it did in Europe. I feel as though we live in a little fortress, bricks and stones forming an isolation from the harsh conditions beyond. We work at the many chores needed to keep the mission functioning, each of us completing assigned daily tasks, scrubbing laundry, peeling vegetables, sweeping floors, and collapsing in exhaustion at the end of the day on our cots. We speak to the others who come and go on a regular basis, but there is no real time to establish friendships between the monotonous work and the transitory nature of those we encounter. Besides, when we have any free time we try to arrange to meet with our family again. Mama helps too, doing the less rigorous jobs of setting tables for meal time and clearing up afterwards with others of her age. She is finding it difficult to adapt to the new life and quite often drifts into depression. We try to cheer her but find it more and more challenging to come up with words of encouragement. She has said she has no more strength left to exist here or to start again somewhere else, that another voyage would kill her.

In despair, I turn to Willi. "What do you suppose we can do about Mama?" I ask him.

"You mean about her mood?" he asks.

"It's more than a mood. Her life has been so changed and she has fought so hard for so long that it seems all of the spirit is gone, used up like firewood." Our trials have worn us all down and Willi has nothing to offer but a shrug.

"What is there to do?" he answers. "We have to worry about survival first. If this damned war ever stops and we can get her to a safe place, things might be better for us all." His voice falters, and I can see he is as uncertain as I am. "If not... I don't know what will happen to any of us."

The most senior and respected of the missionaries is Mother Laula, an American. Her pale blue eyes are buried in a lined face, and her grey hair is pinned up at the back of her head. She wears severe and drab clothing, but her garb is a contrast to her soft smile and the brightness in her eyes. Her age is indeterminate but she seems to have absorbed ages of misery and pain into her very soul. A settled reserve surrounds her like a shroud, a quiet acceptance of the things she has witnessed throughout her life, and an unshakeable faith in her God that give her the courage and strength she needs. Although she has seen hellish things, she devoutly believes in goodness, salvation, and heaven. She has shown us more genuine kindness than we have encountered in a long time, and we have begun to trust her and to value her wisdom.

One day, I find myself seated beside her. We are having our regular break from our routine at midday; it's a quiet time to read or talk. As she and I share some hot tea and a few biscuits, I find myself letting my guard down a bit, which is unusual for me. The circumstances of my life have created a suspicious nature. It is not easy for me to trust, and I tend to keep my feelings to myself, but when Mother Laula asks me how I am dealing with my life here in Shanghai, I speak frankly and ask her the things that are most pressing in my mind.

"How do you live here?" I ask her. "How is it possible to see this bloodshed and agony day after day and still keep your faith?"

She's not startled by my questions. She's heard them before from others who've been displaced, and she's a paragon of patience. She looks at me and I wonder what she must be thinking, that my clothes are starting to show signs of wear, that my fingers are reddened by the harsh soap that we use and the disinfectant that burns the flesh, that my hair needs to be fixed. I soon realize that none of these matter to her at all and I blush at my own vanity. She has gone beyond the outer appearances of the refugees and is looking deeper into our souls, trying to help those who have no one and to offer an explanation for the turmoil of our lives.

"After a while," she responds, "everything becomes commonplace. You have to accept the existence of evil as well as good in this world. For every new day that God grants us, we must do our best to live. Each one of us is destined to die as God sees fit. Our lives are in His hands. You must preserve your faith in His power and give in to His will. There is no other way. Without such faith, there would be no explanation for the horrors that we have seen. Without faith, we could have no reason to live."

"But what do you do if your faith wavers?" I ask.

"You have to bury your doubts as I have done and surrender to a higher power. I still believe in the virtues I was taught despite all I have witnessed and endured. Our lives are meant to be difficult and how we overcome our hardships is the true test of our faith. Charity is a reward of its own, for the pure sake of helping your fellow man."

Her mention of charity is a sudden jolt. It is as if Papa were suddenly speaking to me through this woman.

"That is something which is most important to me," she continues. "When a beggar asks for mercy and a few pennies, I believe that one must give with an open hand and open heart. Don't ask his reasons, for whether his need is food, or liquor, or even opium is not for us to judge. The Lord will judge him when the time comes, just as He will measure each of us."

I am still uncertain. Everything that was important in my life has been cast aside and negated. There has already been so much violence that it is not easy to preserve any faith. We have no time to ponder the mysteries of life and death here where simple survival has become the only possible goal. But, the next day when a ragged child offers his grimy hand to me and beseeches me for help, I drop a coin into it and watch him patter away. I understand the lesson taught to me by Mother Laula and remember Papa once more.

I am soon put to work with Erna, who is already at the Convent, not far from the Missionary Home where we live. I go there every day to teach the skill of European needlepoint to Chinese women. We also help in the kitchen in the preparation of meals for the Catholic sisters and for the many refugees who depend on this food to survive. The fare is meagre. It consists mainly of rice, washed over and over to remove bacteria and insects and then cooked in huge vats. Drinking water must be boiled to make it potable. We are shown the trick of adding a drop of red iodine as a disinfectant to water used for washing food. There are other supplies like powdered milk, dehydrated eggs, coarse bread, and thin jam that are used to feed us all.

One day while I am at work in the kitchen, one of the nuns calls me to come along with her. She needs help with some items to be brought from the pantry. I follow her through some heavy wooden doors to a small corridor and then another set of doors that I have not seen before. When she opens them, I am stunned at the sight within.

Before me is a wondrous cold storeroom, shelves laden floor to ceiling with thick yellow circles of cheeses, pounds of butter wrapped individually in white paper, smoked sausages and hams hanging from hooks, plucked chickens and geese, their necks dangling loosely, all lined up in bountiful splendour. There are cans of Belgian cocoa and South American coffee. The array is dazzling and hardly believable. Not since Vienna, before the war, have I seen such abundance. Here in Shanghai, people everywhere are scrounging for morsels and barely subsisting on the most minimal supplies, yet here, in remarkable decadence, concealed and hoarded from view, lies a feast for royalty.

"Sister," I stammer, "who are all these things for?"

Her grey eyes are steady and bright, her smile unwavering as she replies, "Well, of course, for good and faithful Christians. You could so easily convert here with our help and free yourself from the curse of your birth. If you accept Jesus Christ, Our Saviour, you will find salvation and He will provide all of life's rewards to you in this world and eternal peace in the next, for you and for your suffering family. You will not know hunger again. Think of your elderly mother and of your sister's child, if not just of yourself. Life would be so much easier for you all if you would extricate yourself from the blot of sin and heresy that has been the cause of all your hardship."

Although my stomach, at that very moment, is so torn with hunger that it feels as if wild dogs are tearing at my insides, I face her placid stare with my own. Her words have startled me, torn me from my state of frozen immobility and given me courage. I remember Poldi's brave words and Mama's proud defiance before the Nazis and even my encounter with the girl in the schoolyard who had taunted me so many years before and I respond, my face flushed with rage, "If the Nazis, in their cruelty, could not change me, then you with your oily words and temptations will not either. I was born a Jew and whether I must die tomorrow or in many years as an old woman, it will be as a Jew!"

Her smile turns grim as she ushers me out of the pantry without another word and closes the heavy doors with an unforgiving slam.

CHAPTER 20

THE FRENCH CONCESSION 1939

We have spent merely three months in the Missionary Home but we've found the atmosphere of the place suffocating. Usually refugees are sheltered for just a short time and then expected to make their own way. New immigrants arrive while others are leaving in a constant flow. Because we have resisted conversion, we expect no further contact and no aid from the Church when we go. Despite Mama's worries and foreboding, Willi and I insist that we must leave and set out on our own. We have promised her we will manage to find work and will be able to support ourselves.

The Jewish relief organizations in Shanghai are overloaded with the sudden influx of so many needy. As there is no other solution, we stand in line with the others to ask for initial aid in finding a small flat where we can live and some rations to keep us from starvation. The feeling of such poverty weighs the refugees down like a physical burden. Heads are bent, faces are dour. With the few remaining pennies from the pittance allotted to us on our departure from Vienna, we are virtually destitute. The Nazis have managed, as they had planned, to send us into the world as beggars.

I have been in contact with Herr Berger, and in a brief letter to Poldi I bring him up to date on Herr Berger's progress, as well as our own.

"Dear Poldi,

"I can only pray that you and Dolu are still all right. What a terrible time we are enduring. Will we still awaken in our own warm beds and laugh at the nightmare that we have had? No, of course this is all too real.

"Herr Berger has still assured me he will be able to rescue your parents and that he will get safe passage for them to escape from Vienna. I hope he is right.

"I worry about Mama too. She has been despondent since we arrived here. The pervasive poverty of the Chinese, the overpowering heat that we have never before experienced, the strange faces that surround us are all too much for her. I am also homesick for Vienna, but I am trying very hard to deal with this place.

"We have decided to leave the Missionary Home. The missionaries and the nuns at the convent where we work are kind enough but they want us to convert. How could we do that? They wanted to keep Lily but I was adamant in my opposition to such an idea, and so she is still with us. Now Erna and Fritz as well as Stella and Walter have moved into cramped apartments in the French Concession.

"At this point I don't know where we will be. Willi and I will try to get employment and support ourselves and Mama. We will go to the Jewish relief agencies for help. If you can escape from Italy and do arrive in Shanghai, go to the agencies to look for us. I will try to write again but hope, with God's help, that it will not be too long before I see you here.

"Pray for us as we do for you and one day, maybe we will be together again.

"With love as always,

"Nini"

Without much regret, we prepare to leave the Missionary Home and make our way into the mainstream life of Shanghai. My sisters and brothers-in-law are unable to do much for us as everyone has only enough for himself, so we are mostly on our own to establish living quarters and find a way to keep ourselves fed.

We are overwhelmed by every new sight. We dissolve into the flooding humanity, a population of four and a half million that throngs in the streets, so dense with people that walking through them is like wading in living quicksand. Men balancing heavy bamboo poles with baskets of food swinging on either side rush about trying to sell their wares, and small, thin women tend to cooking odd foods in bamboo steamers, looking as if they never have enough to feed their starving children. Others, more desperate, are offering to sell swaddled babies wailing at their breasts, to be raised as servants or prostitutes by passing Europeans. Poverty and over-population threaten to annihilate them all.

Coolies, wearing their distinctive triangular straw hats, pull bizarre two-wheeled wagons with people sitting inside. Watching them strain every muscle, padding along the streets, I am appalled and believe this to be the most uncivilized country on earth, where people are being used as beasts of burden. They are everywhere, thousands of men pulling thousands of others to their destinations. The carts are rickshaws, we are told, and before long we too begin to use them for transportation. They weave in and out, adding to the mad confusion of traffic that teams day and night in the city streets, among the trolleys, automobiles and pedestrians, always rushing towards their destinations, rushing without a glance, rushing to a better place. Shanghai never rests.

Beggars roam the streets accosting foreigners, hands outstretched, eyes sunken. We soon learn which are the opium addicts who stumble from dark, smoke-filled caverns into the horrid streets and back again when they have scrounged enough for the next heroin fix. Pitiful half-naked children run a jagged course for blocks after every émigré, small dirty palms upturned, pleading and chanting in repetitive monotony the only English words they know, "No mama, no papa, no whiskey, no soda."

Dead bodies litter the sidewalks, having perished from hunger and heat exhaustion or the ravages of leprosy, malaria, cholera, dysentery, or typhoid. Others have succumbed to the numbing opium that has permeated their veins and gnawed at their brains with its poison. Corpses languish like sacks of trash or dirty laundry waiting to be tossed unceremoniously into carts and hauled away. We walk cautiously around the decaying bodies covering our mouths and noses, trying to keep our distance, clenching our lips tightly in determination to be strong despite the horror. Don't look down, I think, just walk on. It's too late for that one. Don't stop.

Mama prefers to stay in the one-room apartment that we have been able to find with the aid of the relief organization but Willi and I set out immediately to explore the layout of Shanghai, walking the maze of busy streets, or riding the crowded streetcars that rattle and chug along the main boulevards. Double-decker buses and cars stream in every direction and horns sound loudly at the many weaving rickshaws that dart in and out along the congested thoroughfares. Pedestrians and bicycles thread their haphazard way through the traffic without apparent concern. The city, we discover, has been segmented, each section distinct and inhabited by different nationalities although the Chinese are everywhere.

The International Settlement spreads to the Garden Bridge. Soochow Creek forms the dividing line between Hongkew District, the poorest side of Shanghai, and the rest of the Settlement. Ruled primarily by British and American interests, the area has become a buzzing cosmopolitan hub where many European and Asian languages are spoken in an agitated cacophony and every shade of skin colour forms a human patchwork. The mixture of distinct and varied cultures is an amazing revelation for me, compared to the strictly homogeneous whiteness of Austria.

Moving from Hongkew, where some of the Jewish refugees have settled, across the bridge, we see the Public Gardens and the extensive British Consulate immaculately maintained with well-groomed lawns and refined facilities. A few blocks farther along is Avenue Edouard VII which divides the International Settlement from the French Concession, so-called because it had been occupied by France and ruled by their consul general. Now though, it is controlled by the Japanese. Within "Frenchtown" can be found the large French Club, called Cercle Sportif Français. Although refugees seldom have access to any of the facilities located within the splendid club grounds, we have been told they house every imaginable luxury from tennis courts to swimming pools.

We know nothing about China and didn't expect to find any Jews here, but we have discovered, since our arrival, that two Jewish communities have already been established in Shanghai. We learn there is a very select group of Sephardic Jews, numbering only about five hundred, who originally came here from Baghdad around 1870. This group consists mostly of very wealthy and influential families who possess enormous holdings, including valuable property such as large deluxe hotels. They are powerful icons wielding considerable influence. Names like Sassoon and Kadoorie are spoken with awe. Through philanthropic efforts, they have set up relief organizations to aid the newcomers being dumped on the shores. Refugee camps, shelters, and basic food are supplied to help us to live. They have established the charity homes where hundreds of people are cared for and fed. Without the generosity and intervention of these people, many of us would have starved to death by now.

The other group is a large one, consisting of about forty-five hundred Russian Jews who fled during the Bolshevik Revolution in 1917. They have also gained social status and respect. The Russian Jews have established themselves in Frenchtown, where there is already an existing community of those from a European background. This is also where our family is relocated in small flats. Avenue Joffre, leading from the heart of the city, is often called "Moscow Boulevard." We are comforted by the familiarity of shops, doctors' and dentists' offices, nightclubs, and a small synagogue, but we cannot forget for one moment that this is Shanghai as Chinese workers of all descriptions fill the streets, vendors and beggars, the high and low churning together in a unique ethnic pot.

A mile farther along, Nanking Road, the main artery heading out of the city, leads into Bubbling Well Road. The British Country Club is there on Bubbling Well and opposite it stands the expansive French Club, the Cathay Mansions apartments, and the Cathay Hotel. We stare in wonder at the splendour of these formidable structures where wealth and power find an ideal home.

Within the French Concession magnificent streets emulate posh Parisian boulevards – exclusive shops sell designer fashion, Chanel perfume, and imported liquor. The Bund is the centre of commercial activity, filled with modern automobiles, chauffeur-driven limousines, as well as the ever-present rickshaws zipping in and out through the traffic, and thousands of Chinese on bicycles or on foot. There are grandiose homes with air conditioning, tropical gardens with swimming pools and every extravagant luxury imaginable, where Chinese servants are employed at a miserly wage to tend to the needs of the powerful. We, as refugees, are not part of that rarefied milieu.

When daylight dawns on our new home, a single room really, with a bathroom and tiny kitchen, one cot for each of us, I stir from sleep and dreams of Vienna, to the realization of our poor surroundings. Mama is still asleep in the corner, Willi is in his bed beside hers. Our cases are lined up against the wall near a frayed and faded upholstered chair beside a chipped wooden table with a lamp and dull stained shade. The task of finding work is urgent, fraught with hurdles. We are completely destitute so Willi and I can waste no time. We kiss Mama on the cheek as we leave her in our little home early in the morning, wishing luck to one another as we set off on a desperate search for any way to feed ourselves. Many jobs require only native Chinese workers, others are out of our reach as we have no qualifications. We are fighting against time. We need some money immediately or we will soon starve.

My shoes are wearing at the heels as I walk the streets in search of some opportunity. Along the cracked and uneven pavement, I hobble alone, fear prickling my skin, my throat dry with thirst and panic. There is not a crust of bread in our poor room and Mama has become depressed, having lost her strength and will to live. Hunger is an aching hollow deep within, a growling voice in my bowels, demanding the food I cannot supply. Lost in worried thoughts of our plight, I almost stumble over a Chinese beggar's lifeless body. He has died in the street, his rags barely covering his pitiful bones. He serves as a further omen, that death is everywhere and that we are treading a narrow pathway through it, easily tripping and falling, to be lost here in this wasteland. There is no time to stop, must go on, can't rest, have to find work, money, food. Mostly I have to keep myself from slipping into delirium.

Trudging halfheartedly along, I nearly bump into another young woman coming the other way. She seems just as preoccupied as I am, looking in shop windows for signs offering employment, her clothes wrinkled and worn. It is Herta, from the ship. We laugh at the near collision and greet one another after the months that have elapsed.

"Where have you been, Herta?" I ask.

"I'm still living in the *Heim*, but the conditions are awful," she says. "We're crowded into dingy rooms in an abandoned building where there is neither heat nor ventilation. In every room, thirty or forty of us are lumped together in barracks, sleeping in rows of narrow bunk beds, afraid of theft, hungry all the time, and waiting like beggars for our handouts, a crust of stale bread or a cup of weak tea. Children are crying night and day. The smells of misery and poverty are unbearable. I can't stand it. I've got to move out, if only I could find some work to support myself. There are so many of us and so few opportunities. The Nazis have sent us to a sure death here. I'm afraid I won't survive."

I shake my head in sad reply, thinking that however badly we are faring at least we are together, but Herta is alone. "I'm also trying to find something to do," I say. "We're living in a little flat right now but the few dollars we have from the things we sold on the ship are nearly gone and we're struggling to feed ourselves. I'm worried about Mama, too. It's so hard on her. But you, Herta, you are young. I'm certain you'll find work and that you'll be all right. And besides, maybe the the situation will improve and we'll be able to find our way out of here."

"I don't know. I hope you're right." Herta's tone reveals a multitude of worries and sorrows. She is distracted and soon makes her excuses for a quick farewell. "Well, Nini, I'm glad to have seen you but I have to rush away now. I'm afraid I can't even afford the luxury of a cup of coffee or the time it takes to drink it. I wish you good luck – maybe we will meet again soon in better circumstances."

"Please, God," I answer. As we hug in a sad embrace, I can feel the bones of her thin body through her frayed coat. Then we continue on our separate ways.

A few blocks farther along, I pass a hotel window and notice a sign requiring a manicurist. Having gone for many hours with nothing to eat, I feel unsteady, worried that I might collapse from weakness and realizing that I dare not do so. I swallow hard and walk into the salon, trying to show a confident demeanour although I have no experience for the job. My English is poor and I wish now that I had paid more attention to my lessons in school. But I must say whatever is necessary at this stage to procure the position. "Yes," I lie, "I am skilled as a manicurist. Yes, I speak English very well." And so I am hired on the spot and put to work right away.

An affluent American gentleman, dressed in a cream-coloured suit of slubbed natural linen, his jacket removed, revealing a matching buttoned vest and an elegant silk shirt with a monogram embroidered on the cuff, is seated in the chair. His wrist is extended over the armrest for me to groom. My hands are trembling terribly as I begin the task. Every time I prick him or poke his fingers with one of the metal utensils, he flinches and groans. Unfortunately the result is a mess, his nails bleeding at the cuticles, cut mercilessly and patched with bandages by the time I'm done. I can only apologize over and over, begging him to understand that it is my first time. He looks down at me with a disgruntled shake of his head and hands me a five-dollar bill, a fortune. The manager, seeing the incompetent effort, fires me without hesitation while bowing in deference and profuse regret to the gentleman. But I am too elated with the faded green paper in my hand to worry about that. I bolt from the shop and run all the way home, shouting breathlessly for Mama, and when I find her, my face beaming with pride, I press the note into her palm.

The exuberance of youth perishes in a slow painful death. We wither in the unbearable summer heat, drenched in sweat without relief, day or night. Our clothing clings to our bodies. When the monsoons come, relentless rain falls in a solid wall, hissing on the broken pavement, turning instantly to steam. We can't bear the sights or smells of the food being cooked and hawked by street vendors. Heaps of croaking frogs, squirming eels, tangles of lazy snakes, and crates of screeching chickens are kept alive in crowded cages and killed just before they are to be consumed. Huge bulge-eyed carp sink to the bottom of wooden barrels, waiting to be devoured in their turn. Piles of living crabs crawl over one another as fishmongers call out in their strange language, and flies buzz over mounds of wilting vegetables.

We have become undernourished, sallow skin pulled tight over our cheekbones, our fingers, nicotine-stained, clutch precious American cigarettes that are smuggled into the country and sold on the black market by clever Chinese entrepreneurs. It is difficult to gather my courage to face every new day, but I feel a different kind of strength building within me. I think of myself as an unborn moth within its cocoon, tightly weaving a crusty shell around my soft vulnerable core. All the misery I have seen, the Nazi torment, the dead bodies stinking on the sidewalks, the brutality of the Chinese and Japanese towards one another, the daily battle with hunger and disease, all are weighing on my mind and all must be overcome. Nothing can permeate the outer layer and destroy my inner self. In the small cracked mirror on our wall I see an older, more sombre reflection although I am still a young woman, but the circumstances that I have already endured have added years to my soul. Joy is rare, hardship is constant, but I am determined to survive.

CHAPTER 21

THE CLUB 1939

After a succession of unsuccessful odd jobs, I am fortunate to have found employment as a hostess in a posh nightclub where I am required to stand by the entrance to a magnificent ballroom, to smile and welcome the well-heeled patrons as they are ushered in. My German language and growing familiarity with English were helpful to me in gaining the position. Shanghai has a well-earned reputation throughout the world for its dark mysteries and exotic allure and here, in the Bolero Club, all of the most outrageous tales of glamorous women and powerful men mesh in a kind of dream world, like a scene from a motion picture.

At the outer doors, under a striped canopy, a red carpet is unrolled to the street. By the doors stands an imposing tan-skinned doorman, a coal-eyed Sikh. He seems a giant, towering above me at about six foot six, with a turban wrapped like a white beehive on his head. He is wearing high black rubber boots and a traditional Indian garment with a long-sleeved tunic and softly draped trousers. He greets me with a kind smile when I arrive for work, and opens the door for me to enter. I think how hot he must be in that clothing, in this heat that envelops us as though we lived in the centre of a furnace.

"Good evening, Missy," he says. "Many customers coming tonight. Maybe good night for tips," he adds, his white teeth bright against his brown face.

"Yes," I reply with a nod, "I hope you're right. I'll see you later."

Stepping into the club each evening when my shift begins, I am always aware of the transition from the mundane life of the masses on one side of the doors to this kind of Shangri-La on the other. Even the air is different. It is cool, air-conditioned, blocking out the stagnant heat outside. I am in a surreal, clandestine milieu that is completely cloistered, an oasis shielded from the effects of the conflicts in Europe and from the wretched misery in the streets just on the other side of the heavy oak doors, with their huge polished brass knobs. Opulent wealth, wealth beyond comprehension, is boldly flaunted inside the candle-lit rooms, their booths lushly upholstered in tufted crimson velvet, crystal chandeliers brilliantly flashing overhead, and music throbbing in the air. The band is playing the popular American music of Cole Porter and Irving Berlin as couples, elegantly attired like actors in Hollywood films, are clicking their shoes on the buffed wooden floor and swaying to the sounds of brass slide trombones, gleaming trumpets, and saxophones.

Our clientele at the Bolero is made up of the same people who frequent the exclusive private clubs during the day. Everyone knows about these places, although they are hidden behind ivy-covered walls, shielded from prying eyes by security gates and armed guards. Social events of special note are described in the newspapers and there, in the smiling photos, we see how another segment lives in Shanghai. The upper class, made up of foreign diplomats, business moguls, and dignitaries, passes the time luxuriating in cool pools, playing croquet or tennis in lush courtyard gardens. Wild orchids bloom around them as they sip afternoon tea from dainty porcelain cups and amuse themselves at billiards or a game of backgammon or bridge. There is the American Club, downtown on Foochow Road, the British Country Club, and the French Club, renowned for its swimming pool, among the largest in Shanghai, each club with precise rules to keep out undesirables. At the German Garden Club businessmen are known to congregate, to raise their arms in national pride, to salute their Fuhrer. Hitler's birthday is celebrated with considerable fanfare.

Behind the solid protected walls, gleaming floors are laid with Italian marble, and the very restricted membership plays lords and ladies. Chinese servants speak in "pidgin English" and remember to keep their place. They are hardly more than slaves, tending to every need and whim, and bowing in obsequious servitude. They pad about in soft small steps, unobtrusive and efficient, made to humble themselves before the strangers who have invaded their land. Within this secluded and segregated world of the privileged, life is lived on a scale to rival royalty, and it is certainly not a place that might welcome impoverished Jewish refugees. We are excluded from that select realm.

For those with the right connections and the money to indulge in the excesses, there is plenty of opportunity to revel without restraint in this city. These people frequent the many nightclubs of Shanghai and find their way into the Bolero, dressed in the most ostentatious flourish of furs and flashing jewels. There is a cosmopolitan mix of British, German, influential "White" Russians, still supporting the overthrown Tsarist regime, and Chinese of unbelievable wealth and influence who spend their nights here and already have become familiar to me.

Shanghai is a sumptuous playground for anyone with sufficient means. The British are living a wonderful life in Shanghai as in other British holdings throughout the Far East such as India, Hong Kong, and Singapore. They have established their clubs, secluded hideaways of rarefied splendour carved out of lush vegetation in steamy climates where an underclass is available to ensure that the grand lifestyle is maintained. Since their victory in the Opium Wars here in China, their position as representatives of the Empire has given them unparalleled freedom and afforded them every luxury. Regularly, they arrive by Rolls-Royce at the door of the Bolero and move among us with a nearly tangible air of superiority.

One of them, Brigadier General Smedley Whitehall, and his party are frequent guests. He is retired from military service, having been sent to Shanghai as a reward for dedicated duty and to enjoy the aristocratic position in which he finds himself in this society. As always, he is dressed in formal military uniform, his impressive array of medals glinting in the reflected light. His wife, in a floor-length gown and mink wrap, chats with their friends. She doesn't acknowledge me, turning her powdered face away, in arrogant disregard. He appears a bit flushed tonight, obviously ruffled about something.

He speaks to me as he hands his hat to the girl at the coat check, smoothing back his thick mane of white hair and patting his moustache into place: "Damn shame about my chauffeur, disappeared overnight, don't you know. We nearly didn't get out at all this evening. Managed to find a replacement in the nick. It's all this blasted nuisance with the Japs. Live and let live, I say, isn't that so? You Jews know what it's about, the war and all. Just an annoyance. It's too much really, isn't it? Disrupts one's peace of mind. Wouldn't you say?"

To him the disappearance of the chauffeur is an irritation, but I know that the man was probably waylaid and murdered. Fleetingly, an image of a severed head, still wearing the chauffeur's cap, flashes in my mind, set among a fresh batch of those chopped by Japanese bayonets and mounted on spikes for the morning's viewing.

"Yes, General, we're so glad that you could come." I smile and nod. This is not a job I can afford to jeopardize and what good would it do to express any indignation? Besides, this man's life is so far removed from the coarse realities of Shanghai that it would be impossible to explain anything to him. What would he care, so absorbed in his petty complaints and spoiled circumstances, so completely untouched by any suffering or concern for anyone else. Why bother? In the Bolero he is free to be himself, which is the reason that he comes here. No, I will not argue with him nor any of his kind.

"You've got our regular table reserved, have you?" General Whitehall asks. "Must have some things to rely upon, mustn't we? Thank heavens for the clubs, only civilized thing about this blasted place. I thoroughly dislike this constant upheaval, not being certain of things. Too distracting really, much too distracting."

"Yes, of course, sir," I answer. "The maître d' will show you to your table, just the same as always."

"Yes, yes, that's splendid. Come along, my dear." He guides his wife gently by the arm, and they descend the steps set between cream marble pillars framing the entrance to the club.

All evening a constant parade of guests swishes through the massive doors to be escorted inside. One particular Chinese man arrives at precisely ten o'clock every night. The source of his money is whispered about discreetly, behind a fluttering fan or into a cocked ear. It is suspected that the opium trade and prostitution, both flourishing enterprises here, have put him into this position, but no one is prepared to judge him or anyone else. Here, in Shanghai, "No Man's Land," a country where there is no such thing as law, tucked away in the most obscure corner of this insane world, who can condemn a rogue when justice and morality no longer have meaning?

He enters. On each arm is wrapped a woman of breathtaking beauty, sultry and elegant, tall and slim, dressed magnificently in fine silk brocades, gowns slit to the thigh, perched on high heels, with dangling earrings and glittering necklaces dipping towards their breasts. They are white women, a sign of power to the Chinese, one blonde, her smooth hair shining and softly sweeping over her left eye like Veronica Lake. The other is a red-head, like Rita Hayworth, her mass of auburn curls bobbing as she walks. It is no coincidence that these women look like movie stars. They have been especially chosen for their resemblance to the screen goddesses of Hollywood. The man himself is garbed in a traditional caftan of ancient Chinese royalty; it reaches to the floor, silken threads woven by hand into the regal garment. Patterns of dragons and long-necked cranes are depicted in emerald green and sapphire blue swirling among the gold, dazzling the eye of the observer. A husky bodyguard, with broad shoulders and thick neck, walks grimly behind, his eyes darting around the room, side to side, and then returning to settle on his charge.

The gentleman nods to me in his now-familiar manner of composed elegance and assurance. He and his entourage are seated at his usual table, the ideal location to view the nightly activity and to be certain that his entrance is observed. From the breast pocket within his robes, he withdraws an intricately carved ivory cigarette holder, inlaid with rubies. The small finger of his right hand has a long, tapered nail, used, it is said, to scoop and sample cocaine. On the finger he wears an entrancing star sapphire ring. Then he removes a gold cigarette case, completely encrusted in diamonds, brilliantly flashing like a handful of stars. From it he selects a narrow white cylinder of wrapped tobacco and inserts it with care into the long holder. One of his female companions lights the cigarette for him, then he contentedly leans back into his plush seat and inhales the warm smoke. Waiters, dressed in tuxedos, hands sheathed in white gloves, bustle about with silver trays and deposit sparkling snifters of French cognac, like liquid topaz, that shimmers in the reflected candlelight as he lifts it to his mouth and swallows it in slow pleasure. An icy bucket of French champagne with frosted glasses and a bowl of Russian caviar, set in a bowl of crushed ice, are placed on the table before him.

There are many others who come to be seen at the Bolero every night, sweeping into the club in grand style, cashmere coats swung casually over finely tailored Italian suits. They emerge from chauffeured limousines, the splendour of outrageous wealth apparent with every gesture. Each of them is preceded and surrounded by uniformed bodyguards, rifles slung from straps on their shoulders. Dazzling perfume-drenched Chinese and European women, swathed in luxurious furs, glide by their sides. The famous Baghdadi Jewish magnates, the Kadoories and Sassoons, and members of the European aristocracy of Shanghai congregate here in the realm of supreme riches that has set them above and apart from the mundane lives of mortals.

Located directly next door to the Bolero is an opium den. This is not one of the lowly hovels for the poor Chinese but instead a grand salon established exclusively for the decadent pleasure of the wealthiest inhabitants of the city. I have watched as patrons leave our club and make their way into the mysterious cavern night after night. There, the heroin is said to be of the purest grade, and pleasures beyond this world are waiting to be had. Curiosity overcomes me one night after work, so, suppressing a quiver of nervous tension, I wander inside. The air is a dense fog of sweet overpowering smoke, so thick that it's difficult to see, and I stumble over a body curled on a small woven carpet, spread on the floor.

As I peer further into the immense building I can detect men and women, puffing on long-hosed water pipes, inhaling the addictive fumes until they attain a state of glassy-eyed semiconsciousness. Chinese servants scamper about, tending to the needs of the rich patrons, who languish in a groggy haze. Bodyguards, standing, arms crossed, watch over their employers, who have fallen into a drugged stupor. They are sprawled on woven rugs or, for those willing to pay the price, on lacquered opium beds, intricately carved of cinnabar and ebony, inlaid with jade, ivory, and mother-of-pearl, piled with puffed raw silk cushions and covers. But as the addicts inhale the yellowish fumes, they are no longer aware of the decadent splendour of their surroundings. The women, in silken evening gowns, are glittering in the foggy darkness, gold jewellery adorning their limp bodies. Men, in expensive business suits, lie in heaps of numb oblivion, having descended into this hazy netherworld, in their quest for elusive pleasure.

Unnoticed and insignificant as a cat that might have strayed into the den, I slip out again as I had entered, wading back through the bodies and smoke. In the early hours of dawn I make my way back to our flat. Out in the real world again, I am keenly aware of the other Shanghai. I am straddling the two opposing extremes. The odours of fine perfume, dusky cigarette smoke, and the pungent scent of opium still cling to my clothing, but my nostrils are already inhaling the foul stench of the streets. From the most opulent display of riches that European and Asian civilization can produce, within minutes, I am cast into such unparalleled poverty that human bodies, ravaged by starvation, are lying in the street. Frozen to death in the winter or rotting in the glaring heat of summer, they are ignored. The newspapers report that the Chinese Benevolent Society picks up and disposes of between 25,000 and 30,000 such bodies a year. Survival in Shanghai is a cruel game that many will lose.

I return to the refugee apartments, separated from the refinement of the aristocratic homes. Here, in the shadows, disconnected from the grandeur, is where we live. We rest precariously on the lowest rung of European society. We are ignored for the most part, here in Shanghai, left alone by the authorities who are unconcerned whether we live or not. Death is accepted and understood so that the demise of Jewish refugees in this overpopulated metropolis is of no note when added to the countless others who perish each day. Besides, the Japanese have more to deal with than the few thousand of us flung on this shore.

Nonetheless, as I turn the knob to the door of our home, I smile. Against innumerable odds, I have earned a reasonable day's wage and carved a safe corner for myself in this unbelievable spot on the globe. Mama hears me come in and mumbles to me from her slumber, "Nini, are you all right? You're home, thank God."

"Yes, Mama, I'm fine, go back to sleep. We will have something nice to eat tomorrow."

As I get ready for bed, I think of my small family, who will soon be starting their working day. Stella has a job in a gift shop. Erna has Lily with her and is still teaching needlework at the convent under the supervision of Mother Laula; Fritz and Walter are employed in a factory. Willi is working in a bar. We are settled here and can support ourselves in this way for as long as it takes. There must be an end somehow, we are convinced, so we are able to live in security until that day. My eyelids shut and my weary mind begins to float into dreams, and I reason that it is better not to worry about the future.

CHAPTER 22

BESHERT 1939

I n the evenings, I write to Poldi by a dim light in our small cramped rooms and beg him to send word of conditions in Milan. I tell him of our plight but assure him that all my family has arrived safely in this strange land and urge him to come as soon as possible. I have not told him that I have received no mail for several weeks from Herr Berger and that I am desperately worried about the Kosiners. I describe where we are in Shanghai and tell him to find us as soon as he arrives.

After I make countless trips to the post office and empty-handed retreats in disappointment, some letters finally arrive. I keep them in my pocket unopened all day and through the night hours when I am at work in the club. I run my fingers over the envelopes many times and smile, thinking that he held them in his hands. When I finally return home in the early morning, I slip into bed and open each one. I devour the words, rushing through them and then rereading them over and over with great pleasure, until every one is memorized.

I feel a lump rising in my throat when I read his words. He is still so far away, and the dangers in Europe seem to be getting worse.

"Dear Nini,

"With all my heart I wish I could be with you now. I know there are hardships in Shanghai and you and your family are struggling. Please be brave and strong and relentless in your fight against the Missionaries. As hard as it is for you, it is still so much worse here in Europe. Have you got any news from Herr Berger about my parents? I still hope that they will be with you in Shanghai by the time we get there.

"The Nazis are becoming more ruthless every day in their goal of ridding the world of us all. Hitler has promised a special holiday when the last Jew has been driven from the continent. Life is a bitter medicine that we swallow each day and pray for a cure to this evil plague, but there is none to be found. The Italians have changed their rules and the Lloyd Triestino Line is no longer permitted to leave from Trieste to take refugees to Shanghai. You might have been on the very last of those voyages.

"The only way out now is by land through Manchuria, which is the route that we must take.

"Dolu and I will make our way overland to Shanghai within another month or two, but I only received one letter from the lawyer Berger and he still has not succeeded with the exit visas for our parents. I cannot discuss it with Dolu. You know what a temper he has and he always rants about Berger, that he should have done more, that he never wanted to help us. I have tried to reason with him many times and have explained that Berger saved you and that he would do all that he could for our parents too, but in truth I am very worried.

"I hope that you, together with all your family, are well. Every night I thank God that I have survived another day and pray that in His Mercy, He will bring me to you again. Although an ocean lies between us, I feel you with me in my small room. Maybe, with God's help we will still unite one day. We should try to keep hope in our hearts, despite the distance and the forces against us.

"My love and devotion always,

"Poldi"

His letters are always a source of joy to me, but now also of growing concern for his safety. After I have digested the words on my own, I share them with my family. We come together almost every day to keep the ties strong. We, like most of the refugees, have developed overpowering fears of separation, imagining that each goodbye may be the last.

It's been weeks since I had any word from Herr Berger when finally a letter arrives. When I see his familiar return address I feel my heart fluttering. In a state of jittery trepidation I tear it open immediately while still in the post office, not even waiting to take it home. When I read the contents I feel weak and lean against the wall, then slump down onto a chair. The letter is not at all from him but from one of his clerks.

"Fraulein Karpel,

"This will be the last correspondence from this office. I know that you were one of Herr Berger's most important clients as he spent so much time on your case. I have decided that I should therefore inform you, in loyalty to him, that he has been arrested by the Gestapo. They have accused him of aiding Jews which is against the law, of using his own funds to work for the release of Jews from the camps, also illegal, and various other crimes against the Reich. The penalty is death.

"Personally, I do not support whatever he did in risking his own life for yours but it is my duty, I think, to let you know that there will be no further aid to you or to any other Jew from this office. In fact, I am losing my job now as the office will have to be shut down. Do not correspond further with us as it will be useless.

"A faithful employee and member of the National Socialist Party."

I scan the words over and over, in stunned disbelief. "My God!" I say aloud. With devastating clarity, I realize at last that they are all gone, Herr Berger and the Kosiners.

For several days after, I cannot eat or sleep much. The news is as traumatic as anything we have experienced till now and I have received nothing from Poldi in over a month. I am certain that he and Dolu are dead, and no amount of reassurance from Mama can convince me that they are all right.

On August 11, the Japanese Naval Landing Party has ordered all refugees already living in Japanese-occupied territory to register. We line up with the rest to sign our names to the list. But by August 21 a new decree is announced. The influx of Jewish immigrants to Shanghai has been halted. Only those already on the high seas will be permitted to disembark here. With the very last avenue of escape plugged, Hitler and his co-conspirators have made certain we are trapped. I am more fearful than ever that Poldi did not escape in time and that I will never see him again.

One evening I am at home with Mama when there is an unexpected knock on the door. Distressed, we exchange a look of concern. Peering apprehensively through the window, I scream suddenly and Mama jumps in fright. "Nini, whatever is wrong!"

"He's here, Mama, he's really here!"

I rush to open the door and welcome Poldi in a tight embrace, drawing him in, holding his hand again in my own. To me it seems as if a light has been lit within the dark room – sunbeams seem to flood through the door. Mama weeps for she is very fond of Poldi and hugs him to her as if he were one of her own children. We sit together until late at night listening to news of Vienna and Milan, telling our own tales. Poldi's face alone tells us his story, for on it is written the harrowing journey he has now completed. His cheeks are hollows beneath protruding bones.

As we talk, I realize how deeply I love this man. I know our destinies have now become intertwined like two trees that will twist and tangle as they grow, indistinguishable from one another, the roots meshing until they are one, to live or to perish together.

Poldi and his brother have arrived in Shanghai together and Dolu is already making contact with some people he knows who live in the French Concession and making arrangements for lodgings for them both.

Poldi has come on his own to see us. After a while I realize I have to tell him about Berger's arrest and the loss of any hope we had of rescuing his parents. I go to retrieve the letter sent from Berger's office and show it to him. Shaken, he lights a cigarette with trembling hands. His eyes mist, he lowers his head and he starts to sob, his shoulders heaving.

Mama gives him a shot of vodka, which he gulps in one swallow.

When he is able to speak again, he describes the image of his parents the last time he saw them before he left for Italy, their hands joined together, tears in their eyes as they waved farewell. He has carried that image with him during the entire trip and it still haunts him.

I had never told Poldi what his mother had predicted years before. He is unaware of her premonition that she and his father would not live to see Poldi and me together again. I still have no intention of telling him this – after all, she might have been wrong. Maybe they will yet escape and make their way here. I manage to smile weakly and touch his hand in an attempt at reassurance. I remember her telling me too about her belief that Poldi and I were destined for each other – *beshert* – and I wonder whether she will be proven right. How very far away those times seem to me now. How strange that she had sensed this reunion that has taken place against all likelihood and in this strange place.

When Poldi has regained his composure, we settle down with hot tea. He removes a small package from his coat pocket. Carefully unwrapping the brown rumpled paper, tied with string, he reveals the contents. In his still quivering hand he holds his mother's gold watch, her most prized possession. We gaze at the smooth disc and long linked chain curled in the paper. How desperate she must have felt to have taken the only valuable in her possession from her neck and pressed it into her son's hand. "I promised that I would return it to her one day when we reunited," Poldi says hardly above a whisper, talking more to himself than to us. "I told her that I would put it back around her neck and she smiled and said, 'Maybe, my son, but if not, keep it and remember me by it.' Yes, that's what she said."

From his valise he withdraws one of his father's small leather-bound books and there on the little scuffed wooden table before us we stare at the only remnants we have of these two lives. The night is not dark enough to hide the loneliest moments of our grief. Tears don't relieve our shared heartache.

After an hour or so, Poldi says, "It's time for me to go. Dolu is waiting for me and I'll have to tell him what has happened. He will be shattered too. But I'll see you tomorrow, Nini. For tonight I can think of nothing but my mama and papa."

I cannot fall asleep. The excitement of his return and the sadness of his parents' unknown fate keep me tossing restlessly until the morning. The next day when I meet Poldi, he tries to suppress the hurt and disappointment he is feeling. We take turns in our efforts at encouraging one another, wanting to make the best of the moment, reasoning that we still have no evidence that his parents are not alive. Maybe the camps are not so bad, and we will still find them safe.

"You know, Poldi," I say in my best attempt at a cheerful attitude, "at least we are both alive. Remember we always said we could accomplish anything if we survived together."

"And," he suggests, taking my hand in his, a smile on his lips, "you thought you would never travel beyond Austria, but the Nazis have given you a chance to see the world."

"I should send them a thank-you note, don't you think?" I say and we both have a laugh.

We walk around the city, stopping for a pot of green tea, which we sip until the last of the leaves remain in a mucky clump at the bottom of the small cups. Being together makes everything an adventure. We joke again and walk along hand in hand, and for the first time in months we talk about the future.

Over the next few weeks, we obsessively follow the news from Europe. Our hope is that Hitler will somehow be overthrown and that the prisoners of the camps will be released. However, the Nazis have brought in a new law, making emigration for Jews more difficult than before. They each need $400 – U.S. dollars – to get out of Vienna. This is a nearly insurmountable obstacle as most people cannot obtain that amount of money and the Germans are losing patience. They are not prepared to wait. Poldi is distraught with the guilt of having abandoned his parents. Without Herr Berger to intervene there is no way to find them and no funds to pay their way out.

Finally in September 1939 we read the headlines: Hitler has invaded Poland, and Britain and France have declared war on Germany. We know then that Poldi's parents are gone forever and an immense grief overcomes us. Poldi is inconsolable. For days he goes without sleep, walking around in a state of shock and disbelief, unable to accept the horrific fate that his beloved parents have had to face. He relives the torment again and again, denying himself any solace. I try to talk to him, to rescue him from his demons. I sit with him for many hours into the night, begging him to hang on to the strength his parents have given him throughout their lives.

His eyes are rimmed in red. He is unshaven and will not speak. Day after day we worry about his survival. Mama goes with me to visit Poldi and Dolu every day, bringing whatever food we can spare and offering our feeble words of comfort. Our hearts break with his and his brother's. We all grieve with them, each of my family expressing sympathy for their terrible loss.

The iron bond Mama has established has held us together and kept us from destruction; now it is extended to include Poldi and Dolu. The lifeline seems to work gradually. Dolu surfaces from his despair more quickly than Poldi. Sometime in October he meets a young woman, Eva, of Russian Jewish descent, who has given him support and encouragement, and he seems well on his way to establishing a new life. As she is a dentist and he had some dental training in Poland, they have set up a dental practice that is prospering and he has told us that he plans to marry her.

Poldi feels the trauma more deeply. Although he has an optimistic nature, this blow has affected his normal disposition. Weeks pass and he is still immersed in a state of melancholy. Just at the point of deepest remorse, there appears to be a gradual improvement in his declining health. Bit by bit he wills himself the courage to carry on. Like a flower inching up toward the light, Poldi slowly regains the spirit of life we feared would be lost. His eyes still betray his anguish, but a weak smile crosses his lips again.

To my great joy, Poldi professes his love for me and tells me that only together will we have the strength to navigate the difficult path ahead. We decide to be married here in Shanghai, to reach for something better. The misery we have already encountered has destroyed our childhood ambitions and every plan we had made for our future. We may not survive to a better time. The road before us remains hidden from our view and will lead us on a journey we cannot foresee.

CHAPTER 23

WE ARE MARRIED 1940

On January 7, 1940, Poldi and I are married. It is the start of a new year and although our lives are far from what we had ever dreamed they would be, at least we are together. We stand side by side, under the simple linen *chuppah* canopy. Fritz, Dolu, Walter, and Willi stand, one at each corner, their hands wrapped around the poles that support the *chuppah*. The rabbi pronounces the words that bind us, and we repeat the ancient vow, "*Anee ledodi, ledodi lee*" – "I am my beloved's and my beloved is mine." When the rabbi pronounces us wed, we kiss and hold hands to the sweet strains of a violin.

Poldi's right foot stomps with a hard crack to break the traditional glass that the rabbi has placed beneath his heel. Everyone shouts, "*Mazel Tov!*" and we feel truly united. The rabbi reminds us of the reason for this tradition, that even the most joyous moment cannot exist without a thought for something painful as well, shattering the happiness like fragile glass, in memory of our own sadness and the sadness of our people. At this time and in this strange place, we hardly need to be told of this fact. It is the joy that is harder to hold tight than the sorrow.

I have chosen to wed not in a traditional white gown but rather in a terra cotta coloured tailored suit and hat. The outfit was made for me here by one of the excellent seamstresses that are quite easy to find, and I am very pleased with the result. With the war continuing, it seems inappropriate to dress as a picture-book bride, though I know many others who do not share this sentiment and wedding dresses with trailing veils are still quite commonly seen.

The family members are dressed in their best clothes and join to share in our celebration. Happiness is doled out in spare measure these days and savoured the more for its rarity. Erna and Fritz offer their wishes and embraces in turn. Lily runs to me and hugs me, her thin small arms clutching me tightly, as if clinging to a life preserver. Stella, her eyes moist, and her husband, Walter, are next in line. My brother, Willi, holds us each in an emotional hug as he comes to congratulate us. Eva and Dolu, who have now been married for about a month, kiss us each on both cheeks, giving us their wishes for many happy years. Mama, unable to control the tears, holds me close and whispers her love and prayers that there may yet be a happy future ahead.

Before I was married, I gave notice at the Bolero Club and said my farewells to all those who had been so helpful through a lonely and difficult time in my life. Now, after the wedding, we have decided to take a trip away from Shanghai for a month or so, but this will not be a simple honeymoon. We are planning a particular journey that may prove to be quite dangerous.

"These are hazardous times, Nini," Poldi tells me. "We need to do something daring if we are to make a decent living here. Poverty is our greatest enemy. We're nearly destitute and it won't be a simple matter for any of us to get ahead."

"What would we have to do?" I ask him, feeling a nervous flutter in my stomach.

"Remember when I told you that I had made a friend named Leon Druck in Milan? He escaped from Europe too and lives in Manchuria now, in a city called Harbin."

I think back to all of the letters from Italy, all the many things that Poldi had written about. "Do you mean that fellow who was learning about the fur trade with you?"

"That's right. We spent a lot of time together in Milan and he wrote to me from Harbin."

And what can he do for us?"

"There is a substantial Jewish community there, several thousand who fled from Russia through Siberia to escape persecution. Leon has written to me with a plan. There are people in Harbin who can help us. He's told me that there is a great demand there for any goods we could collect because the refugees have shortages of everything. So, this is the idea, we'll have to bundle up anything we can spare, anything from Europe that we have managed to take out. They are so isolated there – they're starving for anything European and, most importantly, there is American currency to be had."

I am alarmed and astounded. "I don't know what you're thinking. You know it's forbidden to carry American money. We won't be able to get it past the Japanese. If they catch us they'll drag us off to their prisons, or cut off our hands, or shoot us on the spot." I feel myself getting more agitated and add with greater emphasis, "You know I'm not exaggerating!"

Poldi can see that I am unsettled by this suggestion but is determined to continue with his explanation of the scheme. "I do, but Leon has reliable connections and he will help us. I trust him, Nini," Poldi says firmly. "Do you think we can continue to survive, living hand to mouth? I'm not going to stand in line forever at the relief organizations waiting for handouts like the others. When my pride is gone, I might as well be dead. We're stuck here in Shanghai for the foreseeable future. I don't know when we'll get out and I don't know where we'll end up. I only know that we need the money if we are to succeed and we have to try something bold. We'll deal with the outcome as it happens."

"You really believe we can do this, smuggle American money back into Shanghai under the noses of the Japanese?" I feel the palms of my hands grow sweaty as I fully absorb the danger that we would have to face in this plan.

"Look around you, Nini. We're caught once more in a desperate situation. Think where we have already been, what we have had to do to get here and what will happen to us if we don't get sufficient money. We have no choice. And after all, we have stared down the Nazis and the Italian Fascists between us. We're still alive, right? Are the Japanese worse than their cohorts?"

Poldi has a glint in his dark eyes. He is brave and tough beneath the mild exterior. I know he's right and I'm as indignant as he is that we have been reduced to the level of beggars here. Whatever happens, we will go ahead together.

I nod my head, finally, in agreement as we hold hands and embrace. We have talked a great deal about a possible enterprise we could start. If we can manage to get sufficient capital from Harbin we have decided to open a small business of our own where we will work, side by side. This is our chance to show the Germans that they have not defeated us. I feel the old sense of determination again that I felt in Vienna. We will fight against them in the only way we can and we may succeed, but if we lose the game, we will have to pay the price.

We speak to all of the family together to tell them of our scheme. Mama is against the idea, anxious about the risks we will be taking. My sisters try to convince her that we'll be fine and that there's no other way out of our situation. Reluctantly and with a great deal of foreboding, she acquiesces. Erna and Stella have packed suitcases with fur stoles, needlepoint chair covers, linens and lingerie, elegant clothing from Vienna, cameras, anything they managed to salvage of value and are prepared to sell. I fill another with my own belongings including most of my dowry pieces and also many of Mama's things. We pool our funds so that Poldi and I can buy tickets on a ship from Shanghai and for the train trip through Korea to Harbin. They warn us to be careful. We promise we will and that when we return there will be enough money for everyone to start a new life.

The day arrives for us to set off on our "honeymoon" – the only kind we can have in this war-ravaged world – and we wave cheerfully to the relatives at the pier. Our voyage will take us by ship from Shanghai to Pusan in South

Korea. From there we will board a train that will take us north to Harbin. We will return by train to the port of Pusan and take a ferry across to Kobe in Japan, then make our way back by ship to Shanghai.

We are frugal with our money and manage to book passage on the cheapest means of transport, a freighter ship. By day it's clearly a rather ugly vessel, but we make believe that it turns into a romantic cruise ship by night. We stand by the railing, arm in arm, singing Viennese love songs in harmony and looking up at the black sky with stars that glitter like a pavé of diamonds. The battering waves of the Yellow Sea beat in time with our words, and everything seems suddenly possible, even our most remote dream of a peaceful life together.

From the ship we continue on through Korea into Manchuria in a rumbling train that rocks through the countryside, passing rice paddies where barefoot men and women bend over to tend to their crop or are tugged behind oxen and ploughs. Humans and beasts are toiling together in the same way as their predecessors have done for hundreds of years, muscles strained as they trudge shin deep in the milky water. One after another, the expansive watery patches with sprouting bunches of new green growth flick by the window.

In stations along the way raggedy children, little dirty hands stretched out, beg for coins or food. So many hungry mouths to feed in this country of millions. In the towns the black market business is a flourishing trade. The most prized commodity is American dollars, forbidden as we know, but available nonetheless. Trading is swift for anything that can be sold for the Yankee buck. There is no limit to the range and variety of goods to be had. Everywhere we go we are accosted by vendors who materialize from nowhere with every possible ware for sale. Legality is not an issue. When survival itself is the single constant goal, the means are not to be questioned.

When we arrive in Harbin, Poldi's friend Leon is waiting for us at the train station. He has a motor car and takes us to a hotel where he has booked a room for us. That evening we visit his home for dinner. As in other regions of the Orient, servants tend to our needs, one to cook the meals and another to clean the house. Native labour is cheap and any foreigner even with modest means is able to live very well indeed.

Leon is a congenial man, a few years older than us, now in his early thirties. He is so happy to see us and offers us the greatest hospitality. He and Poldi reminisce about their meeting in Milan, their youthful days of relative freedom and they laugh at each other's jokes while we enjoy the wonderful meal.

"How are conditions here for the Jewish people, Leon?" Poldi asks. Leon speaks German so I can understand what they are saying.

"I can honestly say that the Japanese have tried to do their best for us. You probably don't know that they supported the establishment of a Jewish Council and annual Jewish conferences which began in 1937. They met here in Harbin and brought together Jews from every region in the Orient."

"Why would they bother with that?" I ask.

"A clever wife you have, Poldi. Well, Nini, of course in the end it is for their own interests. The Sephardic Jews in Shanghai are very wealthy and powerful. The Japanese assume that all Jews have economic prowess and more than that they believe that American Jewry has power over the government and economy of the United States."

"Oh, I can't even begin to comprehend such stupidity," I say in disgust. "I think that if the last of us was destroyed, the world would still say that our ghosts were in control of the universe and they would blame our departed souls for whatever befell mankind."

"But Leon," Poldi asks, "what do the people here have to do with American Jewry?"

While we continue talking a Chinese maid moves about silently removing plates and glasses. She is tiny and polite, with a white apron tied around her waist and a blue and white checked kerchief covering her hair. Her head remains lowered. On her feet are the soft-soled slippers that make her movements almost indiscernible. She sets a black lacquered tray with a painted motif of songbirds and blossoms on the table before us. On it are a porcelain coffee pot, matching cups and saucers, creamer and sugar bowl and little silver spoons. She slips out again and Leon pours the dark steaming liquid into the cups.

"I've been told that the Japanese have grander ambitions. Their island is small and their population is bursting – they need to expand and they would like the United States, as well as Britain and Holland which have possessions here, to give them free rein in the region," Leon explains.

"And the Jews, what do the Japanese expect of us?" I ask.

We each have coffee that we sip while we talk. The deep flavour of the strong brew reminds me for a moment of the coffee back home, but then I think again of the situation at hand as Leon goes on with the explanation.

"If you can believe it, the Japanese think we can influence our American counterparts to convince Roosevelt to let them do as they will without interference. Listen, we know all of that is nonsense but it is the word circulating here in Harbin – and the sources are reliable."

The maid appears again, this time with a cut crystal decanter and brandy glasses on a silver tray. She sets it down and removes a full ashtray, replacing it with another clean one. Poldi removes his cigarette case from his jacket pocket and we each take a cigarette.

"We believe that our time here can only be temporary. At any moment the Japanese could decide we are ineffectual and turn against us. Many of us have applied for visas to the United States or South America and plan to leave this country as soon as it is safe, but we can stay here for as long as things remain calm and the Japanese allow us to live in peace. What more can we ask?" Leon leans comfortably back in his chair and shrugs his shoulders in a manner of acceptance when circumstances are beyond one's control. I decide that he is a pleasant fellow with a good heart and generous spirit. He puts me at ease with his relaxed manner and wide grin.

Poldi nods in agreement and says, "That is the lot of the Jewish people. Our lives are always in flux. It has been that way forever and may never change." He takes a sip of cognac and sets the glass on the dining table. We have had a comforting meal and are finishing our coffee and liqueur. Poldi takes a deep draught of his cigarette, sets it down on the ashtray, then becomes earnest and leans towards his old friend. "Leon, you know we have come here for more than a friendly visit."

"I know, Poldi. Well, then listen, this is my plan. Tomorrow you and I will head into the city to meet with a man I know very well. In the meantime, I have purchased a few bushels of crab apples."

Poldi and I look at Leon, then at one another, and break out into laughter so rollicking that we have to wipe the tears from our eyes and hold our aching sides.

"I didn't know that my old friend could get drunk from just a few glasses of cognac," Poldi says at last, still red-faced and grinning. "What happened to my drinking buddy, the one who could go from bar to bar and drain one bottle of whiskey after the other and still walk a straight line? What is that you said about apples?"

Leon has not joined us in the gales of laughter. Through it all he has sat smiling, with an air of concealed wisdom that he is waiting patiently to impart, refilling his glass and continuing to drink in silence. When we are back to reason, he begins to explain. His cook will prepare the apples by cooking them in water and sugar until a thick gooey sauce is produced and the apples are thoroughly preserved. This mixture will be poured into heavy metal cans with handles and lids like paint cans that can be firmly closed. In this dense liquid, rubber packets – sewn by hand, tied with string, and weighted – can be submerged and hidden. And inside those pouches, resting safely on the bottom of the tins, will be rolls of American dollars.

We listen intently, beginning to understand his idea. Leon has another scheme as well. He suggests that he and Poldi leave early the next day and head into the city to meet with someone he knows who has helped others in similar circumstances and is skilled in smuggling techniques. We head back to the hotel and have a good night's sleep in the comfortable room, pulling the covers up over our weary bodies and easing into the clean sheets.

I am still asleep when Leon comes for Poldi in the morning and the two set off. When they return, Poldi tells me what he has been doing.

"Look, Nini," he says, taking off his shoes one by one while seated on the edge of our bed. He holds the shoes up for me to see. "The heels have been hollowed out and in these hollows we can conceal money. There is a false bottom that flips back over and nothing is visible – see?"

I stare at the shoes and see the way the plan will work. Still, I wonder if we will manage to succeed.

"Now, we have to get the money," I say.

"That's where you come in, Nini. We will all head into the city tomorrow. Leon will put us in touch with people connected to the black market, the underground economy. You have to convince them that our belongings are of great value."

"Of course they are," I say indignantly. "After all, we have brought them over eight thousand miles from Vienna, then to Shanghai and finally here to Harbin. They must be worth a fortune just for that alone. Right?"

"Right," he says with a smile. "You were always a good saleslady."

We take our suitcases into Harbin the next day and open them one by one before the purchasers. They are seasoned negotiators but, then, so are we. By the end of the day we go back to the hotel and close the door to our room. We empty my purse and Poldi's pockets onto the bed and stand back in amazement at the sight of all the money, so many American dollars, crumpled dirty greenish paper with English printing. To us this money means the world, every possibility for the future, worth every risk that we will have to take.

We laugh and hug and bounce on the bed in the middle of the bills. Then we get up, sober again, gather up every single dollar, checking under the bed to be sure that we have left nothing behind. We count and bundle them neatly and stuff them back into my purse. We prepare to take all of it to Leon's home, where he and Poldi will conceal it as planned.

Harbin is a small city compared to Vienna or Shanghai and because of its location it is more primitive and less metropolitan. Still, we go out to restaurants and spend a few wonderful days with Leon. We have some money now, enough to feel truly prosperous after so long. Who could ever have believed what we would be doing and where we would be. I feel like the spies in movies, caught in a web of high-stakes intrigue. Cigarette smoke swirls around us, shrouding us in a mist of gauzy mystery. I will play a dramatic role after all.

It is a sad farewell when we finally board the train that will begin our journey back to Shanghai. Leon and Poldi exchange a warm bear hug and Leon kisses me on both cheeks.

"Nini, take care of my good friend. We are like brothers, you know."

"I do, Leon, and I will do my best. Thank you for everything. We'll meet again, won't we?"

"How can we know what the future might bring? But if there is a way, somehow, somewhere we will all be together again. Go in peace."

A porter takes our baggage and the two heavy metal cans of fruit. The train station and our friend grow smaller in the distance and soon are out of sight. Signs posted in various languages, including German and English, remind us that we are not allowed to have foreign currency in our possession in strict violation of the Japanese occupation army. Along the way travellers undergo brief inspections at stations, just a formality – a check of our documents and a wave of the hand sets us off again.

Poldi tells me not to worry, that everything will be fine, but as I lie in his arms I find that sleep will not come. The next day we will be taking a ferry boat into Japan and military police will be inspecting all our belongings. If we are arrested, we are finished. If he is taken away, how will I survive alone? I look at his sleeping face so close to mine, peaceful and handsome, dark curls over his forehead, deep in dreams, and I am comforted. Another tomorrow is all we can hope for. The rest is in the hands of Fate.

The next day, my heart thumps wildly when armed Japanese soldiers enter our room on the train at Pusan. If we pass inspection here, we will be allowed to board the ferry boat to Kobe. The soldiers are stoic, rude, and abrupt. They bark commands in Japanese or Russian. Poldi speaks to them in Russian. I understand neither language but the motions are clear enough. I speak to Poldi in German, telling him to be careful. When the Japanese soldier turns to me and questions me in perfect German, asking what we have to hide, I feel my face turn scarlet.

One officer points to our cans of fruit. Poldi smiles, looking proud of the contents and as if he wants to share the apples with the inspectors. He takes a pocket knife carefully from his jacket, showing it very slowly to make sure they will not mistake it for a weapon. He opens both cans. The Japanese soldiers peer into the thick, dark syrup with the little red apples bobbing around on top. Poldi takes a cup and scoops up some of it, offering it to the men, obviously suggesting that they taste it. They refuse it with disdain. Poldi takes a bit himself to show what they are missing and grins with delight at the taste of the sugary concoction.

One of the soldiers tells him to seal the can again. Then another soldier has an idea. He decides that Poldi should be searched. Again I find it hard to conceal my fear. Poldi, however, seems cool and at ease. They point their rifles at him and demand that he empty his pockets. He smiles at them calmly, shows them his wallet, which holds only Chinese paper money and is of no concern to them. The others ransack our suitcases in a mad search for valuables and tear through my handbag. Poldi removes his shirt and stands, arms raised in the air, legs astride waiting to be checked. A soldier pats down his body, down the length of his pant legs, down to his shoes. Then he stops.

The Japanese exchange a few more words, then leave. When they stomp out of our little cabin, I take several deep breaths. I feel as though the air in my lungs has been constricted and that my chest is being held in a vise. I marvel at Poldi's courage under the rigid gaze of the vicious armed men and at his unflinching disregard for the possible consequences of discovery. We have seen the Japanese beat offenders nearly to death or hack fingers off thieves without a moment's concern. We both know what he has risked.

Poldi looks at me. I look at him. We say nothing, sitting side by side on the lower bunk of the bed, wondering if they might return, whether they might think of something further to inspect. We wait. After some time has passed, I whisper to him, "We did it."

Having passed the border inspection, we can relax and enjoy the beauty of Kobe and also visit Osaka and Tokyo. We have our money carefully hidden and use only the Chinese currency, which we have converted to Japanese yen for our expenses. We do nothing to alert the authorities to our activities. We go about like common newlyweds, simple sightseers, arm in arm, laughing at private jokes, shopping for souvenirs, with no care in the world.

CHAPTER 24

RETURN TO SHANGHAI 1940

The honeymoon and adventure lasted over two months, but now it is March and we have returned once more to Shanghai. Our family is glad to see us again, eager to hear about our success in Harbin and overjoyed that we have managed to bring so much money back for everyone to start new lives. We are beaming as we see them and bask in warm embraces and smiles although for us the trip, despite the danger, was a wonderful dream that we didn't want to end.

It seems that our happiness cannot last for long. The family starts to tell us that developments in Europe have only worsened in our absence. Newspapers from England report nothing but bad news. Hitler's troops, efficient soldiers armed with the most modern equipment and bolstered by the fanatical fervour of their leader's doctrine, have been moulded into a human machine of destruction. Only world domination will satisfy the voracious monster, as it devours people, towns, countries in the gluttony for power.

Since the invasion of Czechoslovakia in March of 1939, then the onslaught on Poland in September, Hitler and the German people have been emboldened by the successes of their army. Diplomatic attempts have proven futile. We are sure that Chamberlain's pre-war slogan "Peace in our time" has become nothing but a joke for the Fuhrer and his men. One by one the flimsy defences of the countries in his path have crumbled.

The year 1940 has been turbulent from the start and so it continues. Germany invades Denmark and Norway in April, then in swift succession conquers the Netherlands, Belgium, and Luxembourg. The world seems hypnotized into submission as these countries tumble like dominoes. We shake our heads as we hear the news and the almost incidental reports that Jews are being herded together and sent away to concentration camps.

The French and English armies are struggling in northern France trying to hold off the enemy. On May 11 Winston Churchill becomes the British prime minister, and we wonder, as we hear his forceful voice on the radio, whether there is the resolve to hold off the onslaught and curtail the bloodletting.

In homes and public places we refugees gather around radios in an effort to get the current news. We hold our heads in anguish, as Hitler's voice thunders with arrogance, making us doubt any possible rescue. We listen spellbound to broadcasts in which Churchill speaks with strength and outrage about the German menace that is eyeing England as another easy target. It is clear to us that a Nazi victory would mark our own doom.

By the end of May the whole European community in Shanghai is in shock and distress as we read the terrifying headline, "France has fallen!" Newspaper photos show the inconceivable sight of German soldiers marching down the Champs Elysées.

It is not just the course of the war that has thrown the family into a state of alarm. While we were away Mama became suddenly ill and in the two months since our return she has deteriorated substantially. I have tried to understand how she could have come to this state in such a short time and am torn with guilt, believing that I might have done something to prevent the circumstances that we must now face.

"No one could have helped her, Nini," Stella says defensively. "Not even you. You always imagine you can solve anything, cure anything, but you're wrong. She is just sick, that's all, and the doctors can't do a thing to save her." Her voice pulls and snaps like a rubber band, revealing her state of tension, a mixture of frustration, anger, and sadness.

"Something should be done," I say in dismal helplessness "How can we just stand by and watch her die?" Fear bubbles up in my throat, making my voice sound high-pitched like a shriek.

Haltingly, Erna says, "We have to accept it. She is dying, Nini. All the doctors in Shanghai can do nothing to save her." Eventually I absorb what they are telling me and acknowledge our impotence. A paralyzing disease has attacked her nervous system, making her weaker day by day and there is no cure.

As we gather by her bedside Poldi and I are distressed, as is everyone. Willi's eyes are moist behind his glasses. Stella and Walter, Erna and Fritz are all pale, drawn, and dismal. Lily sits in her chair quietly scribbling some drawings on a note pad. Dolu and Eva are here too, and all are silent in shared sadness.

Mama is dying and there is nothing to do about it. She lives now with Stella and Walter, so we go there every day since our return to congregate around her. We stand looking at her frail body and shrunken face able only to watch the rapid decline of her energies and physical strength.

We take turns sitting with her, alternating our post with a few hours of restless sleep, after forcing some food or drink down our throats. The vigil lasts for weeks as we watch the heroine of our lives slipping away from us. The woman lying in the bed is a shrivelled shell of what she had been. Her eyes are dulled now, no longer fiery with determination and stubborn resistance. I can hardly bear to see her in this helpless and reduced condition after her courageous struggles and sacrifices.

I am standing by her bedside the next day when she emerges briefly from drugged sleep. "This is the end of the journey for me, Nini," she says, aware now that I am here. Her voice is feeble, her hand reaches to mine. "Some day you will be a mother too, and you will be able to tell your children about me and explain to them what we have experienced. If my prayers are answered, God will allow that my grandchildren will be born in peace. Be brave. Life can still be wonderful for you and Poldi.

You have youth, that is the main thing, and you are strong enough to survive."

My tears turn her and the whole room into a blur of melting images. "No, Mama, don't die. Please stay with us. We all need you so much. Don't leave us alone."

In a weak voice, hardly audible, she replies, "I'm … so tired."

Her words are barely more than a whisper as her life ebbs away. She has slipped into a coma. A constant pain burns in my chest, a hammering assault of anguish, and I can't stop my tears. All of us take turns holding her wrinkled, liver-spotted hand, the blue veins clearly defined under the thin skin. We remember the years that have passed, bend to kiss her forehead and say our farewells. We are waiting for the final breath. The hours tick by and we keep our silent vigil.

Finally, I go to the room next door to try to get some sleep. I have fallen into one of my strange distorted dreams but am soon awakened again. Muffled sounds come from the hallway. I can recognize Fritz's and Walter's voices, and Poldi's. When I go to the door, they are standing together, choking back their sorrow. Erna, Stella, and Willi are convulsed in grief-stricken tears. They look at me but have nothing to say. Words are not needed. I know that Mama has died.

Mama's death has a profound effect on me. I am desperately lonely despite all the others who are still here, even Poldi. Mama meant home to me, my Viennese youth and nostalgic longings. As long as she was alive there existed a bit, just the smallest remnant of the old way of life, a tie to the Sunday teas, the aunties and uncles and especially the connection to Papa. Although I knew that those memories were gone forever, I find this a cruel finality that is hard to bear. The loss of Mama now, so far from our home, destroys my courage and strength. My poor husband tries every means to pull me from my desolation without success. I turn from him and the others in the family.

"Nini, do you think that this is what Mama and your papa would have expected of you?" Poldi asks when we are alone.

I stay curled up in bed, refusing to answer.

"If you were still in Vienna, in the old days, you could pout and carry on in this way, but not here and now. Don't you think the others are mourning too?"

"No," I say in stubborn rejection of his appeals, "not like me. She was closest to Willi and me because we are the youngest and we have been alone with her for so long. They don't feel it like we do."

"Even if that is true, we have no time for self-pity, not a minute of it. Tomorrow we will go and look for a place to set up a business, just you and I together against the whole world. Isn't that what we always have said?"

I nod my head like a child, accepting the words but not able to drive away the grief. I look out the open window at the dark street, the heavy ever-present smells of Shanghai seeping in, the sounds of babies crying, and I feel desperately sad.

CHAPTER 25

TEN GREEN BOTTLES 1940-1941

We are not even allowed the luxury of mourning our loss. With Mama gone, we no longer have an anchor and feel as though we have been suddenly thrust into a hostile environment where we must each find our own direction. I have summoned my courage again and tried to cast the thoughts of depression away. When I hear Viennese music, it conjures up old memories and I want to weep. It would be easy to sink into despair, but I am determined not to give in. Although I miss Mama terribly every day, there remains a force within me that drives me forward. After all, Poldi and I are young and healthy, and our lives still lie before us. Here we are, having outwitted our formidable enemies, and together, we have concluded, we will find a way to survive.

Shortly after Mama's death, with united determination, we set out to look for a way to make a living. Opportunities exist for those who are willing to gamble all they have and who are prepared to plunge without hesitation into the heart of this mysterious city. Jobs are scarce for foreigners, and so a whole spectrum of businesses has begun to sprout around us, owned and operated by refugees. Like them, we have decided it is prudent to put down roots to get us through the time we are here.

Necessity is compelling us to become resourceful, so we immigrants are adapting to the new environment and melding into the cosmopolitan milieu of French Town. We make use of whatever knowledge or skills we have to provide a livelihood. Some cook familiar foods and sell them quite successfully as most of us have not got used to the Chinese cuisine. Others sew affordable European-style clothing in lightweight fabrics, more suitable to this extreme climate than the things we brought from home.

Various possibilities have been discussed for each of us. Using the money we were able to bring back from Harbin, before long everyone in the family has found a suitable enterprise to pursue. Stella and Walter have recently opened a coffee house called Café de Paris where people can congregate as they did at home. Willi and Fritz are selling shoes in another little place, and Erna still teaches needlepoint at the convent, where she can keep Lily close to her.

As for us, Poldi and I have reasoned that a bar would be a good idea. I have some related experience and Poldi has already made some inquiries. He has found that he can negotiate credit terms with some companies that import beer and whiskey from America and vodka from Russia. He has spoken to distributors who provide all kinds of liquor throughout Shanghai, a product that is in constant demand and ready supply. After considerable discussion we have concluded that we could make such an enterprise profitable, but when we set about to rent some space, we discover we really don't have enough money to start on our own. Through those Poldi has met in the liquor trade he has come across a possible way for us to overcome this obstacle. We are told that there is an establishment, a small but reasonably successful bar where the owner is looking for a business partner. We head out to the address we are given.

"Are you sure this is right?" I ask Poldi as we meander into an unsavoury district, looking at numbers on the doors, careful not to collide with any of the seedy-looking pedestrians.

"Well, Nini, you have to expect this kind of place," he says, sidestepping a drunk hunched over on the sidewalk. He takes my hand and we persevere.

When we locate the destination we read the sign above the door, "Marco's Bar," and when we go inside we find the owner sitting at one of the barstools within the dark interior. Marco is a heavy-set Bulgarian Jew with an easygoing disposition. He puts out his large right hand in greeting and slides his bulky body off the seat.

Marco shows us around the place, proudly pointing out all the facilities, including the counter with stools as well as booths. In one corner is a small piano where an entertainer plays each night. In the back is a fully stocked store room and washroom facilities; the liquor licence is displayed on the wall behind the cash register, and brightly coloured prints of the Moulin Rouge in Paris are hung randomly throughout. We agree to buy in with whatever cash we have and make up the rest in worked hours. As we shake hands with Marco, his deep-throated laugh rumbles through his corpulent frame. We agree that this will be a good deal for us all, joining in with his mirth and hugging one another.

We have rented a more comfortable apartment, just one bedroom and adjoining sitting room but we have our own bathroom. The rooms are clean and neatly furnished. It is all that we need. We have become a part of Shanghai, settling here, staying mostly with other European refugees whose faces are becoming more familiar when we pass in the street and meet in the coffee houses. We greet one another in our own language, not mingling much with the Chinese, not accepted by the higher classes of Sephardic Jews or other foreigners, but content within our own world.

By the spring of 1940 the partnership with Marco has come into effect. Even if we are here for just another year or so, we reason, we will earn a reasonably good income. We can put something aside for the future and who knows, we might go to America or England, somewhere civilized, when this seemingly interminable war comes to an end.

For now, there is nothing but Shanghai, a rowdy open port that welcomes ships of all nationalities and the thirsty sailors who man them. During the day a frenzy of commercial activity thrives, but when darkness slips over the city, another side of Shanghai emerges, a sordid kaleidoscope of blurring faces in search of amusement of all sorts. Garish neon lights blink their messages in colours that blare like trumpets, aglow with fluorescent pink, green, and red, a symphony that throbs with raw energy until sunrise.

On the crowded sidewalks we make our way to the bar each evening, passing very young, frail-limbed Chinese girls, their juvenile faces painted thickly in brazen make-up. They sell themselves for the price of a meal or an opium fix and beckon to the uniformed men who carouse on the streets. Their lives are short and horrid, but they are part of the expendable war equipment. Like the ammunition and machinery, they will be used up and discarded as a necessary sacrifice to the war. These are some of the many casualties that will never appear in the lists of wounded or dead.

Our route crosses a street called Blood Alley. Its cobblestones are stained with red and brown blotches of dried blood that has been spilled and has coalesced into a pattern of grisly remembrance. The street itself aches from the skirmishes it has borne. Every night there is some eruption of violence outside or inside the bar. Inevitably one customer insults another's homeland and a brawl erupts. Broken bottles, bloodied fists and faces, screams and threats are the nightly fare. Nearly a year has passed since we started this venture with Marco, and now even these events become routine.

There is a melancholy loneliness among the servicemen that surfaces in their drunken haze. After the fighting, when anger and physical tension have been released, they break into song. Slurred masculine voices penetrate the grey smoky air with tunes of their boyhoods. The British have a favourite that we soon learn to recognize. Arms wound around one another's shoulders, swaying in rhythm and whiskey-soaked nostalgia, they begin,

> Ten green bottles hanging on the wall,
> Ten green bottles hanging on the wall,
> And if one green bottle should accidentally fall,
> There'll be nine green bottles hanging on the wall.

Even the burliest man in a state of inebriation and homesick longing finds himself weeping as the words are sung. For me, the simple
words of the song capture the essence of everything that is lost, broken,
destroyed. From their words and soulful singing, it seems to me that the
sailors are conjuring memories of things they miss, being stuck as we are
in this sordid refuge. Surely they remember the innocence of youth,
surely they are thinking of friends who have fallen in battle, of their
families back home, gathering at holidays, of home-cooking, girlfriends
or wives who are becoming vague memories of tenderness, too far away
and long ago to seem real any more. I picture the connection between
the words and the impact of the feelings. My imagination transforms
the men and their song into a graphic lament where each link to home
smashes to bits like the bottles of the song, tipping, crashing, and splin-
tering into millions of sharp-edged fragments of green glass.

> Nine green bottles hanging on the wall,
> Nine green bottles hanging on the wall,
> And if one green bottle should accidentally fall,
> There'll be eight green bottles hanging on the wall.

The last verse is sung in the slow cadence of a dirge,

> One green bottle hanging on the wall,
> One green bottle hanging on the wall,
> And if this green bottle should accidentally fall,
> There'll be nothing left but the smell upon the wall.

One particularly steamy summer night I am drawn into the mood
of the sailors' sodden tunes. The air in the bar is the usual stale smoky
mixture, bitter with the odour of ale, whiskey, and sweat. The heat
drains my energy. Lethargy and remorse draw me into a sullen mood
and I am uncomfortably hot and sticky as I feel my dress clinging to my
body in the damp heat, perspiration trickling down my back. The som-

bre melody of the refrain echoes in my mind. The clinking notes of the piano fill the air, and the words of the song seem to symbolize my personal struggle. I question my own limitations. How many "bottles" remain in my life? How many more traumas can I endure before I tumble into the final abyss? It is so clear to me at this moment that the song represents my own life. In my mind I go over the words again and again, imagining the jagged glass as my own pile of disappointments and painful separations, losses, and alienation. Smashed, I think, like the glass of Kristallnacht.

I long for Vienna, ache for Mama's arms to cradle me as if I were a baby again. I want the life that I had, the friends, the gaiety and youth that are gone. I sink with the song, drown with the emptiness of our routine, despise the Nazis for what they have done, detest the smells of the Chinese and the omnipresent Japanese soldiers with their rifles and swaggering ways. This is not an evening when Poldi can charm or cajole me into better spirits and he knows enough not even to try.

For many hours I stand behind the counter. The men drink with dedicated purpose, pouring the strong liquor down their throats until they finally fall into the state of forgetfulness they are seeking. Behind the counter the wall is mirrored and lined to the ceiling with glass shelves filled with bottles of every kind, vodka, whiskey, brandy, Scotch, Vermouth, imported wine, and an assortment of sweet liqueurs. There are casks and bottles of beer stacked by the wall.

I am at the cash drawer, methodically counting the crumpled bills and stacking them in order of denomination. Suddenly, an enormous rat leaps over my fingers. In terror, I start screaming and cannot stop. I am convulsing and nausea overcomes me. Still I can't stop the shrill siren that emanates from my throat.

My head reverberates with the relentless refrain of the song. The tune drones on and on, counting down the diminishing numbers of imagined bottles, crashing to bits. Panic and delirium engulf me and I have the sensation of being pulled down into a morass where liquor bottles and faces hover disjointedly all around me. Everything sounds muffled and jumbled together.

Marco has been sitting in one of the booths. When I begin screaming, he is so alarmed that he has tried to jump up, but now finds himself stuck, his wide body jammed into the space. His face is red with embarrassment and he is exasperated as he tries to extricate himself. Others are laughing at him, but I am still screaming. I am vaguely aware of Poldi and some others talking to me, trying to settle me down, but the song fills my mind and the memory of the rat's tail brushing against my skin won't let me go.

"Nini, Nini, please be calm," Poldi whispers into my ear, his arms around me. He leads me to the last booth, near the back of the bar. I sit down, finally quiet but still shuddering. Poldi leaves me for a moment then quickly returns. "Here, *Liebling*," he says gently. "This will help you feel better." He gives me a sip of brandy that streams through my blood and warms my icy veins. He stays with me, insisting that I finish the glass. An hour passes before I stop shivering.

He asks Marco to finish closing up the bar and takes me home to bed where I huddle under the covers, trembling like a child, praying for sleep to soothe my unsettled mind. "Nini," he says, "get some rest. The rat didn't hurt you. You know there are rats in Shanghai. It's at sea level, after all. Just close your eyes and go to sleep and in the morning you will see that things are all right again."

He kisses my forehead and tucks the blanket tight to my body. Drowsy from the effect of the liquor, I pull his arm and ask, "Did you check for bedbugs?" Every night since we've been married I have asked the same question and every night he assures me that he has sprayed to kill anything crawling or squirming in the sheets.

"Yes, Nini. Everything is clean and safe. Good night now, and pleasant dreams. In the morning, things will be better," he says again.

I often awaken abruptly through the night from horrific dreams, wet with cold sweat, my heart racing wildly, my fingers clenched so tightly that my nails have dug red crescents into my palms. Terrible visions drift in my brain of huge hairy rats grown to human size, nibbling at our hands and feet, slowly devouring us as we sleep. Sometimes the dreams are of the Nazis, terrifying in their brutality, slaughtering babies and beating elderly women. Other times the nightmares are of the new horror, the Chinese or Japanese at our door, their narrow glaring eyes condemning our intrusion into their lives.

Violins are playing in the distance, dreamily lilting from scratchy gramophone recordings and my mind floats away in feverish surrender. I can't be certain whether I am drunk, hallucinating, or really hearing the sounds of people playing music outside the window. In our crowded little cells, we displaced Viennese refugees languish in nostalgic homesickness, trying in vain to grasp any fragments of the lost past. Waltzes of Strauss, strains of Mozart, Haydn, and Schubert often fill the hot and humid Shanghai nights. In my mind the familiar melodies merge with frightening images and I struggle again to distinguish reality from fantasy. It would be so easy to retreat into madness. Many have given up the fight, but somehow I battle against the undertow. Unable to surrender to a peaceful slumber, I roll and turn, restless and uneasy throughout the long black night. When the morning sun finally forces its way through the tattered curtains we have hung by the window, I have once more discovered the renewed strength to face the harsh reality of the path placed before us. I am still intact. There are still more "green bottles" remaining in my life.

CHAPTER 26

PEARL HARBOR 1941

Mama has been buried in the Jewish cemetery. After the funeral I often go to visit her grave. At first there is just a mound of freshly dug earth and a wooden marker. She is gone, but I still feel her presence as I always have with Papa. The pain of grief twists like a knife inside, a dull heartache that remains with me every day as I go about my regular activities. Simple things remind me of her – the chair where she used to sit, the coffee house where we would go and gaze at the strange thoroughfare, or someone passing wearing a hat like hers. After a few months my sisters and Willi and I with the rest of the family gather to watch as a headstone is erected. The ceremony is called an unveiling and is considered to be a final farewell.

After that we visit her whenever we can. When Poldi and I go, we see small stones set around the gravesite, mementos from others, messages to show that she is remembered and honoured for the good that she did throughout her life. We each place a pebble on the headstone and shed more tears.

We continue with our lives, managing the bar, spending time with the family, going to the movies or out to restaurants. In fact, our lives are better than they have been for years. The family is well fed and everyone has a reasonable form of livelihood. Despite the sadness, we manage to find a degree of normalcy in this abnormal environment.

"Well, it's not Vienna," we often hear people say in the familiar Viennese dialect, followed by the typical reply, "But we can walk in freedom, for now at least. If we can endure the food and avoid the disease and not anger the Japanese, it's not so bad." The exchange is ended with a smile and a nod.

Emotions sit just below the surface all the time. We are either giddy with a momentary spurt of good humour or depressed by the remembrance of the reason for our exile. These feelings are common among the refugees. Who could remain even-tempered and constantly rational in this chaotic environment? But even in the bible the Jewish people are considered stubborn survivors and are described as "stiff-necked." We mean to overcome the most severe obstacles, even here.

"We are nothing if not an organized people," Poldi says to me one day while he's reading the Jewish newspaper. It's printed in Shanghai now and circulated among most of the refugees, outlining current events, meetings, and gatherings. "I suppose it's a way to replace the structure that's lacking in our lives after all the upheaval." He adds with a wry smile, "Even wandering the desert, Moses had to get the Ten Commandments for us."

The biggest refugee organization in Shanghai is the Jewish Community of Central European Jews called Juedishe Gemeinde. It is an umbrella group encompassing each religious affiliation from Reform to Orthodox and covers a broad range of services and activities. Institutions have been put in place that include Jewish education, Kosher ritual slaughter for our meat, welfare services, and the establishment of Jewish hospitals. Religious ceremonies, marriages, divorces, births, and deaths also come under the auspices of the Gemeinde.

Our group of exiles is not a raggle-taggle company of illiterates and vagrants. We comprise a full spectrum of people with talents and intelligence, who have come from the most civilized cities in Europe and carry our highly organized culture with us. Jewish pride is flourishing once more – although, as might be expected there is bickering about religious practice, whose way is the best way, and so on.

Several synagogues already exist where wedding ceremonies are performed. The Sephardic *shuls* Beth Aharon and Ohel Rachel provide a meeting place for those who were living here before we arrived. As their customs differ from those of our community with European ancestry, we assemble in the Ashkenazi Oihel Moishe Synagogue, where Poldi and I were married by Rabbi Ashkenazi, an interesting name I always think, for the chief rabbi of Shanghai. A Jewish hospital has been opened where doctors who were ostracized and forbidden from practising in Vienna are saving lives and delivering babies.

We have various clubs and relief organizations, including ORT, which was founded in Russia in 1880 to help the peasant population develop useful skills. The letters "ORT" are an acronym of three Russian words that mean "handicrafts, industry and agriculture." In English it is called "Organization for Rehabilitation through Training." In Shanghai, as in Vienna and elsewhere, it provides training to those who need to find useful vocations to deal with transition.

Because Jews are used to being displaced and needing retraining to adapt to new societies, ORT continues to thrive. With thousands of us relocated in China, we need this society more than ever. Trades are taught to those who were musicians or professionals back home but who need more marketable skills here. Men are taught mechanics and women learn the dressmaking trade. In this way our people try to ensure that Jews, regardless of where we might find ourselves, are not a burden through demands on social welfare or, worse, begging for handouts. We try to make our own way and fit in wherever we surface. "Normal" is what we want, but that is not what we can have. "Normal" means peace, and no matter what we do, we are not in a world at peace.

Just as soon as we put the thoughts of war behind us, a news broadcast or headline in the papers reminds us of the events drawing us into the vortex of the storm. It's December now, and the onset of the winter months is sure to put more frozen corpses on the streets. We wear our warm coats and make our way into the cold night air for our regular walk to the bar. As we are up till late hours, we sleep most of the day and only catch up on the latest news when we get to work, but as we hurry along the street on the evening of December 7 there is a different sense of anxiety and we notice a frenzied buzz in the air. We overhear bits of conversations, things like "Can you believe what happened at Pearl Harbor?" and "Thousands were killed." People are bustling about even more than usual and we hear one question repeated over and over: "Will America declare war against Japan?"

Every evening before we open the bar, we and Marco sit and listen to the latest news broadcast. The static crackles, and when the voices break through, they have a characteristic reverberation. When we enter the bar this evening, Marco is seated on his usual stool, his ear cocked to the large wooden-boxed radio by the counter.

"Marco, you heard about Pearl Harbor?" Poldi asks.

"They've been talking about it all day. It happened this morning. *Shh*, I'm just listening to an American news report," he says as he tunes the radio and raises the volume until we can hear the words.

The radio announcer sounds agitated. There is a brittle sound of papers shuffling and a break in the transmission and then he continues, "Ladies and gentlemen, early this morning the American naval base in Honolulu was bombed. At 7:53 a.m. our armed forces sustained the first of two shattering attacks. At 8:55 there was another. Many planes and battleships have been destroyed. We still do not have an exact number of American casualties but the estimate is over two thousand. Our nation is in shock. President Roosevelt is expected to declare war against Japan. Remember this date, folks, December 7, 1941. Pray for our boys and girls overseas and God bless America."

I clasp my hand over my mouth in disbelief.

"Well," Poldi says, "the Americans are in it now whether they want to be or not."

"And right here in our backyard," Marco adds, lifting a glass of beer to his mouth. "The Japs have done it for sure, brought the Yanks into it, the whole damned U.S. army, navy, and marines."

"And now what will happen?" I wonder aloud.

Marco replies, grinning, "Who can say what this might bring to us refugees? In Shanghai, one never knows, right?"

He finishes the foamy brew and sets it down, then lifts his arm towards the entrance, and announces, "My friends, let's open the doors. War or peace, business still goes on."

As a rowdy bunch of soldiers pile in Poldi tells the piano player to play loudly, a quick-tempo upbeat tune to keep everyone amused. All anyone talks about is the war in the Pacific. The European front was too distant to impact on those living in Asia but now it has hit this region with a thunderous blow. We are dead centre in the latest conflict.

At the bar that evening we listen spellbound to the latest from around the world. President Roosevelt's voice sounds strained as he proclaims that December 7, 1941, will live in infamy. He calls the attack premeditated and unprovoked and pledges to wage a righteous fight that will not stop until there is absolute victory.

It seems as though violence and devastation have followed us even to the other side of the world. Pearl Harbor has become another milepost for the refugees – already we refer to this or that happening before or after Pearl Harbor. The very day after the attack, our situation is already beginning to change.

Before Pearl Harbor, the Japanese mostly respected the international zones, though there were incidents from time to time, and we lived in relative peace. But now they are mounting a heavy-handed takeover. Like the Nazis in Europe, they sweep through Shanghai. Private art collections are looted, then in quick succession, the mansions of the ruling class, the stock exchange, and vast factories are confiscated by the Japanese authorities. The glorious and grand landmark, the Cathay Hotel, has been commandeered to house their officers. Residents of the hotel have been evicted without concern or consideration. Many of the wealthy who are Allied nationals are arrested and imprisoned in camps erected on the outskirts of the city. I remember General Whitehall and his haughty wife from the Bolero Club when we read that the British, in particular, have been roughly treated, removed from their ostentatious homes and dragged into the squalid camp. The Sassoon office buildings are converted into a propaganda centre. Everywhere we go we see signs of change, and the ubiquitous flag of Japan, with its radiating rays of the red sun, flutters menacingly wherever we look.

Although life is as precarious as ever, the Jewish refugees in Shanghai see this sudden change as a reason for optimism. In the Jewish papers the news is accompanied by vaguely hopeful editorials. When we speak to other refugees and to our family the same cautious phrasing is heard. Maybe, we hear, maybe this will lead us to a way out. Until now, the Far East was not of much concern to the Americans, and any chance of our rescue was slim, but now that they have been angered and drawn into the war, maybe they will stumble across us, living in this distant enclave, and bring us salvation.

Radio and newspapers are more heavily controlled than ever by the rigid Japanese occupation forces. We get information from outside almost exclusively through the Jewish underground network. From there we discover the effects that the bombing of Pearl Harbor has had, that the entire globe is now at war.

Despite it all we continue with our lives. The bar remains open for business but the British and Americans have gone. Mostly the patrons are Japanese or Korean soldiers.

"I miss the Brits and Yankees," I tell Poldi as we are closing up one night. "I can't speak to the Oriental soldiers or understand what they are saying and I find them rougher somehow."

"They do have a brusque manner," Poldi answers, "but they're heavy drinkers all the same, which is good for business and probably no rowdier than the others."

We make our way home as always at dawn, a time when Shanghai is at its most quiet, just before the early morning activity is about to begin once more. To me it seems that the city itself is as tired as I am, worn down by all the hostility and suffering of the Chinese people. The sun creeps up from the horizon, looking as though it's reluctant to shine once more on this battered and maligned spot on the globe.

In our flat we flop into bed, with a kiss and a wish for a better tomorrow. Fatigue swamps us. Before I fall asleep I say drowsily to Poldi, "Is this bombing a good thing for us? Do you think we might be saved?"

Poldi is already snoring.

The world of the Jewish refugees, or Shanghailanders as we call ourselves, has been altered once more. It is evident that the Japanese government had this scheme well orchestrated. On the morning after the Pearl Harbor offensive, a parade of Japanese forces marches down the Bund. We hear about it on the radio. In a show of impressive might, columns of tanks and armed soldiers and hundreds of red sun flags wave and there is no doubt of the intention. These are the self-proclaimed conquerors taking full and unequivocal control of all Shanghai. Notices tacked to every post and building proclaim war with the United States and Britain.

Although meetings have been planned at the community centre and in the synagogues, we decide not to go. Our family gathers at Stella's apartment. We warm our hands over the radiator but its heat is not sufficient to combat the first chill of the winter months ahead. The room is crowded, for we are all here, even Dolu and Eva, who live in the Russian Settlement. We cling together as a cohesive group. There are no outsiders. We trust each other exclusively.

News is not just a story on the radio to us. History is not something to be read about in books. It is our reality, our life. Our very existence is tied to the political furor that is brewing. Dressed in warm woollens and clutching hot cups of coffee, we also help ourselves to biscuits and some hazelnut torte that Stella was able to get in the Jewish bakery down the street. We are here to discuss the current political strife that has erupted around us and to await Poldi's return. He has been to the Juedishe Gemeinde office, where he usually finds ways to extract the most current information.

When he arrives, I welcome him at the door. His coat is not heavy and he rubs his hands and blows on them for warmth, then gratefully accepts the cup of coffee mixed with three lumps of sugar that I hand to him. As he sips it I see some colour return to his face.

While he removes his hat and coat, everyone starts asking questions at once. "Tell us what you have discovered, Poldi. What will all of this mean to us?" Stella asks.

"And what will the Japanese do now?" Walter adds.

Still trying to shake off the cold he manages to answer, "The Japanese have put themselves into the limelight. They don't want to give Hitler all the glory he's claiming for himself."

"Greedy bastards," Walter exclaims. "Each of them wants more. I wonder if the whole world is enough for them."

"Every time the Nazis swallow up another chunk of Europe their appetite increases again," Fritz comments. "Now the Japanese want a bigger piece for themselves, the game of tug and pull, like little boys in the schoolyard. "

"Except that it is a game of life and death," Stella says, with a sigh.

"When Germany toppled France, Hitler shared his plunder with his Japanese allies," Dolu says. "But, you see, Hirohito's gluttony was only appeased momentarily with his share of Indochina and Thailand. He has wider ambitions."

Eva is sitting quietly next to Dolu. She is dark-haired, slightly plump, well-dressed, well-educated. She speaks German with a Russian accent and is devoted to her husband. She seldom disagrees with him in public. She looks at him with admiration, nodding and smiling when he speaks.

"That's true, brother," Poldi answers, "the Japanese are eager to control the entire Far East. They consider themselves to be a master race among the Asian nationalities. They are determined that nothing will stand in their way, not the Americans, not the British, no one."

"But what about us Jews in all this? We ran from Hitler and now we'll be devoured by a new monster," Erna worries, her forehead creased with concern as she looks at Lily, who is munching some cake. *"Gott in himmel,* what are we to do now?"

"I've been told that the Juedishe Gemeinde will be more than a religious and relief organization now," Poldi says. "The Japanese have designated it as our representative political body. Anything they have to tell us as a whole will be done through this one group. For now, there are no changes for us, but who knows."

Baffled by the new turn of events, I respond, "I can't understand why Hirohito wanted to draw the fire of the Allies. Didn't he have enough of a battle with the Chinese?" Longing for a smoke, I ask, "Poldi, did you get more cigarettes? I'm all out."

He takes a pack from his jacket pocket and lights two, one for me and the other for himself. I inhale thankfully.

"Nini," Poldi answers, "you have to understand their motivation for all of this. Hunger for power is not easily sated. It's like opium addiction, the craving increases and increases, always pushing the addict to demand more to feed his habit until the drug spreads its poison into every pore and finally kills him. Hirohito wants unrestricted control of Asia. The American fleet at Pearl Harbor was an obstacle to his domination of the region."

"But what does it mean to us?" Willi asks. "What will happen to us now?"

Walter replies with conviction, "The Japanese don't care about us. We're insignificant. After all, they don't divide Whites by religion. We're all the same to them."

Poldi disagrees. "I don't know if the Germans won't have something to say about that."

I interrupt, "I can't believe that they would care about us here in the middle of nowhere, so far removed from European civilization."

And so it goes on, the talk, the speculation, the worry. One thing we all agree on is that American involvement is our only hope for rescue. We drink coffee and finish most of the cigarettes before the evening is done. Tension bristles in the room. Erna and Fritz are first to leave. Lily has fallen asleep in her father's arms and they bundle her in her winter coat as they prepare to set out for their own home. Eventually the rest of us leave too.

In our room that night, Poldi and I are still talking about the latest development in the war as we get ready for bed. I ask him, "Do you think we might still be rescued from this place? But where would we go?"

He replies solemnly, "There is nowhere safe. I'm going to write to Leon tomorrow and see if he's all right. Harbin will probably have the same rules as Shanghai, but maybe he has some other information he can give me. I don't really know what might happen to us now."

I sigh. "Well, the U.S. won't be interested in letting in more refugees now that they're at war."

Poldi flicks off the light and we lie there, staring into the blackness. "If somehow Hitler is conquered in Europe and if the Americans defeat the Japanese here, maybe the world will be free again and some doors might open," he says. "For now, we are nothing but pawns in this game. We will be moved by the hands of these giants and can only wait until the play is finished and see who the victor will be."

"Too many 'ifs' and 'maybes' for my liking," I say, yawning and settling into my pillow.

"If my grandmother had wheels, she would have been a bus," Poldi says half asleep. I smile at this old-fashioned saying of his as he squeezes my hand and we drift off to sleep.

CHAPTER 27

HONGKEW 1942-1943

From the battlefields in Europe to the Pacific, the probing tentacles of war are spreading, stretching outward to find the refugees who have sought in vain to escape its grasp. We pray that the Americans will free us, but hope diminishes rapidly.

The strain of daily life in this atmosphere shows on everyone's face. People on the street are always in a hurry these days, even more than usual. They seldom take the time to stop and chat. Coffee houses are often empty and Stella has told me that her business is suffering.

Our business, though, is doing quite well, as people always drown their worries in liquor. Any night a Korean soldier may pull a knife from his boot and slice the air just near a Japanese man in uniform. Many times Poldi has to insert himself in the centre of a free-for-all. He is short and slight but that doesn't stop him. He often has a bruise or cut from the most recent fracas.

"What a business this is!" I say to him, tending to a swelling over his eye.

"Not quite what we had in mind, is it, Nini? Still, the money is coming in and I think we can make a go of it. The war will end one day, *Liebling,* and we'll have a better life. I still believe it."

"You've always been more optimistic than I have. Look, your eye is a red balloon and you talk about a better life. War planes are spinning over our heads and you think about peace."

"Ahh, that iodine stings like the devil!" He winces as I dab at the cut over his brow. "Nini, remember where we are, always keep it in mind. That's what I do to keep me going. I know we have managed, by our wits and not much more, to endure it all – the hostility, the poverty, the food rationing, the shortages, the disease, the homesickness...."

"Yes, all that and more," I say, interrupting his list. "But now we're seeing similarities to Europe, right here. The newspapers have started to carry anti-Semitic articles demanding our expulsion. Every time I read something like that I shiver. It's a repeat of the Nazi propaganda."

Until now we have been treated the same as any other Europeans. The Jewish refugee community has given the Japanese army no trouble, making our way in obscurity, not embroiled in the political strife within China, not creating any new disturbances. As always we are reminded of the ancient shtetl saying, "*Shtill zol zein*" – be quiet, unobtrusive, blend into the background, and the worst will pass. Surely, despite the war in all its fury, the world is vast enough that a few thousand Jews might be allowed to live in peace, asking nothing but to be left alone.

Preserving our routine is the only solution we have to the whirlwind whipping the whole region into a frenzy. The war is encroaching upon us and still we have to put one foot before the other and carry on. We head out in the evening to the bar tugging our coats close to our bodies for warmth against the December wind and walking arm in arm at a quick pace, down the familiar streets to Marco's.

He is always there ahead of us and opens up. We turn the key in the lock and latch it from inside, calling out our greetings to Marco, who is seated as always on his stool by the radio. The cash register is checked, the liquor supply is inspected, and the doors are unlocked for the customers to come in. Marco then leaves us to tend to business and saunters in his usual rolling gait towards the private office at the back of the building. He always bolts himself inside and stays there for most of the night. From the beginning of our relationship with him we have been aware of his secretive ways and just recently he has come to trust us sufficiently to confide in us about his activities. Apparently, he has a shortwave radio concealed in his small room on which he receives news from the Jewish underground.

We have been sworn to respect his privacy and never question him about his involvement with the organization. This has worked satisfactorily for us all. He tells us when there is some news that he is prepared to impart and we demand nothing more of him.

Usually Marco does not make a further appearance until near closing time but tonight, despite the customers seated in the booths, he comes out and rumbles towards us, his breathing laboured, his face sweaty and flushed. Poldi and I are concerned with his sudden emergence from his office and his obvious anxiety. Standing behind the counter, we watch him approach and I get him a glass of water. He plops down on his stool and takes a drink, sighs deeply, then leans towards us.

The Japanese soldiers, already inebriated and still downing more liquor, are laughing raucously. We look around to make sure that no one is interested in our discussion and move closer to Marco to hear his words.

"Things are heating up, my friends, not good this time, not good at all," he says, wiping a large white handkerchief over his face.

I am wearing a woollen cardigan and Poldi is in a long-sleeved shirt with a knit vest, but Marco is apparently as hot as if it were a summer day.

"What has happened?" Poldi asks.

Whispering, he answers. "Hitler has dispatched one of the top Nazis over here to Shanghai, a Gestapo Colonel Josef Meisinger. They say he's one of the cruellest of Hitler's thugs. The word is that he is after the Jews that got away."

I feel the blood draining from my face. I slip a cigarette from the case in my skirt pocket and pull a lighter from the drawer. Poldi takes one too and we begin to inhale. We take another look around but no one seems to be paying attention to us.

"What else, Marco? Do you know more?" Poldi asks, breaking our usual code of no questions.

"Only this. He is coming to meet with the Japanese high command to discuss the 'Jewish problem.'"

"That's enough, isn't it?" I say, more nervous that ever, the cigarette in my fingers trembling as the end forms into grey ash.

"God-damned Krauts," Marco says in a louder voice, "won't let us live in peace, not even here. They'll bust their way in, shoving and stamping, those bloody goose-steppers, you know what they're like, broomsticks up their spines, and who will be safe then?"

"*Shh,* Marco," I say, worried that his words will be understood.

"They want cooperation from the Japs or they will remove their support for the Pacific war effort. Grim reapers, every one of them, and here we sit, caught again."

"Are you sure of this or could it be just a rumour?" Poldi asks.

"As sure as I can be. We'll know soon enough. But what can we do about it? I just don't know. I wanted to tell you. After all, we are like family, right? Keep it quiet though, just for now. I'm going back to see if there's anything else."

We watch him walk slowly towards the back room, his head down, his usually good-natured mood blackened.

It is early morning when we make our way home, talking all the way about Marco's story. We hope that it is just a crazy rumour, but we discover we are not the only ones who have heard the news of Meisinger's arrival and his upcoming talks with the Japanese authorities. Soon the Jewish community is reeling from the news that the enemy is once more on our trail.

That evening Willi drops by. "The Germans are coming here," he says. It has become his habit to visit us on his way home from work before we have to set out for the bar. "What in the world can we do?"

Even Poldi is finding difficulty in coming up with any words of encouragement. We all take cigarettes out and pass around the lighter. "Well," he says at last, "maybe the Yanks will get us out of it this time."

"Are we cats with nine lives?" I ask. "Or are we doomed this time?"

"Who can say?" Poldi shrugs in a gesture of resignation. "But at least the Americans have been angered enough to get into the fight after the bombing at Pearl Harbor. If the Allies win, well, maybe we'll get out of here."

We go to Jewish community meetings where we often meet Dolu and Eva, who are involved with the Russian segment. As in Europe, the Jewish refugees have divided themselves into separate and distinct groups by language and religious affiliations, but when the Nazi wolf prepares to attack, we lambs join together. We listen as the speaker announces some new plans. He is apparently Orthodox, a grey bearded middle-aged man, with glasses, wearing a black hat.

"Things are changing rapidly here, since Pearl Harbor, as you all know," he begins. "In good times – and when you might ask, did we have good times?" He pauses as there is a sprinkle of laughter, then goes on. "Splinter groups were fine enough then, but now we need a united front to present to the Japanese, a group that will represent us all."

He tells us that a group has been put together with the rather unwieldy name the Shanghai United Jewish Committee on Communal Representatives. The group will represent everyone's interests – the Ashkenazi, Sephardi and German communal associations. He has been entertaining but, more importantly, informative, and we leave feeling better. However, what effect this committee might have on Japanese policy still remains uncertain.

The Japanese are besieged on all sides when the Americans enter the war. As occupation troops in China, they are in hostile territory. With ambitions to dominate the region, they appeal to their allies, the Germans, to come to their aid, but the Nazis have another agenda, a preoccupation with the existence of the Jews that extends beyond the shores of the European continent.

We hear rumours concerning the talks taking place between the two Axis nations. The Japanese have tolerated us as a means to ensure economic strength, for the Jews in Shanghai have proven their worth for many years, and the refugees, even within the short time we have been here, have become an asset. In order to rationalize our destruction, the Japanese will need to understand how it could benefit them. We have noticed the similarities of the Japanese and German methods of segregating the Jews. It is apparent that the Germans have explained their methods. It would not be difficult to show that the wealth of their war machine and the personal fortunes of senior Nazi officers have come in great part from plundering Jewish holdings in Europe, without consequence. Perhaps the Japanese will understand this manoeuvre, having ravaged property throughout China as they moved into occupied territories. If they first destroy the European refugees and loot whatever comparatively small assets they possess, the enormous wealth of the old Jewish money in the Far East may eventually lie at their feet. Although the Germans and Japanese have a distrust of one another, they are united in their goal of world domination. As time moves forward, we begin to believe they may succeed. As always, we wait.

Many things changed after Pearl Harbor. All foreign-owned businesses are now supervised by the Japanese. They have frozen bank accounts, and except for limited withdrawals for basic necessities there is very little cash to be had. Gasoline is disappearing quickly and buses have stopped running. The massive traffic jams of the city have been replaced by the slower pace of pedestrians and coolie-pulled rickshaws and carts. Bicycles are the main means of transportation even for the wealthy.

Early in 1943, Poldi and I have to go into the city to the area of the previous International Settlement, now under Japanese control. We have come here to discuss liquor delivery with a supplier who has been unreliable lately. We want to be sure there will be no further disruption of service. We are good customers, paying our bills in cash, so we believe our deliveries should arrive promptly, as promised.

We are walking along the Bund, talking about the meeting, when we hear a commotion and see a crowd gathering. As a first small step into domination here, the Germans are making their presence known. Their troops are putting on a show of strength, flaunting their military might by marching through the main street.

I shudder in disbelief as Nazi soldiers, in their characteristic stiff-legged march, parade down the Bund of Shanghai. But to their amazement and ours, they are suddenly surrounded and disarmed by swarms of Japanese soldiers, who have no intention of surrendering one fraction of their expanding empire to outsiders, allies or not. This is their realm, and they are obstinate and proud enough to thwart any attempt at control.

The representatives of Japan and Germany face one another for an awkward moment. The Japanese soldiers are much shorter than the Germans, but they have their bayonets drawn and their numbers are far superior to the European intruders. The Germans, awaiting orders from their superiors, have come to a stop in the middle of the street.

"This is not your territory," one of the Japanese officers shouts in German. "You will turn around and return to your barracks. Otherwise, we have been ordered to shoot."

The German officer grimaces, seeming to recoil with disgust at the little Oriental man barking orders. However, he thinks better of the confrontation, looks around at the gawking people on the sidewalk, salutes the Japanese soldier, and commands his men to retreat. The crowd disperses and we know that there will be rumours again regarding the outcome of this encounter.

It appears that the Germans are contemplating a takeover of Shanghai but that their allies, the Japanese, are just as fierce in their own tenacious hold on the territory. We are merely spectators in this game although our lives are in grave risk through the slightest change in command or policy. We know that the Germans are exerting pressure for our destruction. The Japanese who, we can surmise from what we have seen, have been unwilling to kowtow to the Germans have however struck a compromise with their persuasive allies.

Poldi learns of it when he heads out for his usual noonday trek for the newspaper; today he's also to get some supplies, cigarettes, coffee, a tin of evaporated milk, tinned sardines, and bread. He is agitated when he arrives home. Pacing our small room, he shows me a flyer he has torn off a post in the city. "Decrees like this are tacked to every pole in Shanghai and blared on the radio," he explains, waving one of the notices. "Every newspaper is carrying the same report, repeated again and again. All 'displaced persons' – meaning Jews – are ordered to be moved into a designated area."

Memories of the past flood into my mind. I remember the Nazi proclamations at home that caused us finally to flee. I remember the horrors of Kristallnacht and once again my heart flutters in apprehension.

I take the ripped paper and read the edict:

"Due to military necessity, places of residence and businesses of stateless refugees in the Shanghai area shall hereafter be restricted to the under mentioned area in the International Settlement. East of the line connecting Chaoufong Road, Muirhead Road and Dent Road; West of Yangtzepoo Creek; North of the line connecting East Seward Road and Wayside Road; and South of the boundary of the International Settlement."

"But why?" I ask, horrified. "I thought they didn't concern themselves with us. We've mostly been ignored until now. What harm can a group of poor civilians do against their strength?"

Willi is at the door. "Have you heard the radio broadcast?" he asks, his face ashen.

"No, the radio is at the bar, but Poldi just brought home this pamphlet." I draw him into our apartment by his arm.

"These aren't just rumours any more," Poldi says, his face reddening with anger and frustration. "The Germans have really made an impact on the Japanese and we are targets again. Bastards! We're going to be herded into a ghetto."

I am frozen in shock. A ghetto is as good as prison.

"How could this have happened?" Willi asks, distressed.

"News has obviously reached Berlin that a community of Jews is surviving and prospering in Shanghai," Poldi says, lighting a cigarette. "I can only imagine that it must have driven Hitler into a rage. He wants us all dead. What other explanation is there?"

I pull the last cigarette from his pack and draw the smoke into my body, deep, deeper into my lungs and feel a slight relaxation of my limbs, but my overall state is panic.

Unceremoniously and without warning, the Japanese, on February 18, 1943, urged by the Germans, have ordered us into the Shanghai ghetto called Hongkew, a cramped section of about one square mile where all of us, some 18,000 people, are to be relocated in May. This is to be a more stringently regulated and heavily guarded enclosure, the new Restricted Area. In what we fear could be a first step towards our demise, we are ordered to give up our quarters to Oriental families who have been living in the still shabbier section, and to trade places with them.

We go over to the Café de Paris where Stella and Walter are sitting at a table, coffee cups and an ashtray overflowing with stubs before them. When they see us come in, Stella jumps up and rushes towards us.

"Can you believe what is going on?" She is distraught and grasps my hand. "Why don't they leave us alone? They are planning to take over everything that we have, the shop, the apartment, everything."

Poldi and Walter shake hands, chairs are pulled up for us, the others move to make room and soon we are drinking coffee with them. None of us can think of what to say. Finally Walter, rubbing his hand up and down his cheek, says, "You know, do you, that we have three months, to move into this designated area?"

Three months, I think, that's all we have before we go into the enclosure. In that time, we have to close up our business, pack all our belongings, and make arrangements to exchange our apartment for one in Hongkew.

Poldi adds, "We need permission and approval from the Japanese for any of these transactions. That's part of their decree. And anyone who arrived after 1937 is to move. We'll be separated from the rest of the Europeans, those who were here before."

"But Hongkew is so small," Stella says. "And there are thousands of Chinese there. How will we all get in?"

"A squeeze, my dear," Walter answers, "a tight squeeze."

Not long after this, we begin to see queues at the offices of real estate agents in Frenchtown. The Shanghailanders want to list properties for immediate sale, apartments and businesses that have taken penny-by-penny savings and ceaseless labour to establish. Now we will have to take any offer just to get out.

Most of the purchasers are Japanese. The plan is that we are to trade places with them. The Japanese who lived in the dismal and neglected dwellings of Hongkew will abandon them and move into our nice clean homes, homes where we have managed to install indoor plumbing and telephones, furnished with things we dragged across the ocean from Vienna or purchased here.

Gleeful Japanese citizens are already mounting the steps into vacated homes. They offer the most paltry sums for our best china or pieces of treasured jewellery, hidden from the Nazis at risk of death. At the same time, now that the United States is an enemy, American aid has dried up. Relief funds, including supplies from private American Jewish agencies, which have been a great source of help to us, can no longer enter occupied China. We will have to sell anything of value just to feed ourselves.

The bitter truth is underscored by an item Poldi reads to me from the newspaper. "It's all here," Poldi says, folding the pages back with a noisy flourish. "There are 811 apartments, divided into 2,766 rooms that are outside the designated area. In addition there are 307 businesses owned by the stateless refugees. These will now be exchanged by official order of the Japanese Authority for homes and locations inside the designated area. The move is to be completed by May 18, 1942. Those who do not comply will face severe punishment."

By April we have lost our business. Marco's Bar is under new management; a Japanese man stands behind the counter. We shake hands with Marco when we meet at the bar for the last time. It is disconcerting to see the sadness in the big man's fleshy face. He manages to say a few words to us. "I am going to Harbin tonight. I have approval from the authorities to stay with my brother there for now. After that, I don't know. Will you stay here?"

"Our family is here, Marco," I say. "Besides, we have no documents to travel. We have no choice but to move into Hongkew. We'll miss you." Sadly, we say farewell.

Our apartment, which we have been renting, has been accepted by a Japanese couple, and we have been assigned an address in Hongkew where they lived and where we will have to move. They have offered us a small sum of money for the few things we have managed to accumulate so we sell our rug and bits of furniture to them. After all, how could we carry it all with us? We look with consternation at the money we are given for our valuables, a pittance that will buy little more than cigarettes and a few bags of rice. The rest, including my precious skis, is packed into our big trunk, the one that we salvaged from Vienna, and we arrange for coolies to carry it along to our new location.

Because the Russian and Sephardic early settlers are exempt, Dolu, married to a Russian, is allowed to remain in the French Concession. He has never done a thing to help us although he was always in a better financial situation. Now that we are at our lowest point, there is no word from him. I resent his selfishness and say as much to Poldi. "Leave it to your brother," I say grimly, "he always manages to look after himself above all." Poldi shrugs. He loves his brother but has never expected help from him and would not ask.

Heavy-hearted, we bundle up our few possessions in bags and suitcases and carry them with us to our new home. A Japanese soldier, a rifle slung across his shoulder, stands at the entrance to the ghetto. We don't understand his language, nor he ours, but he makes himself clear with rough commands and signals, and once again we have no choice but to obey. We show him our documents, duly stamped and signed. Poldi and I, with two coolies who are burdened with the weight of our trunk, make our way to the address we have written on a small scrap of paper.

We trudge along until we arrive at a dilapidated area, abandoned and desolate except for the poorest Chinese in Shanghai, and homeless vagrants seeking shelter wherever they can. Poldi and I wander through the warren of streets looking for signs and asking other refugees for help in locating our new address within the makeshift settlement in a bombed-out ruin. We make our way through the rows of ramshackle tenements, flimsy structures that remain hardly standing, with shingles torn off roof tops, windows cracked and broken, loose planks hanging by rusty nails. Within the patchwork of streets that is Shanghai, this is the lowliest part. We are within the burnt remains of a ferocious conflict between the Chinese and their invaders, the Japanese army.

Hundreds of Jewish refugees plod with us through the barren waste, grim and frightened. We are in what is called Lane Housing, a collection of shaky shells of dismal one- and two-storey shacks, lining both sides of a maze of narrow alleyways.

Poldi and I continue through the broken streets in search of numbers or some indication of the location we are seeking. Finally, "Here, this is it," he calls and we head into the crumbling structure. This is where we must live, in the rubble left from the violent door-to-door combat. Looking at the squalor that surrounds us, I mutter sadly, "Thank God Mama didn't live to see this. Her heart would have broken in two at the sight of this misery."

In the entrance to the building, we find a ragged Chinese man sleeping in a curled lump. A passing Japanese soldier shouts at him and gives him a hard kick. The man rouses from his sleep and stumbles away, yelping like a dog.

We head up a flight of rickety stairs and at the top we find just one small, dingy room that is ours. The smell of mildew welcomes us into the hovel, dank and musty, without ventilation, dark, and oppressive. It is the middle of winter and the weather has turned icy cold. There is no heat, and the wind is howling through the cracked windows and crevices in the walls. We wonder whether our family has fared any better; they have given us addresses for where they will be settled so that we might find one another.

The coolies take the money we had promised them and mutter some grumbling words. They are glad to set their load down and leave us to ourselves. We remain alone in the gloomy room, looking at the four shabby walls that will be our enclosure. I drop the bundles I've been carrying and go towards a wobbly chair in the corner. With my sleeve I brush away some of the grimy surface and plunk myself down. My head lowered in my hands, elbows on my knees, I stare down at the filthy floor. "How can we live here? What have we come to? Were we fools to imagine that the Nazis would allow us to escape? I have felt that they were chasing after us all along, lurking somewhere unseen, ready to smash us to dust." The words come out in bitter spurts.

Finally I look up to see Poldi, standing by the little window, the glass cob-webbed, cracks forming a pattern of radiating lines and pierced with missing pieces through which the wind is whistling. He is examining it, considering how it might be repaired. I know he will soon become busy as he has done before. He will absorb himself in comforting tasks, hammering crooked old nails to straighten them, rummaging in trash to retrieve bits and scraps that can be fitted together to mend rusty hinges, warped doors, and uneven walls so that the gusting wind will be kept out. Somehow he will manage to put things together and so, by focusing on the little things of normal life, he will be able to preserve his sanity and hope. This is his method of dealing with the succession of demoralizing events. He turns towards me then. "Nini, you know that we have to make the best of the situation. We'll clean this room and disinfect it and then I'll find a way to make some money. We will be all right. Don't give up."

But as I survey the space that we are to call home, I find no comfort, only disappointment and more cause for distress. Leaving my perch, I walk towards one dark corner where I have noticed something I can't recognize. Revolted, I have discovered our one toilet is nothing more than a bucket with a lid. "Look at this, Poldi. My God, is this a toilet? In Frenchtown there was indoor plumbing, at least. In my wildest imagination, I never expected a place so vile and low."

I wander about the cramped space and stop at the window. From our second-storey room, I can see the tangle of alleyways spreading out in twists and turns. Our neighbourhood is a jumble of unlikely residents thrown together to live or to die. The Chinese are obviously stunned by the sudden influx of foreigners, parading into their ramshackle area. The refugees in turn are bewildered and distressed, all their belongings stuffed once more into threadbare bags and battered valises. They gaze up and around in disbelief as they make their way into their quarters located somewhere in this crooked little part of the city into which they've been thrust.

"Here we are, Poldi, not so very clever after all." I'm dejected and fatigued by the latest set-back to our lives. "And I guess the Nazis have won. What did it matter that we could run from them, when they have the might to destroy us anywhere, even here?"

"I don't know any more," he says, sadly, "I don't know." And suddenly I feel worse than ever. If Poldi has given up, what more is there to do? We have no comfort to give one another. After some time in lonely silence, he comes to where I am sitting by the window and pats my shoulder. Without a word he has brought a little courage back to me.

All the family is relocated in Hongkew and have met the deadline of May 18. Erna and Fritz are a few streets over from us, in a building that is one of the better ones which they were assigned because they have a child. Stella and Walter are in another, and Willi is living with them.

A number of refugees have already been living in Hongkew for years, those who were the poorest of us. Now we will all be together. This latest move into Hongkew for those who were just beginning to accept conditions in Frenchtown has been a mortal blow. Morale has sunk to its lowest level, and many have succumbed to chronic depression complicated by a greater susceptibility to physical illness.

Somehow Poldi and I, and the rest of my family, are strong enough to adapt to our surroundings, and to accept the circumstances we must endure. We believe we are more fortunate than most as we are young and resilient, but youth is our only resource. Despite my despair, I try to believe that we can overcome the obstacles although the effects of this newest dislocation show on each of our faces.

The morning after our first unsettled night here, we are awakened early by a sound that soon becomes as familiar and anticipated as a cock's crow: coolies pulling a cart that clatters down the narrow winding streets. Going from door to door, they perform their lowly job, and we soon recognize and welcome their daily sing-song greeting that alerts us to rush out with our toilet pails. Into their carts they pour the stinking mess that leaves a trail of putrid brown liquid whose stench attracts swarms of buzzing flies. Repulsed at first, we gradually become accustomed to this routine as we must to so many things, sights that we had never imagined in our home in Vienna.

We scrub and scour our dreadful little rooms and make the best of it all. We discover the ways of Hongkew, living here, side by side with the most downtrodden of society. They are industrious, never seeming to squander time or money, always rushing from one spot to another with some purpose that will better their own lives or, at least, those of their children. They find uses for everything and nothing is wasted. Groves of bamboo grow quickly and can be found everywhere in the tropical climate. We discover that this magical plant is used for everything imaginable – from long sturdy poles that are stronger and more flexible than steel and are used for construction or for carrying goods slung across shoulders; to woven bamboo baskets for cooking; to food, as the young shoots of the bamboo plant are cooked and eaten with bowls of rice. The soy plant also has a multitude of uses, from a kind of nourishing milk to sprouts, cooked as a vegetable, or compressed into a salty dark liquid that preserves and flavours food at the same time.

A mutual respect is gradually nurtured between us and these strange people, although it may never develop into complete trust. We have heard the Chinese refer to us as "White Devils," and we have seen their caricatures of the intrusive Caucasians depicted with long pointed noses, round fiery red eyes, and flaming hair. For our part the differences between us are just as frightening, yet we are able to live with them in peace.

We have discovered the primitive cooking equipment set outside the kitchen door. It is a round clay drum, about two feet high, with a square hole cut out at the bottom. Halfway up, a metal grid is welded to the sides. The technique of using it is a baffling procedure that we must master if we are ever to eat again. To start the fire we have to build a little mound of crumpled paper and kindling wood. On this scruffy nest, we place some rough coal briquettes formed from a mixture that is mostly mud with some coal dust added on top. To ignite the fire we use a match to burn a bit of paper or rag that is meant to set the whole mess afire. The flame seems always reluctant to catch, so we take turns squatting by the stove and furiously waving a bamboo fan, trying in frantic desperation to cause the flames to rise and glow red hot. The sight of a flickering ember causes us to shout in fits of jubilation, but more often than not, it is soon extinguished and the entire thing must be cleaned out and the whole task started again.

Nothing is familiar in this place. Everything is new and difficult or frightening. We are terrified of the spread of virulent diseases that surround us in the sub-tropical climate. We learn to wash our hair and bodies in disinfectant, scrubbing our skin raw to rid ourselves of lice and other insects and bacteria that are agents of contagion. Wails of agony filter through the flimsy walls or even out to the street, and we know that it is from the stinging pain of harsh chemicals burning human flesh. We are obsessed with cleansing ourselves, trying with limited success to purge our squalid accommodations of the germs that are seeping into our air, food, water, everything that we touch.

Thousands of us are crowded into this slum. Shouting, sobbing, slamming doors, muffled sounds of pathetic love making, and frustrated cries of despair fuse together to become the discordant song of Hongkew. As I lie awake on our wooden cot, shivering in the cold damp room, my mind slips back again to the verdant hills of Vienna. What is there to do but to add my tears to the many others being shed around me?

Turned on my side, lying in bed next to Poldi, I can see our food storage area lit by moonlight and casting shadows in the corners. Sleep does not settle easily in this hideous place. I listen in the dark to the scraping, scratching noises of cockroaches and watch the black hard-shelled beetles scurrying up and down the greasy walls in search of grains of rice that we have tried so hard to hide in firmly closed containers. My skin prickles at the sight. Mosquitoes are buzzing around my ears and I know that we will have fresh welts in the morning. These mosquitoes can be more than a nuisance as they can carry malaria. I will have to find some netting tomorrow, I think, to protect us.

Sometimes when the night is still, I can hear another sound, the plaintive chant in Hebrew known to every Jew, that I first learned as a child, "*Shema Yisrael, Adonai Elohanu, Adonai Ehud.*" Other voices join the first and repeat the solemn words slowly, over and over. Poldi is asleep, snoring loudly, overcome by fatigue, but I whisper the familiar prayer in the ugly darkness of our room. Sleep won't come. My eyes are burning and sore so I lie awake staring into the black space. The ancient words return to me, a desperate prayer in memory of Mama and Papa and of Poldi's martyred parents, in hope of salvation, in fear of death, in dread of our enemies, and finally in supplication for peace and the slim possibility of rescue and a real life once again.

CHAPTER 28

SURVIVAL 1944

We are aware of our imprisonment now more than ever before. Even here in Shanghai where thieves, pimps, drug peddlers, and murderers walk freely in the streets, subject to no laws or restrictions, we, as Jews, are condemned. Outside of Hongkew we are required to carry a blue card that can be demanded by any Japanese soldier. The exits are guarded by armed military patrols that restrict our movements.

"Did you see that grotesque little man at the gate," I ask Poldi, "swaggering around in his uniform, barking commands at us, treating us as though we were inferior life forms?"

"That's Goya," he answers. "

"Like a Japanese Hitler," I say, with disgust. "Just what we needed."

"As long as we're under Japanese occupation he will make sure to cause trouble for us."

I see the anger spark in his eyes as he says, "Nini, I hate this whole thing, begging him for favours just to get the food in our mouths. What have they made of us now – beggars, prisoners, not free men any longer."

"Never mind him," I say, trying to settle him down. "We'll keep out of his way."

To make certain we adhere to their rules, the Japanese have installed a commander in Hongkew, General Goya, who has proclaimed himself "King of the Jews." His office is here, and each of us soon becomes familiar with this short, skinny man in military uniform strutting among us, always with taller soldiers for his protection at his side. His face is pockmarked and broad, propped on a short, spindly neck and looking like a misshapen melon perched shakily above his narrow shoulders. He is bitter and cruel, revelling in his position of power over the struggling European refugees who must beg him for the favours that he withholds without reason. He is prone to fits of rage, irrational bouts of anger when any of us may feel the weight of his hand on our cheeks. His disdain for us is tangible. Some say that he detests the women most of all, and that he enjoys physical abuse, his face twitching with obvious pleasure at the chance to personally and brutally punish anyone for an infraction of his many rules.

Goya stands on a podium raised above us as we approach, caps clutched in our hands as a sign of humility and respect, to beg for a day pass out of the ghetto. In order to leave to seek work or to carry on any trade, we must apply for special permits that have to be renewed each month. Early in the morning the queues have already begun. Standing in the wretched heat or fierce cold, we look up eagerly anticipating his appearance. He purposely forces us to wait, never arriving before noon, so those at the end of the line have to come back another day. He refuses to see everyone who's standing before him. At any moment, he may turn his back on those waiting for work permits, the only means of freedom from starvation, and declare the day done.

He seems to detest us all. It is not uncommon for him to strike anyone, young or old, with an unprovoked slap across the face.

"Go home," he commands, a smile of contempt twisting his face, "I will see no one else today. You have tired me with your pathetic complaints and endless badgering. Come tomorrow, and arrive early if you want your family to eat and don't tell me of your misery. You wretched beggars are getting what you deserve."

Poldi stands in line once a month with the others to beseech a stamp on his pass. Each encounter is an ordeal because he's risking so much. He might be beaten or worse, and if his pass is denied we will have no food, but he has to go into Shanghai to make a living in whatever way he can. He has decided on a reasonably good enterprise of buying and trading, getting what he can from wholesale suppliers and then carting desirable items aboard the vessels anchored in the harbour. He trades with various nationalities and finds his facility in languages useful. Always a skilled negotiator, Poldi manages to barter for goods such as cigars and brandy that are in demand by the servicemen. If he finds a deal on souvenirs that the sailors will buy to take home for girlfriends or family, he picks those up too. Mostly he is on the look-out for American cigarettes, which are scarce and highly valued. He hustles about on a bicycle to factories in the city and then takes his finds on to the ships at the dock. He has made arrangements with the captains, who are not above taking a cut, to let him come aboard. In this way, Poldi is able to bring some money home each day, if only enough for basic necessities.

We go about our lives despite Goya's cruelty and the deprivation we have come to accept. In Hongkew we all trudge about in a fog of worry, concentrating on how we will supply the next meal. One day, as I am trying to purchase some wilted greens from a little Chinese vegetable stand, I notice a woman beside me, bent over to inspect some of the scraggly produce in the cart. She seems familiar, but I cannot quite place her. I finally draw her attention to me and as she turns her face, I can see it is Herta Weinstein from the ship. She glances at me but doesn't smile or betray any recognition. She seems so different. Her pale blond hair has been dyed to a wild orange red and her make-up is thick and hard-edged. Her cheeks are garishly rouged and the lingering smell of her perfume is strong and potent. I notice her fingernails and cuticles, still bitten to raggedy bits. She tries to hide her hands when she sees me examining them.

"Herta," I say, "is that you?"

"No, you are mistaken," she replies nervously. She pays her money to the vendor without looking directly at me and turns to hurry away.

I watch her scurry into the thick crowd and soon she has disappeared, but I cannot forget the harshly outlined contours of her face nor the dull downcast eyes. Herta is not the only Jewish woman in Hongkew who has descended into prostitution. Poverty, hunger, and fear have forced many to make a living in this way. Her obvious shame at the position in which she has found herself saddens me. Within the ghetto there is little chance for anonymity, and I see Herta many times after this encounter, accompanied usually by Japanese soldiers, their arms roughly draped around her shoulders, as they weave drunkenly through the street. Herta has found a way to survive and I will not judge her, but she never greets me and I try to look away quickly when I see her, knowing she is ashamed of her situation and that my glance in her direction will cause her more pain.

I can understand Herta's choice, although I am concerned about her path. I am aware of the violent beatings that prostitutes are known to endure and the exposure to venereal diseases that have already debilitated and killed many. Still, I understand. Death is our mutually sworn adversary. In this battle, each survivor has succeeded in staying alive by a strong will, determined to defeat our foe by whatever means available. We have become hardened in a way we never believed possible. We have been able to watch horror upon horror unfold before us, able to turn away from corruption, bloodshed, and injustice and still to go on. Adversity has fuelled our hunger to survive.

Herta has no family, and that has made the difference between her and me. Without the support of a husband or any relatives, she has had to rely only on herself, and who can blame her for that? For us it is different, we have one another. Mama believed that family was of the greatest importance and the only thing to count on. We cling together and derive sustenance from our proximity to one another. We have escaped as a unit, and there is an unspoken belief that we need each other to exist, each member a remnant of our lost home, each one incomplete by himself.

Our food consists mostly of boiled rice, soya beans, and scrawny greens that look like weeds and are tasteless. We no longer expect three meals a day, and just like the other refugees, we manage to exist while in a condition of perpetual hunger. This is a time of great desperation. Within the maze of twisting streets of Hongkew, Jewish refugees have no shoes, improvising with rags bound to their feet. Daily, thin fingers scoop bowls of rice into mouths, as our Chinese neighbours do, trying in vain to stop the relentless ache within our bellies.

We are prepared to sell all the scant belongings we still possess. Japanese soldiers, revelling in their position of superiority, purchase for miserly sums whatever the impoverished refugees have salvaged. Precious pieces of jewellery, winter coats that will be sorely missed when the wind howls, anything that can be spared is bartered. The gloating grins of the soldiers and the sadness of the Hongkew inhabitants tell the story. Poldi has found a way to bring razor blades into the ghetto and to sell them for a few pennies each, but the money is hardly enough for us both to subsist. We can scarcely afford enough food to live from day to day. Cigarettes have become a rare luxury, and each puff is inhaled and expelled in slow wafts, shared and smoked down until the very last whiff of tobacco has filled our lungs. We have reached a plateau of destitution and poverty not much different from the beggars scrounging in the street for scraps.

Sometimes I find myself staring off into space, no tears left to shed, no feeling but the hunger rumbling inside. Then an image of Papa, faded and out of focus, but recognizable all the same, comes to me. He looks at me gravely, but I can't hear any words of encouragement or hope. He has nothing to tell me now, now that we are poorer than any soul he ever met or could imagine, and his advice of offering charity rings hollow and forlorn. There is nothing to give, I think, nothing for us nor for anyone else. This is a situation he did not foresee, that we, his children, might come to a condition of such devastation that we must ask for handouts, stand in line at a soup kitchen for the most meagre sustenance simply to survive. I feel ashamed and degraded.

Many times Poldi has taken his mother's gold watch from its hiding place and rubbed it gently, caressing the smooth round contours and running the long chain through his fingers. One day, at the time of our greatest hunger, he asks, "Do you think we should sell it, Nini?"

"Never!" I reply without hesitation. The small shining disc in his hands has become a symbol for me of the family dignity that existed before this horrendous time. As long as we have it, I still can preserve some shred of hope that we will return one day to that former state, to become whole again. If we lose that hope, we will truly be finished.

"Somehow we will find enough to eat," I say, finding some of my old defiance that I thought was gone, "but that is all you have left of her. We cannot sell it. Imagine how you could live knowing that one of those Japanese bastards was carrying her precious watch, touching it with his fingers. No. Never."

Poldi holds me close to his chest and I feel his heart thumping in quick rhythm against me. I close my eyes as tears trickle down my cheek. His pain is mine and mine his. We infuse one another with the strength to continue in our daily battle of endurance.

We often share our simple supplies with the family, but there is never enough to satisfy our stomachs. Tonight, however, there is to be a special celebration, and we are eagerly anticipating a dinner with meat. Erna is cooking a fine beef tongue that she has been able to purchase with money earned at the Catholic Convent where she is still teaching her needlepoint skills to Chinese children. Goya has reluctantly given her the necessary pass to leave Hongkew every day, having been pressured by the nuns to do so. Mother Laula herself had to come to see him to persuade him to allow the daily release.

We are invited to Erna and Fritz's flat where we will share the long-anticipated delicacy. The Japanese have erected a radio transmitter in Hongkew, and next door to that is where they live. The area is considered the most secure in Hongkew as it is protected fiercely by the Japanese. There is even a residence there for a number of Jewish families that we call "The Safe Place."

"I'll go over to Erna's to see if she needs help," I say to Poldi on my way out. He is working on some repair job as usual. "Remember we are going there tonight for dinner, a real dinner with meat."

"How could I forget? I can't remember when I last ate meat."

Squatting by her Chinese stove, Erna is trying in vain to get the stubborn flame to catch.

"It's no wonder the Chinese are so thin and dying of starvation," she says, wiping away the sweat of frustration with the back of her hand, her hair sticking in moist strands to her forehead and the nape of her neck. "They can never get their stoves to light."

I smile at her joke but she doesn't notice and continues to wave the bamboo fan in a rapid upward and downward motion until the coals finally begin to glow red hot.

"Look, Mama is cooking on the flower pot stove," Lily says, pointing at her mother, who is straining to master this primitive cooking method. We all laugh and agree with the child, that the stove does resemble an inverted planting pot.

Having successfully lit the flame at last and set the pot boiling for hours to soften the meat, she turns to prepare the table for us all. "I'll be back later with Poldi. Do you have everything you need?"

"Yes, Nini, it's all fine. We'll have a good dinner tonight for once."

When everyone arrives later in the evening, the delicious smell is almost too much to bear after such a long deprivation, and we glance longingly at the big metal soup pot, steaming and bubbling, rocking gently from side to side on the flimsy cooking device. We try to ignore the rumbling complaints from our stomachs and to have patience.

"This feast is worth the wait, you'll see," Erna tells us. "I chose the juiciest, fattest beef tongue in the butcher shop and spent all the money I had put aside for this one dinner."

"When will it be ready?" Fritz asks. "I think I could eat it raw after waiting so long for a bit of meat again. I can taste it already dipped into the mustard sauce you've prepared." He laughs as we all groan at the anticipation he is building up.

"Soon, soon, it's almost soft enough. After all this time we can wait a little longer to make sure it's just perfect."

Fritz used to be a husky man, fond of good food and in his best mood after a plentiful meal. In Vienna we shared many dinners and his round freckled face always beamed with pride at his young wife's ability to provide a satisfying repast. But since we have been in Shanghai, he, like the rest of us, has suffered deprivation and grown thin. We all miss Fritz's contented chuckles and good humour after one of Erna's special feasts. Tonight will be one of those occasions again.

We are gathered together, cramped into the small space, squeezing, elbow to elbow, on the extra chairs we have brought along. The table is tiny but there is a plate for each of us and we are in the cheeriest spirits since we moved into the ghetto. Conversation is lively, and laughter ripples through the air once more.

All of a sudden, we are shocked by the sound of a howl and screech. We jump up in alarm and rush to the cooking area, just outside the door on the little open porch. We stop in disbelief at the sight before us: the steaming water has been tipped and splashed out of the pot, and a huge stray cat from the alley, obviously starving and attracted by the tantalizing aromas of the cooking, has plunged its paw into the scalding water, managed to extract the whole tongue, and run off with the prize clenched in its jaws. Erna, her apron flapping around her, a ladle clasped in her fist, chases the culprit down the stairs and through the lane, distraught and screaming wild abuse at the terrified animal: "If I catch you, you demon from Hell, you'll go into the pot with the tongue! Come back, you ungodly creature, you stupid black monster!"

Although we are famished and disappointed, we explode in uncontrolled fits of laughter. We can't resist the sight of the scrawny wayward cat, its teeth tight around the hot beef tongue, driven by a hunger more fierce than the pain in its scorched paw or the fear of being caught by its enraged pursuer, and Erna chasing it wildly down the street. We watch them as they race in and out of doorways, and under lines of flapping wash hung on ropes strung from one post to another. Our neighbours, eyes wide in amazement, peer out their windows, taken abruptly from their duties by the sounds of commotion, and even grimy Chinese workers stare in wonder, fingers pointing at the sight and laughing uproariously.

"There it goes!" Willi shouts. "Look, it's gone behind the vegetable cart! Run, Erna, run, you'll get it back."

"And then," I say, turning to my brother, "do you expect us to eat what the cat has had in its mouth and dragged through half of Hongkew?"

He shrugs, but is intent on watching the chase.

We wait, standing bunched together by the doorway as they vanish around a corner. Fritz, with a white napkin still tucked under his chin, and the rest of us in various states of anxious dismay are straining forward to see whether Erna has been able to retrieve the piece of meat. We're arguing about the possibility of boiling it again so that we might still have something to eat. At last we see her trudging sadly towards us and we know what has happened.

"I'm so sorry," Erna says, out of breath when she finally returns, shaking her bowed head in frustration, her face flushed and damp, "I couldn't catch it and our dinner is gone."

We try to comfort her as Fritz leads her back into the house with his arm around her shoulder, his fingers brushing a few stray hairs back from her face. We return to the table at last, and begin to eat our ever-present bowls of plain cooked rice. This time, however, the discussion is animated, interjected with bursts of merriment, and we don't grumble about the miserly fare before us. There will be another night of aching stomachs when we go to bed, but the tale is told again and again, eliciting the same hilarity each time. In some ways that is better nourishment than the meat might have been.

CHAPTER 29

LIFE IN HONGKEW 1944-1945

From our room we are able to see through the barred windows of the Japanese prison where howling Chinese are being beaten and tortured. Despite our efforts to pass by without looking, our eyes seem to turn involuntarily towards the sight of increasing cruelty and unbelievable suffering. Boiling oil is poured over arms and legs, fingers are chopped off, and the screams ring endlessly from behind the walls of confinement. We observe, sometimes frozen in petrified horror, or covering our eyes and then glimpsing bits of the horrendous scenes as we look again. Poldi pushes me aside at one point telling me not to look. He continues to watch for a little while as one of the prisoners, bound with ropes, shakes and screeches until his mouth is forced open with a hose and water is poured down his throat. Poldi grimaces and turns his head away. For just another moment he turns back to see that the water is pumped and pumped until the prisoner seems to bloat up and burst from the pressure, his eyes bulging until his breath is gone and he finally expires.

Poldi has seen some terrible things since we arrived in Shanghai, and so have I, but this is more than we can bear. He heads for our toilet pot to heave. I am nauseated too but rush out into the air to take deep gulps of breath until my head stops spinning and I can stop trembling.

We try to compose ourselves but the sights of grotesque terror continue to haunt us. There is no way to intervene, no police to call, no authority to condemn the perpetrators. New and more heinous methods of torture are performed daily. Death arrives through various means in this strange land and we can do nothing but accept our roles as silent observers. The cries of agony are only another melody in the song of Hongkew, the opera of misery that floats, reverberates, and finally lulls us into numbness.

"You know, Poldi, there are times when I become absolutely terrified of this place, times when I wonder how the horrors must be affecting us, as human beings. Can we still have sensitive and tender hearts after we've seen the things we've seen?" I ask one night as we hold one another in bed and try to push aside the day's sights and sounds to settle into sleep. "Are we the same as we once were or will we ever be that way again?"

Taking my hand, he says, "Inside, Nini, inside we are still the same — loving, feeling, hoping — but outside we have to be hard, like a crust of bread, to protect the soft middle and keep it from crumbling to bits."

I shake my head. "I don't know, I feel as though I'm drowning, like the time in the bar when the rat jumped over my fingers. I'm afraid, always afraid. Fear has become the only certainty in my life."

"We are still together," he says firmly. "We will survive all of this yet." He takes me in his arms and holds me tightly in the dark until our shuddering bodies melt into one.

Plague after plague befall the Jews of Hongkew. During the summer we witness a natural catastrophe, a typhoon. Although it is midday, the sky turns to sudden darkness as the storm advances towards us. We stand by our windows, staring agape at the black sky, frozen in fear inside our pathetic rundown homes, and watch helplessly as the wind begins to rage. It is unlike anything we have ever encountered or could imagine. This storm of biblical scale demolishes everything in its path. In its vengeance and fury it rips through Shanghai, as though God, Himself, could see the Earth's turmoil and is unleashing His anger at the dangerous folly of humankind. The ferocious wind bellows like packs of wolves starving for flesh, and the rain pounds in a flood from heaven, as if the entire ocean were being dumped upon us. Raw sewage and debris swim in the street. Torrents of stinking water gush and with it comes disease and death.

When the rain ceases after days of endless downpour, we look out at the streets that have been washed away and are now rivers, hip-deep in putrid water. To go out to buy a bit of food from one of the street vendors, I must hike my skirt up and wade into the swishing filth. The smells are sickening. I shudder and close my eyes, trying to ignore the dead rats and garbage. Reaching a dry area, I pull myself up and take a breath. The sight of my legs, my skin coated in slime, makes me queasy. Then I notice the welts, puffed and red. I rub my swollen legs and begin to weep. When I finally arrive home with a few scraps of food, I am shivering in my damp clothes and soon have a fever from the infection that has spread through my body.

Within a few days the sores have become pussy globules. I apply salves to heal the ugly mess, but the disease of my terror isn't so easily cured. On my body, scabs form within days and eventually the crusty patches disappear. Blotches still remain, however, scars that will never go away.

Our rabbis are kept busy, scurrying up and down the little streets, visiting one home after another to offer good wishes and to recite Hebrew blessings for recovery from whatever scourge is currently most prevalent. But most prayers are left unanswered, and then they are off to the funerals. More and more of us are ill, having contracted dysentery, and still others are already buried in the ever-growing cemetery of Hongkew. The plaintive wails of grief are common, accompanied by another familiar sound that is ever present in Hongkew, *Kaddish,* the prayer for the dead.

As the months become years, we adapt to the world into which we have been cast. The war appears destined to go on forever. We are still forced to live in the designated area, to carry passes, and to check in and out of Hongkew with the Japanese guards standing firmly at the gate, but no matter how grim, we rationalize, there is more freedom here than we were allowed in Vienna under the Nazis.

Within the enclosure of the ghetto we are free to do what we choose. Ingenuity and willpower have carried us through, and somehow that is enough. Because we long for the basics of the civilization we knew, small enterprises once more are established to replicate in some way the only life we have known.

Before long, incongruous European-style cafés spring up on the sidewalks. Chinese labourers work alongside the immigrants, hammers and nails gripped in sweaty fists, piecing together salvaged lumber, scraps, and remnants rummaged and reused, more by determination than the strength of the supplies. Nothing is discarded. Everyone works together to restore a bit of the broken dreams. We cling to the hope for a better life against severe obstacles.

There is a little bakery, then a patisserie, with sweet smells caressing our nostrils once again. There is a tailor, a hairdresser, a restaurant serving authentic home cooking like sauerbraten and goulash. In the midst of this chaos we have tried to rebuild the Vienna that we knew. People are talking and laughing again, but whenever the discussion grows serious, we ask, "When will the war ever end?"

A row of pretty shops has appeared, one by one. Chusan Road has become a little oasis of home in the very midst of the Chinese squalor. Food shops with Viennese and Bavarian sausages hang in the windows in chains of tempting fat links. Dress shops display modern Chinese and European fashion, then coffee houses, shoe stores, liquor stores, all are here. If this is to be our home, not for months, but now as it seems, interminable years, we are determined to live as the educated human beings that we are.

Every weekday my little niece, Lily, goes to a school now established in Hongkew for Jewish children. We sometimes see her skipping down the street, hopping over the cracks, her hair braided in pigtails and fastened with ribbons, flopping up and down on her shoulders. The children seem to have adjusted to their world, and Lily's bright freckled face wears a smile despite the shabby surroundings and poor conditions we are enduring. She remembers little else. For the adults, happiness is more difficult to attain. We have already seen so much that is harsh and painful that simple naive pleasure is a rare gift.

Sometimes when Lily, who is now nine years old, comes home from school, she and I go out for a treat. We have a favourite spot where we like to go, our own secret place. We hold hands, whispering and giggling like co-conspirators, as we head out to find a Chinese street vendor who is usually positioned around the corner from where we live. We are the only ones in the family brave enough to eat the dumplings that are sold. Lily jumps over broken pieces of the pavement as we make our way. Although Poldi has told me not to take a chance on this strange food for fear it might be contaminated, we sneak out all the same and hurry to the spot to eat our forbidden delicacy.

"Auntie Nini," she says, "look at the hat in that window, with the great big red flowers on top. I would like a hat like that when I grow up. Don't you think that's a wonderful hat?"

"Yes, a wonderful hat," I agree, smiling. "In this place I hardly think you'll need one. But maybe we will be living somewhere glamorous like Paris or New York and then you would absolutely have to get one just like it."

"Where are those places, Auntie Nini? Are they near Hongkew?"

"No, Lily, there is nowhere near Hongkew. This is a place that is alone, near nothing, like an island in an ocean. Outside these gates there is Shanghai, but that is still like Hongkew. If we are to go somewhere really different, it will have to be far, far away from here. We will go in a very big boat and travel for a long time until everything here is left behind us."

"And will all the family be together forever?"

"Forever, I promise." I pause in reflection, wondering if that could be true. I decide I don't want to think about it any longer. This is to be a special time, a day for pleasure. "Let's go, Lily. I can almost taste those dumplings now."

The old Chinese woman smiles her toothless grin when we approach her. She knows us and seems to like the fact that we are willing to trust her cooking when most of the refugees would not. She scoops two hot doughy lumps from her pot and hands them to us, nodding her head in delight as she watches Lily take her first bite, tasting with pleasure the sweet mixture buried inside, a juicy trickle running down her chin.

In one of the little alleyways, Wayside Road, the Wayside Movie Theatre has been created in the hollowed cavity of an old warehouse. It is here that so many of us go and pay our hard-earned pennies to escape into a world far removed from the one we inhabit. Seated in the dark we are transported to the glamorous locations where beautifully dressed people glide across the screen. We are as addicted as the Chinese. We distance ourselves from our own painful reality through the artificial world of films, while they drown in the euphoric oblivion of their opium dens.

Sometimes Poldi and I go on a Saturday night when we have enough money set aside; sometimes I take Lily and just the two of us go to an afternoon show when she is back from school. The admission is only pennies but even so, it is a special occasion when we can spare the money. I rationalize the expense, thinking that there are so few diversions from the tedious daily activities and so little to make us forget our imprisonment, so I try to put enough aside to go at least once every other week.

We have no special clothes for going out. The days of finery are behind us now and who knows if they will ever return. I try to keep clean above all and fix my hair in the style of the movies, pinned up in a wave in front and off my neck in the back. This evening Stella and Walter will join us and we will walk along the street together, talking and joking. We will put our worries away, at least for a few hours.

I'm becoming more familiar with English words as I watch the flickering old Hollywood movies. I know they are escapist fantasies. Attractive heroes and heroines burst into song or dance, anywhere at all. I'm not alone in losing myself in their perfect pretend world. Within the musty little theatre, gazing up at the screen, I know that the other patrons are imagining themselves strolling nonchalantly with these perfect beings. We are enraptured by the clicking shoes of Fred Astaire and Ginger Rogers, Bing Crosby's warbling voice, Clark Gable's debonair grin, and Greta Garbo's mysterious smoky allure. Screen goddesses drift ethereally across the screen, draped sensuously in satin and chiffon evening gowns accompanied by tall handsome men, stylish in top hat and tails. And every story has a happy ending. That is what we want. What do we need with fictitious accounts of starvation, brutality, grief, or betrayal when that is our life?

My favourite, however, is a saga that has a special resonance, a movie that involves alienation and loss of home and family. It is the remarkable Technicolor marvel, *Gone With The Wind*. I have seen it again and again, usually going by myself into the darkened theatre, not needing anyone to share this experience, and each time, I imagine myself as Scarlett O'Hara. I know the story by heart and mouth the heroine's words, feeling her emotions as my own. I accept her philosophy of life. The past must be drowned out so the future can exist. "Tomorrow is another day," she says, and I say the words with her. She shakes away the tears that pool in her eyes, tosses her hair back in a wonderful display of petulance and determination. I believe in her fortitude and ability to surmount her travails, and I transfer that resolve to my own circumstances.

Food is scarce and physical hunger is always foremost in our minds, but our souls have been starving too. Who are these people now living like peasants and beggars? Many of the exiles are multi-talented and educated although their skills and passions have been submerged.

Poldi is more likely to make friends than I am. I feel shy or intimidated by strangers while he is at ease with new people and can charm them effortlessly. He has introduced me to a young violinist, Kurt Guttenberg, and his wife, Elsa. They have also come from Vienna, and we have met them a few times in the coffee houses, so when they suggest that we come to hear Kurt play in a special concert, we are eager to go.

"Kurt was a gifted musician in Vienna," Elsa has told us. "He was just beginning to make a reputation for himself when Hitler came along and everything changed. He had to leave the Vienna Philharmonic after the Nuremberg Laws were initiated. He managed to work at manual labour, washing dishes in a restaurant and the most menial type of jobs to keep us alive, and then even that was impossible."

"Oh Elsa," I say, trying to make her feel better and to forget the pain that they had experienced, "think about tonight and how wonderful it will be for everyone to hear him play."

Poldi and I are seated beside Elsa, all of us dressed in our best clothes. I have worn my wedding suit and feel quite elegant. Elsa's auburn hair is swept up in a twist at the back and in it is a jade clip. Her dress is faded green brocade, once beautiful and opulent but now worn and patched. Nevertheless she has a glow on her face when she spots her young husband on the stage, tuning his violin, the very one that he rescued from Vienna and carried with him in its special case.

"Look, Nini, Poldi, there is Kurt. Wait until you hear him play. He's so good."

As the music begins we are captivated by the performance but focus mostly on Kurt. He adjusts his wire-rimmed eyeglasses before he settles the precious violin on his shoulder. He runs his bow gently, then with more energy across the strings. His eyes close. The music moves him so that his whole body seems to be playing. All the hurt of the past is infused into the instrument, the slow melody of pain. Then the sound lightens, as if expressing freedom from confinement, and a release of his passion for music, his determination to survive and to play again. Each of the refugees in this room, in his own way, has overcome such obstacles and has persisted in the struggle. As the power of his music fills the small space, many in the audience, just like us, are in tears.

I close my streaming eyes for a moment and pretend that we are in the velvet seats of the Vienna Opera House again, but when I open them it is still Shanghai, still the hard chairs set up in a dingy hall, still far from home. The gifts and talents of these musicians and other professionals here in Shanghai were not enough to save them. But the finer spirit of humanity has not yet perished. Although it was driven from Europe it has re-emerged in Hongkew.

The strains pouring from the violins are all the more potent as they echo the melancholy of the players. The instruments themselves have been salvaged from Vienna and forced to endure the journey. Scuffed, dented, and bruised, they were allowed to accompany their owners only if they were deemed useless. Sometimes the violins served to conceal a few items of sentimental value, a wedding ring, a pair of earrings, a watch, things that were used to buy food and preserve life. Finally, here, in Shanghai, the cherished reminders of a better time are finally given the chance to do once more what they were crafted for, to sing.

People from outside the ghetto have heard about the changes we have made and have begun to come to "Little Vienna" to enjoy the civility we have created. The advent of a chamber orchestra has caused a stir of excitement, a chance to fill another hunger that we endure in Hongkew, the deprivation of culture. Something beautiful and inspiring has sprouted from the very midst of misery and decay. Even Goya and his henchmen have attended our soirée, making their entrance as if they were royalty waiting to be entertained by their slaves. With bravado, dressed in full military uniform, medals of war glistening, they make their way to the front seats. Despite the discomfort that their presence instills in us all, the glory of the Viennese music soon overcomes the tension, and by the end of the performance the Japanese soldiers add their applause to the rest. We rise to our feet as the last note is played and hug Elsa, who is crying with joy. We clap and clap until our hands are sore and all of us have wept in a shared pleasure for once rather than our usual sorrow.

Viennese and German Jewish expatriates congregate in the coffee houses just as they did at home, to talk in their own language, simply to play a game of cards or read a newspaper, and to pretend that life is normal. I love to inhale the aromas of home baking that mingle with smells of Oriental cooking. The human spirit is flourishing despite everything that has occurred to destroy it and to demoralize us. We are still very poor, suffering from lack of sufficient food and living in horrid conditions. But there is laughter and music and family gatherings, and we dare to feel that life will be fine again.

But our lives never seem to go on undisturbed for long. In 1943 we first see American airplanes, circling overhead. Poldi believes they are on reconnaissance flights, pinpointing targets, and photographing strategic Japanese military installations. As we gaze skyward, many of us whisper prayers for our salvation. But the occupation forces are enraged and nervous. They immediately round up more Chinese prisoners than before to be tortured and murdered and become more rigid with the Jewish captives of the ghetto.

Quickly and without warning, we descend into a precarious state as before, working for pennies, starving for morsels of edible food, terrified of disease and daring to hope for rescue. A few days after the American planes are first seen over Shanghai, Willi arrives at our door with some news. His shirt sleeves are rolled back and as always he has a cigarette wedged between his fingers.

"This is the latest development," he announces, showing us a scrap of paper. "All able-bodied male refugees are to take their turn in duty to protect the designated area of Hongkew," he reads. "Each man will be given a whistle, a baton, and an arm band to take his watch in the 'Pau-Chia'."

"The what?" I ask.

"The Pau-Chia," he explains, "is to be established as a group of Jews, to take turns in watch over the entrance to Hongkew. We are to work with the authority to report on the comings and goings of the inhabitants through the check-points and to help the Japanese keep order. If anyone becomes unruly or if there is a breakdown or, I suppose, a riot, we have to enforce control."

Poldi appears concerned by the news. Frowning, he shakes his head and says, "I can't believe it. The Japanese must really be getting jittery to want our help or even to think that we could possibly be of any use to them. I don't like the whole thing. This is a way to pit us against one another, to spy for them and to betray our fellow Jews to them. You'll see, it will lead to disputes among us."

"I don't think we have much choice," Willi replies. "It's hard to disobey their rules. They hold our lives in their hands." He shrugs. "I think it's best to go along with this latest idea. What good are these weapons anyway? What can we do with a stick and a whistle? They must be mad."

"Or will they use the Jews as human shields if there really is trouble?" I ask, anxious again.

They stare at me for a moment in grim silence. The Jews being put forward as protection for the Japanese seems a reasonable strategy. They have allowed us to live and now they will find some practical use for us.

Sure enough, the next day each of the men in a family is provided with the makeshift tools of the Pau-Chia "army." Together the Jews of Hongkew form a raggle-taggle troop of pretend soldiers, each carrying a stick and wearing a white cotton rag wrapped around his upper arm. Like children playing with toys, up and down the streets they march, trying to keep peace among the refugees or interrupting arguments among the coolies, taking turns at the gate and staying out of the glaring watch of Goya.

Poldi's concerns prove to be well founded. Constant bickering, disagreements, and struggles break out among the Pau-Chia men. If someone arrives a few minutes late for guard duty, the others are required to report the infraction to the Japanese command. We have been caged here and treated like dogs, and now we have been given the unsavoury occupation of informants, bringing discredit to our friends.

CHAPTER 30

THE WAR CONTINUES 1943-1945

Our lives are connected as always with the events unfolding in Europe. Our estrangement from the continent of our births has not released us from the destiny of our people. We are bound together through the faith that has been both our heritage and the cause of persistent persecution. Despite the trials our people remain cemented together by our deeply rooted respect for Jewish life. A kindred link binds us, a link I felt first as a small child in Vienna, standing in the synagogue, watching those around me engrossed in prayer, understanding even then that we are somehow all the same.

We devour the news about the battles that have torn Europe apart and watch, with personal concern, the latest developments. Hitler's victories have seemed inevitable. His evil grin splashed across the front pages fills us with renewed anguish. The twitching small black moustache and arm raised in victorious arrogance beneath a flapping swastika flag cause us endless dread.

Every evening Poldi gives me the information he has heard during the day. One night he says sadly, "There is no good news coming from Europe. We know that much of what we are getting is propaganda, fed to the Japanese by the Germans, but even our sources have nothing hopeful to report."

"Do you really believe the Nazis will win?" I am alarmed at his tone.

He bites his lip, then answers, "I don't want to believe it. All we can do is hang on to the thin possibility that they might still be defeated."

"But with the Americans in it now too, won't there be more hope for our victory?"

"Nini, we have experienced so many disappointments and setbacks that it is hard to truly believe in salvation. We are all asking for a promise that no one can give, that we might be liberated."

"And even here, the Germans would try to kill us?" I ask, fearing the reply.

He answers, "Already concentration camps have been set up here in Shanghai – I have seen them myself – where the Japanese are interning their Chinese prisoners. I'm afraid that it won't be long before they round us up, each one of us in Hongkew, and drive us in there." I understand his meaning, once in those camps there would essentially be no further hope.

Miraculously at the time of our weakest resolve and darkest fears, there seems to be a change in the direction of the war. The Axis armies are beginning to fail. The Americans' entry into the war does seem to have made a difference, and we are beginning to hear of Allied victories. Small bits of encouraging news sift through the ranting propaganda from Berlin, and from this we derive courage to hope for a turn of fortune. Now, with cautious smiles, we listen to a different tone in the newscasts and hug one another for support and encouragement.

In 1943 the Russians are able to win the Battle of Stalingrad and to defeat twenty-two divisions of German troops. D-Day on June 6, 1944, brings millions of American, British, and Canadian soldiers to the shores of Normandy. Italy has signed an armistice agreement. By August, Paris has been liberated. On the Russian front the Germans have been pushed back, and in a fierce struggle the occupied countries, one after the other, are freed. With the combined might of the Allied forces, tons and tons of explosives are dropped on Germany, and finally on May 7, 1945, there is unconditional surrender. Word spreads quickly of the German defeat. Hitler has been found dead, having committed suicide in his bunker. Mussolini has been hanged in public.

We hear of the tyrants' ignominious deaths and are struck dumb with disbelief. We rejoice in a kind of trance. After the years of suffering, we are unable to fully comprehend the end of our flight. Are we free? In Hongkew the news is greeted first with some jubilation, then sombre disappointment. The Japanese have refused to surrender. They are still at war, and we are still captives.

CHAPTER 31

BOMBS FALL IN HONGKEW 1945

On the wide khaki-coloured waters of the Yangtze River a number of barges stand empty, swaying, awaiting cargo. What are they waiting for? Ordinarily the commerce is swift with loads of goods transported without delay. Hundreds of coolies, bandannas tied around their foreheads, toil for endless back-breaking hours, lifting sacks and crates, grunting and moaning under the weight of their burdens. Their singsong working chant, "Aaay ho," is a familiar sound echoing from one man to another, along the length of the docks. It is unusual to see vacant boats anchored and immobile for any period of time.

Whispers and hushed rumours are circulating within Hongkew, and people are panicked with fear. We are told that the barges are meant for us. They are death ships. This time there will be no escape. We are mice caught by the hungry cat that has wanted to devour us from the start. Each time we have narrowly escaped its grasp but now it can taste our blood in its gaping jaws, hot and sweet. Before their defeat the Germans suggested this plan to the Japanese, who now seem prepared to comply. Gradually, we learn the full extent of the scheme for our extermination and in disbelief, the word spreads throughout our community.

An underground communication network equipped with shortwave radios has been set up among the refugees to receive the current news from Europe and the Pacific. Throughout the war spies, even some among the German officials in Shanghai, have dispensed bits of information. The Germans have now disappeared, racing away to find hiding places in the Orient or, we have heard, in South America. But the Japanese are still in power here and we remain in Hongkew, awaiting our fate. The news this time is terrifying. Can we believe it?

Those with day passes from the ghetto have clandestine meetings in Shanghai to try to find out the latest information, then pass it on when they return to Hongkew. Poldi has made friends with some of those involved and tells me there is limited hope as the Japanese are tenacious and unwilling still to capitulate.

Truth and conjecture mix in a frenzied outpouring regarding the plans for our fate, talk about concentration camps and gas chambers. We know that at least some of what we hear is factual as Poldi has seen such structures himself. He has told me they are already erected and standing vacant and ominous, across the Whang Po River on an island called Woosung, where the Jews of Hongkew might be transferred en masse and annihilated. Lists of Jewish names have been posted for all to see. For us this is a haunting repeat of events in Vienna. We are told by the Japanese authorities to sign up but Poldi and I decide to wait. If this is a death list, we are in no hurry to add our names to the roster. Where to run this time? Some are trying to hide illegally in Frenchtown or in the International Settlement, sneaking out at night like criminals, hoping to dissolve into the dense crowds of Shanghai. But if they are caught, they will have to deal with the wrath of Goya, who is forever watchful of the comings and goings of the prisoners under his command. Those found in hiding are beaten severely and returned to captivity in Hongkew with no allowance for exit passes. Their fate is meant to be a warning to the rest of us. The bruises and welts on their faces and arms are clear enough to make the point. Our family has no safe place to hide outside of Hongkew, but we are still together and are not prepared to separate.

Every day, the hostility of the Japanese occupation forces is increasing towards us but even more towards the Chinese. At the same time, the Chinese are feeling more confident and are aggressively attacking their enemies. Japanese officers are disappearing mysteriously, murdered in gruesome ways, and in return there are horrendous reprisals. The Japanese are worried, afraid of a revolt. If the Chinese take to the streets in a blind rampage, a deluge of blood will flow through all Shanghai.

It is July 17, the height of the scalding summer heat. The rising sun of the early morning amplifies the heat of the preceding night. By noon it is unbearable. Poldi and I are sitting on two wooden stools out on the small porch where our cooking implement is located. Sweat trickles into our eyes and down our necks. Clothing is merely wet rags hung on our drenched bodies. We drink boiled water and wipe our foreheads and arms with the fluid, but the heat is oppressive, steady, day and night, without the relief of a breeze. The air is thick with smells of rotting garbage and decaying human flesh, buzzing with flies and with mosquitoes carrying malaria. And still, we are holding on, unwilling to give up. Poldi is wearing just a sleeveless white undershirt and shorts. I am in a thin summer dress but it is clinging from the streams of perspiration. Our hair is damp, sticking to our skin. I flick a Chinese pleated paper fan across my face but the air doesn't seem to move. Sleep will be fitful this night.

Time is against us if the Japanese are truly prepared to exterminate us by September as we have heard. The most frequently circulated rumour is that we will be rounded up, most likely during our High Holy Day of *Rosh Hashana*, when we will all be together and easy prey, vulnerable, huddled in the various synagogues where we congregate to worship. Then every man, woman, and child is to be herded onto the barges that stand silently on the water. The boats are to be sent out onto the river, and there we are to be set on fire, burned alive.

Poldi is talking about the latest information from outside the ghetto, wiping the sweat from his forehead with the back of his hand. His face is grim as he says, "Our only hope is the Americans. The Japanese attack at Pearl Harbor brought them into the war, seeking revenge. But they will need determination to overcome these enemies. The Japanese are not prepared to surrender. That is not their way. There are kamikaze pilots by the hundreds on suicide bombing raids, blowing up American ships, killing as they are killed. That is how they die with honour."

"Honour through more bloodshed," I reply in disgust. "The Earth should be soaked red by now. Nothing has been achieved – just more human misery."

We become aware of a distant rumbling noise and the walls quivering. The sounds are growing closer and closer until they erupt in a violent burst. I scream in terror – is it an earthquake? We rush inside and crouch down on the floor.

The roar of war planes zooming overhead is deafening. We throw ourselves to the ground in our little room and lie sprawled on the floor, Poldi's arm wrapped around my shoulder, our hands clasped together. The screeching bombs tear through the sky, followed by a loud thud as they hit their target. We can hear wild shouting outside. Incredibly, amid the horrific sound of the aircraft, we can hear cries of celebration from outside.

"It's the Americans!" they are saying. "They have come to save us at last!"

"Poldi," I whisper from our spot, still on the floor, "is it true? Do you think we will be rescued in time?"

"It's our last and only hope," he answers, standing up slowly with caution, and peering out the window. "If we're not found and released now, or if the Americans are defeated, I don't think there will be another chance."

"God help us." We feel the floor below us quivering again and Poldi throws himself down, next to me again.

Bombs are falling everywhere in Shanghai. Explosions are crashing in violent retaliation against the Japanese who dared harm American citizens. We, hardly noticeable specks, are caught in the line of fire, hanging on for bare survival.

The Americans are bombing directly on Hongkew, aiming to destroy the strategically placed Japanese radio transmitter. Before long we may be washed away in the tide, killed by one side or another, it doesn't matter which. The thin walls shake as though thunderbolts are colliding within our very rooms. Plaster is crumbling, falling in chunks, with clouds of dust filling the air. Pieces of the patched ceiling are littered around us. Windows are rattling and cracking and splintered glass is everywhere. "I thought the Americans were going to rescue us. Why are they trying to kill us?" I ask Poldi my voice hoarse with fear.

"Keep down!" he shouts.

"But, why are they bombing us?"

In the midst of the chaos, he shouts over the noise, "We're not the target, Nini. We're just stuck in the middle."

I can hardly make out what he's saying. I press my hands against my ears to block out the sound. He puts his mouth closer to my ear, trying to explain the fierce battle around us.

"The Americans are trying to destroy the Japanese. Who even knows or cares that we are here? "

All night bombs continue to crash in ear-popping explosions. The sight from our window is a wonder to see. Chinese men are squatting, bare-chested and cross-legged on the shattered rooftops, pointing upward, waving their spindly arms at the American bomber planes. They are shouting their greetings as well. Having suffered for years under the rule of their oppressors, they too are hoping for an American rescue. They have lost so much that caution is not a concern. We understand the purpose for their reckless actions. They must have felt as invisible and neglected as we have. They want to be seen.

We can see and hear them as they shout up to the sky as the bombers soar overhead, "Amelicans, Amelicans! Kill bad Japs. Save China people. Yanky, save us! We wait too long. Time is now!"

Our flimsy apartment walls are beginning to buckle from the tremors. "We'd better get out!" Poldi shouts above the clamour.

He takes my hand and we manoeuvre our way down the loosened planks of the stairs. We have decided to stay out in the street with a number of others who have left their homes in fear. Buildings are tumbling like sand castles amid the screams of those taking flight. We don't know which way to turn, but then there is more noise overhead.

The red flares of Japanese anti-aircraft tracer shells float skyward, and the cacophony starts again. Beneath the bombs' crashing blare, muffled human wails can be heard. Many of the Chinese, caught in the line of fire, are hit as they perch on the rooftops. Jewish doctors are rushing around in the streets, amid the confusion and shrieking voices, trying to save the lives of those who have toppled to the ground. People scurry about in delirious fear mixed with the intoxicating hope of freedom.

Fire is raging through the ramshackle buildings. In the streets screaming Chinese and terrified Jewish refugees alike scatter in every direction, scrambling for shelter. People are frantically trying to douse the flames, to preserve whatever still remains of their homes. A few blocks away we can see the flames rising. There has been a direct hit on "The Safe Place."

"We have to go to Erna's house to see if they're all right!" I shout in alarm to Poldi, over the clattering noise.

He doesn't answer at first, listening and waiting for a break in the bombing before he replies, "All right. It's quiet now. Let's go."

We run in spurts, then stop and hide in any small sheltered spot we pass, wait a minute or two then move again. Parts of walls have been blown away, as if sliced through like a melon, and the intimate lives of the inhabitants are exposed. Once more privacy has been violated, belongings destroyed. Some 100,000 Chinese live in Hongkew crammed together with the refugees. Now we all share this latest devastation.

Adrenalin pulses in our veins, and once again fear is as ripe as harvest fruit. We dash towards Erna's flat but as we approach our hearts leap in terror. We see only a mound of rubble and people running everywhere. Bodies in various states of injury are being pulled out of the wreckage. We can see Willi, wearing his Pau-Chia arm band, tugging someone's limbs from beneath the heap of ruins. His hair and glasses are coated in dust.

"Willi, have you seen Erna? Are they safe?" I beg him, pulling at his sleeve.

"I don't know." He doesn't take a break from his struggle to release the half-living body from its trap. Walter comes racing towards us, along with other men, ready to help drag the shocked victim from his near-grave.

"We've already found thirty-one Jewish people, dead from the attack, and many more Chinese. We hope there won't be others." Willi, short of breath, struggles with the weight of the motionless body, covered in plaster dust.

Poldi joins them, clawing with bare hands at the piles of rubbish, searching in desperation for any sign of someone still breathing. Others are running from all directions to aid the rescuers. The men, their backs bent, join together, calling out to the victims, trying to offer encouragement to anyone caught under the rubble, frantically pulling them out and finally dragging the injured and dead from the ruins.

I can't find the others and decide to try Stella's place. Heart pounding, I run into Stella's apartment house, up the broken steps.

"Auntie Nini, did you hear all the noise?" Lily calls out. "I was scared and the whole ceiling fell down on the floor and Daddy told me not to cry but I cried anyway."

I kneel down and hug the child, who rubs her teary eyes with the back of her dirty hand. Erna and Stella are quiet, trembling and staring into space, still in shock from the proximity of the hit. I try to comfort them, insist that they each swallow a bit of boiled water to settle them down. Fritz is here too. "Nini," he says, "where is everyone?"

"Down in the street. There are bodies everywhere and they are trying to help."

"I'm going too," he says, remembering to kiss Erna and Lily who starts to cry again. Before he rushes out he says, "Tomorrow it may be our turn, but today we are still alive. Be brave my ladies."

Some ancient words come suddenly into my mind: "In every generation an enemy will arise to destroy us." So it is written in the Passover *Haggadah* that we recite every year. "And in every generation the Lord will reach out His hand to save a portion of His people to carry on." But this time, I think to myself, He has abandoned us.

I leave my sisters and Lily after a while. The bombing has ceased for now and outside there is a frenzy of activity.

The day is long, as we try to sort the living from the dead and to save whichever lives can be salvaged. The whole community has united in this battle. We are mobilized as one, all the factions coming together in the face of such an ordeal. I see Elsa Guttenberg among those who have come to lend their hands to the needy. She has brought torn night-clothes and sheets to make into bandages. "Elsa," I say, "give me some of those so I can do something."

She is kneeling on the stoney mounds her face and hands coated in a mixture of dirt and blood. Her red hair is a muddy mop and she, like everyone else is a frazzled mess. She hands me some of the makeshift bandages. I bend down beside her and begin to tend to one of the wounded people lying on the ground, an old woman whose leg is cut from some falling debris.

I can see Poldi lifting rocks with the others of our family who are searching for survivors and I realize I haven't seen Elsa's husband. "Where is Kurt?" I ask her.

"Kurt was injured but the doctors have been to see him. I've left him in our room. At least the place is still standing. He's asleep and I wanted to come out and help some others. His left shoulder and hand are broken but the doctors believe they will heal so he can play his violin again – that is if we survive this. I pray they are right."

I also have seen Herta wading through the wreckage, carrying decanters of boiled water for the injured. She is too far away to hear me if I were to call to her – besides we have lost contact – but I am glad that she still feels a part of the community and that she has not become so hardened that she would turn her back on those in distress. Every muscle is strained as we finally retreat, weary and drained. That night we stay at Stella's home, collapsing in the meagre comfort of the rooms, in one of the few buildings remaining intact. We say *Kaddish* for those whose lives were lost.

"Will we ever get out of here alive?" Erna asks, in a whisper trying not to wake Lily who is sleeping in her lap.

"Don't talk like that," Stella says, tears soaking her cheeks. "It's not over yet."

Exhausted, slumped on a chair, I say, "How ironic – we escape Hitler only to be bombed by the Americans. My nerves are too strained and my courage is at its limit."

But Poldi is not ready to surrender, and he grips my arms firmly. "We have to be strong, now more than ever. Maybe we're the ones meant to survive. Have faith. I believe it still, and so should you. Don't give up now. I need you. I love you."

He is stronger than I have ever seen him, stubborn and relentless in his belief, and as I look into his bright eyes, I believe too.

Willi and Fritz fall asleep on the floor, Poldi and I are on chairs. Stella and Walter are in their bed, Lily is sleeping with Erna on the sofa.

By the next day we know that the Jewish victims have already been buried in our cemetery, whisked away in haste during the night to prevent desecration of the bodies. We have no dead in our own family, thank God, but those who have had losses would have stayed with their deceased overnight as is the ritual. The body is not to be left alone until the soul has had time to depart to the next world.

As daylight breaks it is still quiet. We look out our window at the broken heaps of debris of the aftermath; we see patches of dried blood, stained reddish-brown blotches on the dusty street. The whole of

Hongkew is a web of partially standing structures. We see people out in the street rummaging through the waste, searching for bits of their lives, any fragments that might have survived the bombing.

On the road outside our building and against the backdrop of devastation, the Japanese have laid out the bodies of dozens of dead Chinese. The soldiers, standing guard over the corpses, are burning an American flag and shouting slogans against the Allied forces who, they say, are responsible for the carnage. The surviving Chinese eye their oppressors with renewed hostility as they grieve for their lost family members, dumped like animal carcasses on the street. Their eyes reveal hatred for their enemies. This violation of the dead is a great dishonour, more painful than the actual death. Over this period of bombing, the Chinese and the refugees have formed a new bond of friendship. The Chinese offer their help and smile with gratitude at the Jewish doctors and volunteers who stood with them.

For weeks the bombing continues with quiet spells between. Morale among the refugees is as low as it has ever been. Finding food and clean water occupies our time. There are no movies or musical performances, no diversions. Everyone sits in the ruins of the formerly rebuilt structures waiting, waiting and wondering what to do next. Poldi has tried to get out of Hongkew to find some rice and cigarettes but it is getting more difficult. The Japanese authority is not about to grant passes. They are concerned with the attacks on our ghetto and are not favourably disposed to the refugees. People are no longer smiling. If this lasts much longer, we will starve to death and there will be nothing left to save in Hongkew. For now, though, a soup kitchen has been set up and whatever food can be found is stored and shared so that at least the children are fed. We stand in line with the others and wait for some rations to sustain us.

We don't know when to expect another hit. It is August now. The heat is oppressive, water and food are in increasingly short supply, and every new day may be our last. My courage is waning, despite Poldi's efforts at encouragement.

The sweltering heat does not abate. Each new day is as brutal as the one before. Our nerves are fragile, ready to snap. On the fifth of August we are awakened again by the crashing sounds of another air raid. I cry hysterically as the bombing continues around us. I shake with fear, hunger screaming in my stomach, thirst tearing at my throat. Then, there is silence again. We wait, unable to move for hours, looking up at the ragged ceiling, expecting a new barrage to begin again at any time. We are back in our old apartment – that is, what remains of it. Our furniture is damaged and even more pathetic than before. We look into the darkness, numb and immobile, then finally fall into the sleep of exhaustion on our bed. All our clothing is covered in a layer of dust from the falling plaster. The lamps are smashed and we have only a few candles that we are hoarding.

Word of what's happening outside our small world filters in to us. Despite the devastation of the bombs, the Japanese have refused to give up, hitting back with endless storms of suicide missions. They are resisting the Allied forces with relentless determination, ordered to carry on by their obsessed emperor. Inflamed by nationalistic fervour that goes beyond reason, driven by blind obedience and faith in his holy wisdom, they proceed in their crusade. More and more of their young men are sent to their plummeting deaths, taking countless lives along with them to early graves.

I still can't comprehend the seemingly unquenchable thirst for power that is driving this war and the suicide attacks that don't relent. "Why don't they surrender now?" I ask Poldi.

"That is their way," he answers. "The Japanese have a different philosophy of life and death than we do. Death is a certainty but the form of death is of the utmost importance."

I shake my head. If they don't value their own lives, then what chance do we have to defeat them?

CHAPTER 32

VICTORY 1945

All day long tension bristles in Hongkew. Poldi and I meet with the others to exchange information. Wherever there is a functioning radio, we huddle around to learn the latest developments. More frantic Japanese suicide missions are reported, as well as further destruction and fatalities. Finally the Americans lose patience. The next day, we can hardly believe the newscasts: the United States has dropped two atomic bombs. The first explodes on August 6, on Hiroshima, the second on August 9, on Nagasaki.

All of us in Hongkew are thrown into a state of confusion, vacillating between exhilaration and anxiety. Is it really over? On August 9, the very day of the bombing of Nagasaki, the Russians declare war on Japan, flinging their hat into the ring of battle at the last minute. On August 10 newsletters appear from nowhere and are dispersed all over the ghetto. Someone tells us that Allied flags have been seen flying over public buildings in Shanghai, and there are bursts of rejoicing, but this elation is soon dampened by bad news – refugees living in Manchuria are in danger of reprisals from Japanese authorities.

Poldi looks concerned as he scans one of the most current flyers. "What about Leon Druck?" he asks.

I hadn't thought of Leon for a long time. All through the bombing raids and the devastation of Hongkew, we had no chance to write and no way to receive any communication from outside Hongkew. Now I am reminded of Leon's help and courage, his devotion to Poldi and kindness to me, and I become as worried as Poldi is.

"Is there any way to get word to him? What can we do to help him?" I ask.

"I don't know. We're still prisoners ourselves. I can try to speak to someone in the underground. If there is any way to help him, I'll do it. He has been like a brother... well, in some ways more than a brother to me," he says, making an oblique reference to Dolu, who has been silent through most of the latest turmoil.

For another two weeks life is uncertain. The British and American flags that had been hung briefly throughout the city have been torn down from their perches. Sporadic shows of victory celebration in the streets of Hongkew have been curtailed by the increasingly forceful Japanese command. The Japanese government has officially surrendered but paradoxically we remain under siege. Again we wait, and each day our situation is more precarious than the one before.

One early morning in mid-August, just after daybreak, we are awakened by the sound of a whistle and the shout "Wake up, wake up! The guard is gone! The Japs have left! We're free, we're free! The Yanks are coming. It's over, it's over at last!" Rushing to the window, we see a young man, wildly blowing his Pau-Chia whistle and running up and down the street, still shouting.

We burst out into the street with many others, half-dressed and rubbing sleep from our eyes, to discover what has happened. Sure enough, there is no guard at his usual post, at the end of Tong Shan Road. The Japanese flag, its dreaded red rising sun insignia familiar to us and despised, has been removed. Marching boldly down the main street are soldiers, bearing the unmistakable air of victors, calm and confident. To our relief, delight, and incredulity, they are Americans.

The strong young soldiers are striding casually towards us, tall, smiling, and relaxed. We overwhelm them with our welcome. Women and children rush towards the uniformed Americans and throw their arms around their necks, or tug at their sleeves, kissing their hands. Old men, hands clasped together, pray in gratitude, eyes upturned to the sky. Joyful tears flow. We are dancing, twirling on the crumbling pavement of the street, laughing and crying at once, unable to bottle our emotions for one moment longer.

Poldi grabs me in his arms and swings me round and round. The world is spinning around us and we are giddy with the pleasure of freedom. We kiss and passers-by shake our hands.

"Victory! Victory! At last it's over," Poldi shouts and others respond with calls of their own, and fingers raised in a "V" for victory symbol. Our Chinese neighbours bow to us and we to them and there is so much joy that we feel we might explode.

"I love you," I say to him and he responds, "How wonderful life is. How grand to be alive!"

We go to find the others in the family, feeling the lifting of the burden that has weighed us down for years. Willi, Walter and Stella, Erna and Fritz with Lily, all are there in the street and we embrace, surrounded by ruins, with no thoughts of the future, nothing but this one moment of unrestricted joy. Kurt, his hand nearly healed, and Elsa are there too and we embrace them.

Like children, we enthusiastically hug friends, family members, and strangers who emerge from bomb-ravaged homes. We clutch one another in long, tight embraces, wanting to hold on forever.

The sounds of our joyous celebration are interrupted by the welcome rumble of army trucks. As they roll into sight, we see their characteristic splotches of camouflage paint, now splattered with mud, their red, white, and blue Stars and Stripes flags waving as a freedom banner. All around us everything is in shambles. The painstaking work we had put in to repair and restore the dilapidated structures has been demolished again. Now, the conquering heroes march into the midst of our incarceration and appear baffled by the sight of us here, a secluded community of malnourished Europeans tucked away in this forlorn corner of Shanghai. We are caught in the throngs of barefoot Chinese, children in rags, shell-shocked men and women, the old and the sick, all making their way towards the Americans, our skeletal arms outstretched. I grasp Poldi's hand tightly for fear of losing him in the crowd.

The Americans have brought food such as we have not seen or tasted in years. Glowing with joy, we surround the soldiers, eagerly anticipating our share of their plentiful supplies. At last we believe that the war is over and that we have truly been saved.

American aid flows once more, and within a few days the United Nations Relief Agency, UNRA, begins to supply vast quantities of food. Soon we have chocolate bars, tins of cooked chicken, butter, biscuits, cured ham, instant coffee, canned milk, cocoa, and fruit. After the hardship and deprivation of the past six years, we are overwhelmed by the arrival of so much at once.

Over the following days, people talk of the future – where they will go, what they will do, and most importantly, how they will do it. But most of the inhabitants of Hongkew decide to stay where they are. The community has achieved a solidarity that we did not really anticipate. This ghetto and the organizations formed to deal with life in this tiny inhospitable patch of Shanghai have united various groups who had nothing in common. The Orthodox Jews with their characteristic black hats, beards, and sidelocks have merged with the least religious factions among us, melding us into one people simply because our enemies threw us together. The foundations of a community exist here, and there is already a movement underway to begin rebuilding.

As a sign of returning normalcy, mail delivery begins, though it is sporadic. "Nini, I have a letter from Leon." Poldi waves a battered envelope as he rushes in the door. "The Japanese didn't have a chance to retaliate against the refugees in Harbin, and he has just received confirmation from New York that he has a visa to go there. He's leaving soon and wants us to apply as well."

I am happy to have Leon's news but so far Poldi and I have no such prospects. We don't know anyone in New York who would sponsor us, and it is too soon to think of future plans. We want to revel, at least for this moment, in the pure joy of peace.

We are still discussing the letter when we hear shouting in the street and go to the window. We can see a crowd gathering near Goya's office. Poldi says, "Let's go and see what's happening."

Goya has been caught while frantically pulling papers from office cabinets, trying to destroy evidence of the injustices and cruelty committed under his command. He has rushed out into the street, a valise clutched tightly in his hand. A group of young Jewish men are waiting for him. With bare fists and the miserable Pau-Chia batons he forced them to carry, they start to release their hatred. "This is for my mother – you slapped her across the face and broke her teeth when she asked for a pass!" one of them shouts as his knuckles smash Goya's disfigured face. He cries in pain as a red trickle drips from his lip.

As we watch the fight, I feel no compassion for the man who was our tormentor for so long. Like the others, I want revenge for the pain, the years of anguish, the fear and the death. Mama lies in the cemetery. Poldi's parents are dead. Why should this miserable little man get away? If I had the courage I would join in the pummelling.

"This is for my sister, who begged for help and was beaten for it," screams another, flailing his stick against Goya's brittle bowed legs, making him crumple to the ground, his arms folded over his head, amid pleas for the mercy that he never offered to his victims.

"This is for my father who was denied medicine and died because of you!" shouts one more, tears of hatred and frustration wetting his face.

A mob has gathered , cheering on the beating, shouting in anger at the despised, squirming little man who caused so much misery for so long. Each time he is knocked down, he rises again, each time more shakily, and attempts a defiant military salute. He is still a Japanese soldier, trying to save face. On it goes until he is lying bloodied and bruised, but not dead. They have not killed him. That is not our way, even now, after the agony and torture and years of confinement. Even now we keep the commandment "Thou shalt not kill." We turn our backs on him in disgust and revulsion. The "King of the Jews" has been overthrown.

"Enough," I say to Poldi, "I can't look at the blood any more. I want some quiet at last. Let's go home."

Sounds of revelling fill the narrow alleyways and broad boulevards of Shanghai. There are no longer divisions or segregated areas. There is only one city, gone crazy with a euphoric energy. Many are drinking and singing in inebriated glee, weaving joyously through the streets, arm in arm, bottles of whiskey and gin dangling from their hands. The American soldiers are a raucous bunch, carousing from bar to bar, and then like mischievous children, they dump the coolies and beggar children into the seats of the rickshaws and race excitedly up and down the roads, zigzagging through traffic, making a game of it all.

The Chinese are baffled and uncomfortable with this behaviour as it seems that the Americans are mocking them and the tedious work that has been their families' livelihood for generations past. They consider it "losing face" but the Yanks are oblivious to the Oriental customs and sensibilities and carry on. We watch horrified, expecting a Chinese reaction to the blatant show of disrespect. After all these years, we have learned a few lessons about the reverence for tradition and honour. But there is no outcry, just some shocked faces and disapproving glances. After all, it is only the Americans having some good-natured fun and everyone is so grateful for the long-awaited freedom that these violations can be forgiven.

A new prosperity washes over Shanghai. Businesses are flourishing. The Americans have brought the precious commodity of U.S. dollars with them and are spending wildly, purchasing everything from hand-painted porcelain vases to fur coats that they will take back "Stateside." They fill the restaurants, bars, and brothels and everyone is suddenly prosperous. An abundance of food fills the marketplaces with fresh produce. Rows of roasted red ducks and suckling pigs are hanging upside down in the Chinese shop windows or can be seen rotating on barbecue spits, fatty juices dripping, appealing aromas filling the air of the streets. Steamed dumplings are hawked on the sidewalks from huge boiling pots and bamboo steamer baskets. We have become accustomed to the smells of the local cooking that repelled us when we first arrived, and now the European refugees are even scooping rice and exotic delicacies into their mouths with chopsticks, in the Oriental style. A cosmopolitan banquet is available in Little Vienna, where Eastern cooking exists side by side with our familiar European foods. The Viennese cuisine in Hongkew these days is richer and finer than we have seen since we left Austria, and we all indulge. We eat and drink in a gluttonous orgy and vain attempt to fill the emptiness that characterized so many years.

It is the fall of 1945, and as we approach *Rosh Hashanah,* our New Year, the time we had previously feared we would be destroyed, we have reason to rejoice.

Poldi and I have started repairs on our room, trying once more to create a habitable space after the most recent destruction, but today we are visiting Stella and Walter's home. The whole family is together again. There is a feeling of relaxed good spirits that has been missing for so long. For once there is food, real food, not the morsels and scraps that have sustained us through years of deprivation.

"I feel as though I've been dropped into a barrel of honey," Poldi says, smiling and munching on a piece of fresh fruit. "There's so much of everything now that the famine is over."

"What should we do to celebrate?" Walter asks, eyes gleaming with anticipation.

"Something wonderful!" I say. "We must all take a holiday together now while we're still so full of this feeling. We'll go away with no care in the world and not talk about the future, only this precious moment."

Everyone is inspired by my buoyant spirits. Then Willi says, beaming with delight at his idea, "Let's go to Moka Shan, you know the place that everyone talks about, up high in the mountains, away from the heat of Shanghai, a paradise, they say. There are hotels up there with swimming pools and cool shady glades. It will be heaven."

We all go together, even Dolu and Eva. Now, all the friction that our separation had caused is put aside. We are alive and longing for peace and harmony above anything else. In reckless abandon, we leave plans for future enterprises behind, longing just to escape from the chaos that we survived and the scorching heat that seems to come from the centre of the earth, seeping up through the cracks of the sidewalks.

CHAPTER 33

THE SHOCK OF THE HOLOCAUST
1945

When Allied troops marched into the Nazis' hideous concentration camps in the late stages of the war, word of the immensity of the horror was released to the world. From newspapers and through radio broadcasts, we become aware of the unspeakable atrocities, the torture and deprivation, the gas chambers and mass graves. Now we know what became of our revered aunties and uncles, of Poldi's beloved parents, and of so many other dear friends and family members. Each life was torn from a warm home and normal civilized existence, and taken to its doom. They and hundreds of thousands of others were thrust into the most unholy terror ever conceived. Innocent and unwary, they were tortured sadistically and murdered for no cause but their faith.

The photos in the papers reveal the extent of the unthinkable. Haunting faces glare back at us from images of living cadavers. Dull eyes, sunken within skulls covered by sagging skin, peer straight ahead. Toothless grins of the forsaken, their gold teeth having been extracted by their tormentors or fallen out from gum disease and malnutrition, reveal the undying spark of human hope, treasured and preserved even in a man-made purgatory. On their emaciated forearms tattooed numbers can be seen, seared into pallid skin, branding them like cattle for slaughter. American, Russian, and British troops are shown wading among piles of skeletons, and we are sickened. Only then do we com-

prehend our own good fortune, despite the hardships, having survived
as we have done. Suddenly we feel guilty to have complained of our circumstances, ashamed of our comparative ease.

The accounts are precisely detailed. We find that we had only the
briefest taste in Vienna of the barbarism of the Germans. We learn that
every day some 20,000 naked starved humans, more than the Jewish
population of Hongkew, were led into the gas chambers in Auschwitz
alone, just one of the many camps scattered through Nazi-occupied
territory. In all, six million Jews were murdered, more than the teeming
masses of Shanghai. We look at the numbers in horror and disbelief and
try to absorb the enormity of the sin, six million... six million... six
million. How can this ever be understood?

Beyond the sheer volume of innocent wasted lives, we discover that
simple murder was not sufficient for the Nazis. Sadism and bestiality
were daily practice in the concentration camps, and as we read of the
disgrace, we weep. They, our people, were drowned in cesspools, choking to death on their own excrement. They were violently raped,
maimed, injected with poison, and observed as they died in distortions
of agony, ripped apart by vicious dogs or electrocuted on barbed wire
fences. Nothing was too cruel. And as we read and reread the words, we
are left incredulous, unable to comprehend such hatred.

We, along with the others in the ghetto, listen to the frightening
news of discovery as Allied troops enter one death camp after another
and recoil from the horrors they must witness. We scan the newspaper
photos with numb disbelief. Names are listed on boards, rows and rows
of names of those senselessly slaughtered. We search for those whom we
knew, especially Poldi's parents.

We have begun to spend much more time now with Dolu and Eva
as all of Shanghai is open again; we can move freely from Hongkew
and the others can come through the open gates to visit us. The lists
of those murdered in Europe have dredged up all the grief that we and
especially Poldi and his brother had already endured. They speak of

their parents with respect, reverence and, above all, love.

"We have searched through all the lists, again and again but haven't found their names," Poldi says, when he and Dolu return from another heart-wrenching search. Eva and I do our best to alleviate the sorrow. She pats Dolu's hand when he sits down beside her.

"I don't know if we'll ever find out what really happened to them." Dolu shakes his head in frustration and sadness. "These lists aren't complete and the enormous number of victims is staggering."

"After all we've been through, it appears that we had the easiest time of it." Eva dabs her eyes with a handkerchief. "I can't bear to think of all those who were tortured and burned alive like that and there was no one to stop it."

"If I'd known what could happen, I would never have left them," Poldi says, still tormenting himself with guilt. "I can still see Mama and Papa the way they looked the last time I saw them, the last time. I know I could have gotten them out if I had stayed behind in Vienna. They must have been sent to Dachau as we were told, but will we ever know for sure?"

"Poldi," I say, trying to lift his spirits, "they wanted you and Dolu to go on and live your lives. Life in Shanghai has been a constant battle – they might have died here like Mama did. Your mother told me once, years ago, that things are *beshert*, you know, meant to happen in a certain way. She believed in the hand of fate. Allow them to rest in peace now. They deserve that at least."

Grim-faced, Poldi and Dolu hang their heads. In the morning, they plan to go to the small synagogue where Poldi and I were married, to say *Kaddish*.

Already we have seen refugees attempting to bury the nightmares so deeply that they will never have to be faced. We are no different. We have vowed to ourselves not to tell the children we may nurture one day, nor anyone in the outside world, what we have suffered. No one needs to know. How else can we go on? If we have to relive it, we will all go mad. Better to let it go, to create a rock-hard shell, a protective fortress against all that has happened. Forget the torture, forget the Nazis, forget the cruelty of the Japanese. Forget it all.

All our energies are directed towards survival. Poldi and I are ready to concentrate on the prospect of a new beginning. Whenever a break has come in our lives we scan the global prospects. Where to go? Poldi has made inquiries about the possibility of leaving Shanghai. Throughout the war we often dreamed of returning to our homeland if the Nazis were ever defeated, a dream that sustained us during that hard time, but we realize that we can never return to Vienna. The cobbled pavements there are permanently stained with memories of brutality and hatred. Now that we have put that behind us, as much as possible, we are prepared once again to start anew.

We meet often with the others in the family and there is an excitement about our prospects. We have been stifled for so long and have so much pent-up energy that we are anxious to make our way to an improved life. At the same time we are caught once more in uncertainty. I ask Poldi, "Is there any news of where we might settle? Where should we apply?"

He shakes his head and says, to our amazement and distress, "It appears there is no country eager to let us in. For now, this remains our home, still… Shanghai."

CHAPTER 34

LIFE AFTER THE WAR 1946

With the opening of the city, we visit Mama's grave in the small Jewish cemetery, and once again I find myself repeating the ritual that has become so familiar. I place a stone on her marker and say the few words of prayer I have kept since childhood. My hand touches the roundness of my belly to meet the rippling movement from inside. I am expecting a child.

Standing by the silent grave, I speak to a stone but envisage a face, lined with worry, smiling despite all the adversity and anguish, and as I speak to her, tears stain my cheek once more. "Mama, I miss you so much. I wish you could have lived to see this day, to see that, by God's will, we have lived through such unbelievable turmoil and have survived. Look, I am going to have a baby, a grandchild for you. How wonderful it would have been for you to see a new life now, after all this pain and death. Although you are no longer here to give me the guidance and reassurance that I need, I see you still in my dreams and wonder if you can hear me."

Although we face uncertainty ahead, we are happy in a way we feared we could never be again. There will be a child to care for and there is peace at last. For now, we are prepared to remain in Shanghai. After all, we have nowhere else to go but we reason that things may be all right here. There has been such longing for an end to war that we want only to immerse ourselves in the reconstruction of normal life. We don't ask for more.

Simple peaceful existence, which we doubted would truly return, is being devoured with eager enthusiasm. Food and wine taste better than ever before. Music plays with renewed joy, and the curtain of despair that had descended upon us is finally lifted. We have even gone to a symphony concert and were thrilled to see that our old friend Kurt was there with his wife, Elsa. We soak in the atmosphere of serenity, absent for so long. We are going to have a child, start a family of our own, and become complete people once more.

Shanghai is freer for us than it has ever been, and although we can come and go as we please, the family is staying in Hongkew. We are used to its sights, sounds, and smells, and it is being rebuilt once more to its status as the "Little Vienna of the Far East." Scruffy rooftops have been brilliantly transformed through hard work and unflagging determination. They have become enchanting roof-garden restaurants decorated with potted plants, bright Chinese lanterns, and little tables topped with clean tablecloths. We, along with other Jewish Europeans, sip brandy or Viennese iced coffee, topped decadently with fresh whipped cream. Even those from the wealthy unrestricted French Concession and International Settlement are coming here to partake in the European ambience. The restaurants, cafés, and cabarets are beginning to flourish. What a waste of time, I think. For all those years there could have been peace and a civilized life and so many would have lived to benefit.

Expensive new automobiles soon appear on the rutted streets, and in the cool months ladies wrapped in the most luscious fur creations, Russian sable, mink, and fox, step daintily on to the cracked pavement. Poldi, having spent so much time studying the fur trade in Italy, remarks in awe on the sumptuous quality of the pelts and obvious wealth pouring into our poor little Hongkew. We have decided to open a fur salon, a business venture in which Poldi is at last able to use his skills. Energized by the current circumstances of renewed life and liberty, we are prepared to gather up the bits and pieces of a tattered life and try once again to build a future.

With the influx of American currency into Hongkew, prosperity has become a possibility once more. Because Poldi was able to sell his goods more easily than before, without the restrictions that we previously experienced with the Japanese, we have accumulated enough to establish a new business.

"This will be so much better than the bar, Poldi," I say with enthusiasm. "No more rough customers and late nights. No more drunken carousing and smashed bottles. I'm looking forward to a civilized way of living again."

"I know," Poldi answers. "That business was hard on us both, but it kept us fed for a few years. Nevertheless, I'm glad we can start something new. Maybe this will give us the foundation for a good future. "

Poldi has contacted his old friend Leon Druck again. Leon, with his many connections in Harbin and knowledge of the fur trade, has been invaluable in setting us up with contacts. He is still waiting for his passage to America but for now he has done what he can to help us. The best fur pelts come from Russia and Manchuria, and we have been able to get suppliers who will give us goods on consignment so that we don't have to pay until the pieces are sold. Skilled workers in China will make the coats and hats, stoles and wraps that we are sure will do well here. We have found a lovely little shop on one of the main streets of Hongkew, and we have begun to set up the business and plan to work at it together, no partners this time.

At seven months into my pregnancy, I'm feeling the physical discomfort of my changing body, the aching back, swollen ankles, and weakened bladder. I'm aware that I have become a cocoon, sheltering within myself the kernel of unformed life. Bulky and unable to easily rise from the soft, cushioned chair, I finally push myself up from my seat, then pad around our apartment in the Chinese embroidered slippers I like to wear. I can feel my face relaxing into a smile, experiencing contentment amid the new whirlwind of our lives. We have moved into a larger apartment with room for the baby and for a nanny to stay with it when I go to work at the store. This time, we may allow ourselves the pleasure we have not had for so long. I try to shake off the superstitious taboo of feeling too much happiness for fear of bringing bad luck and some new sorrow.

When the time comes for the birth, I feel estranged again. I had always relied on my mother, the heart of the family, and expected her to be with me in this crucial moment. Now she is gone. When the labour pains begin I think of her and believe it is her strength that will guide me through. In my mind, I hear her trying to comfort me as she would have done if she were here. She tells me everything will be all right.

Our daughter is born in the small Jewish hospital in Hongkew in 1946. We name her Vivian, after V for victory, *vivre* to live, and for my favourite movie star, Vivien Leigh, and Jeanette after Mama's name, Johanna. Our daily prayers are simply that she may know peace in her lifetime and never suffer the agony of war. Our child becomes the centre of our lives and the focus of all our dreams. For me, she is the salvation that can pull me from dark thoughts and melancholy. I want to be strong for her sake.

Poldi and I are thrilled with our little daughter. Poldi's eyes glisten with joy when he holds the baby in his arms for the first time. He kisses her on the forehead and on the tips of her little fingers. How much greater is happiness, I think, when sorrow has been so immense. I feel the most serene and content I have been for years.

"Some day," Poldi says, "when she's grown, we'll give her the gold watch from my mother. We'll save it for her as we've done until now, and she'll be proud to wear it. We'll tell her the story of her grandparents so she may know her heritage."

When we bring Vivian home, a Chinese nurse – an *amah* – has already been installed to care for her. We treat the baby with the utmost care and despite the difficult conditions in Shanghai, where disease is prevalent and infant mortality is high, she grows and develops well in her first year. She is always dressed in pristine white linens, embroidered by hand, with matching bonnets framing her small heart-shaped face. The *amah* washes and irons her things and makes sure that she is perfectly clean. Ash blond curls peek out from under the wide brims shading her from the harsh sun. She has bright hazel eyes with flecks of green. Encircling her little wrist is a bracelet strung with beads of red coral. Both the Chinese and the European Jews are superstitious people. We believe evil spirits are hovering over human beings, ready to create havoc, to derail happiness, to cause illness and death. The colour red is worn by Chinese children to prevent harm from these supernatural forces, and coincidentally, Jewish babies often have red ribbons tied to wrists or ankles to combat a *"Gitoig,"* or evil eye.

We have a fine navy blue English pram, a gift from the family. All the relatives dote over "Vivi," and she loves the attention. No babies have been born into the family in years. Lily is eleven now and is delighted with her new cousin. She learns to speak in an infantile version of German words mixed with Chinese, taught to her by the *amah*. She is our cherished angel. We have nicknamed her "Poupie," or little doll. Everything that has been taken from us, we plan to restore to her. It becomes our driving obsession to give her the life we have lost. We allow ourselves to contemplate a better life, to make plans now that peace has returned, and to laugh again. On her first birthday, we invite all the family for the afternoon to celebrate, just like we did in Vienna, with hot coffee and fresh pastry and a reason to be happy again.

The paralyzing heat and primitive sewage disposal make hygiene in Shanghai nonexistent. We boil all water that is to be consumed. Vivi's room is kept scrupulously clean, and anything she is to touch is meticulously sterilized. Every possible precaution is taken to safeguard her from the rampant bacteria and disease that have brought so many European immigrants to devastating illness and death. Insulated within this pure scrubbed world, our child is sheltered, protected and apart from the ravages of an unsanitary environment. We are determined in this way to keep her secure and safe, unaware that we are preventing her from building any immunity to the inevitable intrusion of any malady.

Every night I awaken several times to check that she is all right. One early morning, before dawn, I discover a change. Alarmed, I call Poldi in wild fear. "Poldi! Look at the baby. Something's wrong. Her whole body is burning with fever. Get the doctor – he has to come right now!"

Poldi runs out into the dark street and down the narrow lanes to the doctor's home, and within an interminable hour they are back. As the doctor examines her, we can hear only her weak cries. Poldi puts his arm around my shoulder as we stand waiting for the verdict. The doctor's grim face prepares us for the news he is about to deliver, and before he can speak, I feel myself shivering, my knees ready to buckle. He approaches us, trying in some way to soften the impact of the words that he must say: "I'm afraid that she has contracted typhoid fever." He has told so many others the same thing, for this virulent illness has spread mercilessly through Hongkew, infecting and killing many of the refugees.

"What is there to do?" Poldi asks anxiously.

"We have very little for it," he replies, "but I will consult with some of the other doctors from the hospital in the morning and see if there's anything they can suggest. Try to get her to drink the boiled water, so that she doesn't dehydrate. Sponge her body with cool damp cloths to bring the fever down. I'll speak to you again tomorrow."

As Vivi lies in her crib, limp and pale, we face a terror that surpasses everything we have encountered before. In her feverish state, no smile crosses her dry lips, no sparkle gleams in her eyes. Every day the doctor arrives to visit but has no encouragement to offer. He hangs his head in solemn sorrow and apology.

Once more, I begin to succumb to the ever-threatening lure of madness and feel that whatever fragile sanity yet remains is slipping away. Of all the obstacles that I have had to face and conquer, this one seems beyond my limits. A consortium of European physicians, dressed in black coats, each carrying a small leather satchel of supplies, converges at our home. They whisper at length, leaning over the motionless body of our little girl, then emerge in silence from her room. They have concluded that the situation is hopeless. The eldest of the three doctors, a man of about sixty, is the spokesman. He adjusts his spectacles, rubs his bristled grey beard, and announces, "There is nothing more that can be done. Now, we can only pray."

His words hang in the air like a death sentence.

"No!" I scream, consumed by an overwhelming fear. "You have to save her! She is all we have in this world, all that means anything to us. You can't walk away from us."

"We're sorry. We have nothing more to offer."

"Poldi!" I scream again. "Tell them to do something. There must be something!"

Poldi is devastated and speechless. He retreats slowly, shuffling his feet like an old man, hunched and forlorn. He goes to a little wooden chair beside a small round table set in a dark corner, and sits down, his back towards us. Shoulders heaving in despair, he weeps in silence. He reaches for a half-empty bottle of vodka and pours some into a small glass on the table. He stares vacantly into space, unable to speak. Our previous worries about running the business have been pushed aside. The doors of the shop remain closed. We have no cares but one.

Out of control with despair, I scream deliriously and pull my hair. Tears burn my face. I try to attack the doctors with my fists as they rush out the door. I want only to die.

How can we give up when there is still life? We have fought to survive to this moment and place. By sheer determination we have escaped the death camps that were meant to be our fate. Surely there must be a way to defeat this foe no matter how powerful its grasp.

I run out of the house and down the street to Erna's home.

"Vivi is sick. She's dying," I weep frantically. "What can we do? What can we do?"

"Did you try to get advice at the hospital?" she suggests, in helpless concern.

Erna watches me rush madly out of her house again and down the narrow streets. To the Chinese coolies, who look up briefly from their tasks, I must appear to be insane, ranting, running with my hair tangled and wild.

I fling open the door of the Jewish Hospital, the very hospital where my baby was born just over a year ago.

"Please," I beg, "please help me."

The nurse behind the desk looks up from her papers but doesn't seem particularly surprised or alarmed. I'm sure many hysterical parents have come here before, hoping for some medical miracle to save their children from the scourge of one of the lethal tropical diseases so common in this place. "What can I do for you?" she asks matter-of-factly.

"My baby is dying of typhoid. The doctors have said there is nothing to do, but they must be wrong. They are wrong!"

She sighs and pulls out her pad of paper and pen. "Give me your name and address and I will see if there is anything else to be done. There are always new drugs, but you must accept the reality of Shanghai. Don't get your hopes too high. I'll do what I can."

Beaten and demoralized, I leave the hospital again. Walking around aimlessly, I wander, dazed, up the alleyways and down again, nearly stepping in the path of a truck rumbling by. Why, I think, why is this happening? Maybe this is a punishment for something I did wrong. But what could I have done that was so evil to have this thrust upon us? I think of all the family superstitions that could bring retribution. What have I done?

At last I reach our home again and open the door to see the same dismal sight before me. There is our baby lying still and silent in her crib and Poldi sitting in the corner. The sun is starting to set and the room is in shadows. I go and sit opposite him.

"I went to the hospital. They'll let us know if anything can be done."

He nods his head in understanding but neither of us says any more.

The night is long and quiet, disturbed only by shallow breathing and the sound of our whimpering sobs.

Early next morning, there is a hard knock at our door. When we open it we see a stranger at the threshold. He explains he has been sent by the hospital. "There is an experimental and very costly new drug, called penicillin," he says, "but its success is not assured. Many have already died of these diseases and we have been powerless to prevent them. We're hoping this will be the miracle drug we have been waiting for." We can scarcely take in his words – all we know is that he is giving us hope. "If you give your permission, I will advise a doctor to come today to administer it to your child. We have nothing else to offer. I suggest strongly that you agree before it is too late."

We are prepared to try anything. Vivi is hovering at death's door. Later that day, the medication is administered to her with warnings that she has only twenty-four hours to live in her present condition. If the crisis is not averted by then, she will perish. Through the night, we remain hunched over the side of her crib, which is swathed in mosquito netting. We fall in and out of tormented, unsettled sleep. I have a recurring dream in which I am running desperately, carrying something in my arms, glancing behind me again and again, to see the vague figure of a stranger whose footsteps are coming closer, pounding with increasingly louder thuds against the pavement. I can't see his face in the dark but I know I must keep running. Then I look down at the bundle in my arms, the lifeless body of my child. I awaken suddenly in a startled jump, soaked in cold sweat.

I flutter a paper fan over my baby's body and sponge her with a damp cloth, in a vain attempt to cool the raging heat on her skin. Hope has been reduced to the fragile thread of a spider's web. We are in shreds, fragmented and lost, but our thoughts are as one. If the child dies, we will not go on.

In my delirious state, half-conscious, half-dreaming, an image returns again and again: a vision of green glass at my feet, shards and splinters piled up to my ankles, cutting bleeding tears into my flesh. I see before me a brick wall where one single bottle, the last of the imagined ten green bottles, remains precariously tipped on a ledge. I have come to the last of my travails, the last that I can endure.

The room is hot and achingly quiet. A ceiling fan churns the stagnant air with a dull whir as the minutes of our vigil click by, measured by the clock on the nightstand. Despite the heat I find myself shivering. A mound of curled cigarette butts in the ashtray reveals the only thing we have been able to put to our lips.

My mind wrestles with doubt and dread, resorting at times to desperate prayers, mumbled incoherently, "Please God, with all my heart and everything that I have in this world, I implore You, don't take this child from us. We have suffered, You know how we have suffered. We have gone through fire and water, blood and tears to come to this point.

"What can I offer but my own life? I beg you, take me instead. If only you save her to live and to see freedom, to grow up in peace, I will gladly die. Please give the disease to me. My God, for the sake of my father and mother already buried and gone, and Poldi's parents tortured and murdered in Dachau, allow this one child to survive."

As the first rays of dawn streak rose-pink through the window, we are startled by a sound, weak and barely audible. At first we believe ourselves caught in one of the many disjointed dreams that have filled our minds throughout the night. Vivi speaks for the first time in days. Her small, white forehead is moist with perspiration as the fever breaks and she lifts her tiny hand up to our incredulous faces. She asks for something to eat, her favourite, tomato soup with rice.

CHAPTER 35

ALL'S WELL 1947

We have experienced nothing less than a miracle. Our child's life has been restored to us, just when we believed all was lost. It is as if all the springtimes of our lives have exploded in one glorious burst. We feel as though we had been deaf and blind and are suddenly whole again. The wonder of every day is bestowed as a gift and we revel in the bounty of life as if it were meant for us alone.

"I can endure anything now, I think," I say to Poldi. "Nothing could compare to the nightmare we've been through."

He answers with resolve in his voice, "If we can accept this as an omen, then we should go ahead with our plans. We'll build up the business and provide a good future for our little girl. It will be all right for us yet."

The store has been closed for a week, the one week of hell when Vivi was so sick. We return to it with renewed vigour and a new dedication. We work long hours, and deal with all the setbacks that apparently are routine in Shanghai. We discover that bolts of lining disappear now and then, sometimes stolen by our own workers, sometimes by skilled thieves who make them vanish before our eyes. We are always perplexed when we come across one of these losses but in the end we accept the problems as we must, and conclude that this is the best time we have experienced in years.

When the heat of Shanghai's summer becomes unbearable, we close the shop for vacation. In any case, it is hard to sell furs at this time of year, and we welcome the break. Most of the refugees have done well enough in their trades that they can afford to get away from the city to the mountain resort at Moka Shan, which is typically packed with Europeans. We plan our holidays and arrange to meet with the family, including Willi and his bride Susie, who will all make their way there later.

We leave Hongkew, taking a four-hour train ride up into the mountains. We disembark at the final stop but it is only partway up the mountain slope. At the station, located deep into the green hills, crowds of coolies call out to us. They are competing for passengers to be taken further up by foot, on the only pathway to the Chinese village where we are headed. I am seated comfortably in one of the upholstered sedan chairs, with Vivian on my lap, as we are transported along hazardous twisting paths. The chair is supported on two heavy bamboo poles, held by one man in front and another at the back, as they carry us higher into the lushly vegetated mountains. Dressed in loose-fitting white cotton shirts and shorts and in bare feet, they tread cautiously on the narrow walk. Somehow they manage to balance their heavy loads and to place one foot before the other without losing grip of their human cargo.

Partway up the mountainside, the men set the conveyances down and there is a sudden fracas of shouting amid hand gestures. Confused and alarmed, I call to Poldi, who is behind us in another sedan chair, "What is happening now? What do they want?"

"We should have expected this," he answers. "Don't worry, Nini. They have decided to bargain for more money than we agreed upon. Just a negotiating tactic. They have us at a disadvantage and know it. We have no choice now. We will have to pay more before they continue further up."

Poldi's experiences in the fur trade of Italy have prepared him well for this encounter. He argues and gesticulates until the bargain is set and then we continue on our way. When we reach our destination at last, we are relieved to see the accommodations are better than most we have previously experienced in China. There are a few individual cottages, a common shower house, and, of course, the traditional toilet bucket in the corner of our room. The place has been converted from a typical

Chinese village into guest quarters, and although it is primitive, we are delighted. Everything appears clean and wonderful to us, surrounded by the clear mountain breezes gently rustling the leaves. For once we can enjoy odours that are fresh, appealing, and revitalizing. For the first time in many years, we feel as though a burden has been magically removed.

The rest of the family has come up from Hongkew to join us. We swim in pools, rock in hammocks among the leafy trees, and regain some scraps of our fractured humanity. We rejoice in the simple fact of our survival. We trek along the walkways and, for the first time, are able to truly appreciate the beauty of the country. We pass ponds covered with huge floating lotus leaves, wide splotches of leathery green with thick stems sprouting from their centres and lemon-yellow petals opening and arching up to the sunlight.

Splendid ancient swoop-roofed pagodas tower unexpectedly in the midst of the thick forest. Wafts of pungent incense rise dreamily into the air from the ornately carved and gilded altars in the temples. Tangerine-robed monks with shaved heads, bowed in piety, kneel on embroidered cushions before an enormous statue of Buddha. They are praying in gratitude for the salvation of their people, now that they are finally free from their hated oppressors and are at ease in their own land. Signs of the battles that had been waged are everywhere we go, in the bombed-out buildings and demolished statues. But in the shining eyes of the people one can see that a decade of anguish has now been replaced by serenity.

The holiday over, we return to Hongkew and open the fur salon once more. It is just a small business but it is ours. Fashionable clientele soon discover us, though, and we are busy. The shop has a European flair evident in its displays, the style of garments, and decor. The windows facing on to the street show the most modern designs fitted on mannequins. On the counter is a large wooden abacus, with round wooden counting balls that slide along as the adding process is done. It is the Chinese method of calculation. Poldi is especially intrigued with its mathematical principles and has become proficient in its use.

We are feeling more secure than we have in years – Fritz, Willi, and Walter all have jobs at the American military base; we have enough food after years of deprivation; and civilization is beginning to return to Hongkew. Normal life is being restored once more to Little Vienna. Music drifts from the windows, and an order of sorts is restored in the midst of the ruins.

The family gathers at outdoor coffee houses. Dolu and Eva often join us – they have prospered as dentists and live a relatively comfortable life. We chat and laugh, at ease with the German language surrounding us, the familiar food, the good-natured camaraderie of all the refugees who have shared the same upheavals and still are able to carry on with an appearance of normalcy. We dress in European clothing and fix our hair in the European styles. We have always maintained a separation from the Chinese and they from us. To them we are white foreigners. We employ them as fur finishers and as servants, as have the others who have come before us. Although we are aware of the injustice in this, we accept it. Things do not change easily.

Despite the relaxed mood and certain prosperity that peace has brought to us, and although we have spent years living in Shanghai, we still feel like outsiders, never truly integrated into this part of the world. As Europeans, we are still trying to understand and adapt to the environment and the people who inhabit it, the customs, the dangers, and the taboos. Shanghai remains a no-man's land, a place where the bizarre is the ordinary, a place where corruption at all levels is commonplace and where survival is achieved at all costs. We have done things here that we never could have imagined and yet the ceaseless machinery of life in Shanghai has never absorbed us as its own. The mysteries of the Far East remain elusive to the refugees who are passing through it.

CHAPTER 36

THE COMMUNISTS 1948

Engrossed in the new freedom of our lives, the ability to move about without restrictions or fear of persecution, we are reluctant to pay attention to signs of a new menace edging over the horizon. We are aware that yet another brutal conflict has erupted in China. We hear reports regularly of the hostilities and renewed violence in Manchuria, far to the north, but reason that this is one confrontation that will not affect us. It is so far from Shanghai and the possibility of a Communist victory seems remote.

The 1945 surrender of the Japanese had been followed by withdrawal of their occupation forces from China. The vacuum of power resulted in an immediate renewal of another struggle for domination between the Nationalist troops under Chiang Kai-shek, with the support of the U.S. armed forces, against the Communist guerrillas who were eager to gain control. This country of unbalanced fortunes has proved to be a fertile environment for left-wing ideology. We believe that the combined strength of the Americans and ruling Chinese will be sufficient to ward off any attempt at a military coup, and choose to ignore the underlying reasons for the flourishing new movement.

We have seen enough of the injustice and decay to realize that a mighty revolution may be inevitable. The huge population of beggars and illiterate peasants has been waiting for a release from the bondage that has made them slaves. Subjugated by a corrupt and greedy bureaucracy and reduced to the level of a servile majority by detested foreigners, they are willing to die for the cause of liberation. Communism has promised them equality and justice, a China for the Chinese. What lies ahead can only bring destruction and more torrents of blood.

We are beginning to realize that we face another uncertain future. Poldi makes it clear he's worried. "This talk of Communism in China is bad for business," Poldi tells me, as he reads the newspaper one morning. "The whole premise of class distinction may be headed for extinction...."

I interrupt him, quickly seeing where he's leading: "And then who will buy furs?"

"Exactly. Wearing furs will be seen as the decadent flaunting of bourgeois oppression. Our business would be one of the first to go and if the Communists come to power they will take over all free enterprise."

I know that he is right and view the imminent threat as another frightening reversal of our recent prosperity and well-being.

As word of Communist victories reaches us, we also become aware of their avowed agenda. In order to sweep the country clean and establish a new order, they have decreed that all foreigners, either on their own or by force, will be evicted from the country. It is a mad scramble once again.

Panicked, owners are closing shops one by one, and homes are abandoned and dark. Massive warehouses called "go-downs" stand silent and vacant. People are being uprooted abruptly, gathering belongings in a hasty departure, running once more in fear. The wait for immigration to the United States is four years. Some are seeking a haven in Australia or Canada but one needs a resident sponsor. Others are trying to make their way to the new State of Israel, known to be a hostile desert in the Middle East where thousands of Arabs angrily resist the arrival of Jews.

Poldi and I have started talking about the future again in earnest. We have a child to think about now and we must prepare ourselves for yet another disruption of our lives. Now that there is something ominous brewing and becoming a more likely threat, I press him to write once more to his relatives in Canada – his cousins Nathan, Joe and Czarna Coopersmith and their families – to describe the urgency of our predicament. They have been there for years but have not been able to give us aid before now.

"Well?" I ask, impatient at the delays and worried about our future. "Have you heard from your relatives in Canada yet, or is there word from Leon? He went to New York, didn't he? Could we get in there?"

"Yes, Leon is in New York, but he's a new immigrant himself. He couldn't help us. I think our best chance is Canada. If the Canadian government relaxes its quotas, my cousins might have some luck in getting us in there as landed immigrants."

"And what about all my family?"

"We can try."

Time is pressing. Every day news of the Communist offensive becomes more alarming. It is apparent that the country will soon be embroiled in an immense and violent civil war. The Communists have successfully captured the railways and a number of cities. They are moving south. By the end of 1948 it is obvious that nothing will stop the invasion of this new force that is strengthening in support and numbers as it floods the entire country.

It is clear we will lose every scrap we have managed to accumulate since the end of the war. Our lives will be in grave peril if we cannot find a way to leave. Already the troops have been marching through the streets, and door to door, into the houses. It is a familiar nightmare being repeated. One night soldiers barge in and ransack our home searching for valuables. Poldi has hidden some money in his shoes. He stretches his arms in mock surrender and offers himself for search. I recall another time like this one, Japanese soldiers then, Chinese now. His courage and nerve – *chutzpah* – frighten and amaze me. I watch, apprehensive, as the uniformed men dig into his pockets but don't detect his hiding place. We have also concealed some valuables in a hollow table-leg. Our little girl, playing on the floor and aware of the secret spot, in innocence points to the table, and in her baby language announces to the soldiers that the treasure has been hidden there. We stare at Vivi in wide-eyed shock, our voices constricted, fearing the consequences. The soldiers, however, ignore her infantile babble and leave in an angry huff as we sigh in relief.

We are weary of running, aching for permanence and a sense of belonging. Yet it is impossible to stay in Shanghai. We will have to flee to an unknown land where we will be strangers again. We don't have the luxury of choosing a suitable destination, or time to settle our affairs in an orderly way. We will go wherever we are allowed entry and salvage whatever we can in the frenzied escape. My nostalgia for Vienna, blending with the torment of estrangement, is with me constantly. Even the sound of German, our mother-tongue, which is the main language we still speak here, reminds us of a place from which we have been ostracized. It hasn't been necessary to learn any other language, just a few phrases in Chinese, not really anything much. But we have picked up some English from the British and Americans we have encountered which we hope will be helpful if we ever manage to make our way to Britain, Australia, the United States, or Canada.

We write letters abroad to these countries and others, even to South America where we also have relatives. We are desperate for some news, a small crack through which we might slip into an accepting port. And what about our family here in Shanghai? We will not betray or abandon any of them. We have come this far together and so we will continue.

Finally, Poldi makes contact with the Coopersmiths, his cousins in Canada. They are prepared to sponsor us all, the whole of my family and, of course, Dolu and Eva. Although the Canadian restrictions for new immigrants are still very stringent, there is a way for us all to enter. We have to send enough money to purchase a piece of farm land that we are to work. Having lived only in large cities, we know nothing of agriculture. Somewhat daunted by the prospect of farming, we are nevertheless prepared to take our chances and to set out on yet another challenge. Once again, there really is no choice. The family gets together to discuss the prospect. We joke as we look at one another, as urban as can be, the men most comfortable in suits and neckties and the women in dresses and high heels. How are we to become farmers? We can hardly imagine the possibility, but necessity will once more dictate our future path.

Poldi and I set about in our plan of liquidating our fur business and putting all the money to use. Before the workers are paid their last wage, Poldi designs a red coat and hood with white fur lining that is made for Vivian. We bundle some of the furs into one of the large steamer trunks. Maybe they will be of use to us, we think, planning once more for any way we might find to convert assets to cash. The one thing we know about Canada is that there are cold winters. The others in the family also assemble anything of value they have accumulated. We send as much money as we can to Canada, for our share of a piece of land in a place called Richmond Hill, not too far, we've been told, from Toronto. The names sound exotic and foreign. Then we purchase tickets aboard a ship that will take us on another long voyage to another new life.

We have managed to book passage and so have the others, although not all at the same time. Poldi and I with Vivian are to leave in January. The others will follow in the next month or so, taking whichever ship is available. Once again we are to be separated from one another with the hope and promise that we will all be united once more. We will leave Mama behind in this foreign resting place, so far from Papa, knowing that we will not be able to visit her grave ever again.

There is a reason that we are going aboard the first vessel we can book; I am pregnant again. Before it is time to go, I visit Mama one last time and place a remembrance stone, and speak to her as before: "Mama, in my heart I know we're not leaving you. I believe you will travel with us and that the memory of your wisdom will guide us. Papa's spirit has never deserted me." Rubbing my fingers over the headstone and thinking of all we have endured, I go on, "I know he is always with me and his strength has pulled me through the harshest ordeals when there was nowhere else to turn. Please, Mama, stay with me too. I need you especially now. I am so frightened and I will be having another child." I feel the baby kicking and put my hand to my stomach. "I implore you to give me the courage that I need." For the last time I touch the etched words above her grave and whisper, "I love you both so much."

With our little girl, dressed in her new cherry red coat, now two years old, we will set out for another unknown land on the other side of the world, across the vast Pacific.

CHAPTER 37

THE SHIP 1949

The sudden and massive exodus of refugees, this time from Shanghai, is a reminder of our previous emigration. We've seen hundreds of them bundling themselves and their belongings together and preparing for final departure. Things are changing rapidly and the face of Hongkew is different once more. Shops are being taken over by the Chinese. Final dispersal sales are common, and many people are hustling around trying to pick up bargains and collecting treasures they have purchased.

A bristle of excitement floods through the Hongkew laneways these days. Soon we'll leave Shanghai behind, a ten-year sojourn that extended much longer than we had expected, believing that it would be just a short stopover on the way to somewhere else. The ships in the harbour are destined for various ports of call – Israel, Australia, the United States, South America, and for us, Canada. We are heading for a place whose soil has been untouched by the war. We are still refugees and will arrive on those foreign shores as outsiders, but our hope is for the next generation, that they might live peacefully in a hospitable homeland where they can feel accepted. Poldi, Vivi, and I are sailing aboard the American vessel SS *General Meicks*.

Like the others, we are sorting through our belongings. What should we take and what should we leave behind? Now we have more things to gather together, including many items of Chinese origin, reflections of our changing understanding and feelings towards the country that has been our home and haven for the past decade. We have learned something of the ancient civilization of the Chinese and have come to appreciate their artistry. Our first impressions of this land had been of a coarse people, uncivilized by European standards, but we have come to respect their ancient culture and customs.

Into our trunks go starched tablecloths, and matching napkins, embroidered by hand with tiny red, pink, and blue flowers with trailing green vines, stitched with care and perfect detail onto ivory linen. These will replace some of the things stolen by the Nazis. The Canadian government has allowed us to bring household items in duty-free as we are to be landed immigrants. We reason that we will be able to use these things ourselves but if we need cash in a hurry, we will have something to sell or barter. This is the method we have successfully used before, so we take as much of the Oriental handicrafts as possible, including hand-carved wooden cabinets, finely worked pure silver figurines, and ashtrays embedded with Chinese silver coins. So many thoughts race through my mind as I carefully fold our Japanese kimonos, hand-painted on heavy silk, and ornately embroidered *obis* sewn with threads of silver and gold among the brightly coloured patterns. What, I wonder, am I preparing for this time? Will we truly find a home? Among all the Oriental treasures we have accumulated are still the few pieces salvaged from Vienna and never unpacked. At the bottom of the case, I uncover the petit point rolls and the heavy woollen sweaters packed away in pungent mothballs. Finally, there are my skis and poles, never removed from this trunk and now preparing to journey somewhere new.

I glare threateningly at Poldi when he sees me repack these things. I can see he believes it's foolish to drag these useless items across the other half of the world but he doesn't dare complain. After all, he has his books, his own bits of strange nostalgia that tie him to his birthplace in Poland, school books from the courses in engineering he was not permitted to complete. He also has saved his father's books, memories of the relationship of admiration and love and of the precious lives that were senselessly destroyed. And there are new books, ones about China he has purchased here to learn about the land we have inhabited and are now leaving behind. Then there are his Hebrew books of prayer and learning, still preserved and treasured, and finally English-language books to prepare us for our next destination. I, with my Austrian skis, and he with his cartons of heavy books – what a pair of fools we must seem!

Three boarding passes have been issued, but all the forms clearly state that pregnant women beyond the first few months are not allowed on ship and will be turned back at the ramp. I am nine months along, a state difficult to conceal, but we can't wait for a better departure date or until the baby is delivered. We have to go. It is January 1949 when we prepare to start off on the voyage. I am wearing a wide flared coat, my hands hidden in a huge fur muff to try to conceal my swollen belly. Poldi carries Vivian, who is dressed in her red coat and hood. We board the ship filled with many other European Jews who are leaving Shanghai. A nervous electricity runs through the refugees. They are laughing loudly and speaking in a mixture of European languages, German, Russian, Polish, Hungarian. We all face uncertainty but a new spirit of freedom is in the air. Around me I note the hopeful expressions of fellow passengers although, like us, lines of pain are embedded deeply into their faces. We are alive but our lives have not been easy.

We wave to our family still standing on the dock, shouting farewells and promises for a reunion in Canada. As the ship slices into the massive ocean, parting the waters before us, we look back for the last time at the misted harbour with its strange water dwellers, unchanged from when we first arrived. The sights and smells have become familiar, but we were never a part of this land, and now that we are finally leaving forever, we are glad to see the outline of the shore diminish until it is out of sight.

Leaving behind the suffocating heaviness of air that always hangs over the vastly overpopulated city of Shanghai, we can breathe freely again. In our cabin, Poldi and I watch Vivian sleeping in her crib and turn towards one another in a long embrace. We clutch each other tightly without a word, our hearts beating in unison, our thoughts as one. Finally, Poldi says, "Do you trust me now? Do you believe that we will be all right after everything we've endured? You have to believe now. I love you, Nini, with all my heart."

"And I love you, but I'm still afraid, Poldi. I'm still terrified of the new world, arriving with nothing, and then there will be four of us, God willing. Even now, every time the baby moves inside me, my heart leaps with worry for the obstacles still ahead. I can't let go of my fears."

The ship rises and falls in heaving spasms through the dark waves. When the labour pains begin, my body convulses with the same fervour as the ocean's rolling fury. When the ache becomes unbearable and I beg for relief, Poldi searches in vain for the ship's doctor. I am shrieking for help as the throbbing intensifies. My anxiety mingles with the wrenching pressure from without and within. I imagine my body being ripped apart.

We have docked in Guam harbour, a strategic American naval base in the Pacific. Our child will be an American, I think, and will have something we have been denied, a nationality of which he can be proud, a country to call home and freedom to grow up in peace. The doctor finally is located but he has drunk himself into a stupor. His watery eyes are sunk into a red swollen face that registers only bewilderment and anger. The heavy odour of stale whiskey hangs in the air as he weaves unsteadily into the room. Accompanying him is the ship's captain, a bulky man who rages and storms, ranting that the child just emerging into the world is a castaway. We must placate them both, offering a bribe we cannot afford. We beg for their understanding and commend their compassion, dreading that somehow they will detain the baby and not allow it to disembark.

My labour is a torturous agony, dragging on for hours of sweat-drenched pain. The doctor, meanwhile, is trying to revive himself with cups of black coffee. His shaking hands betray his addiction and incompetence. Poldi has told me so often that I am strong and that I can surmount any obstacle, but I want to give up. I feel unable to gather the necessary fortitude.

"Push," the doctor shouts, "push, for all you're worth! You had enough nerve to come on board this ship ready to pop and now, for God's sake, push it out!"

Finally the baby's first wails ring in my ears, pulling me back from semiconscious exhaustion. The child is a boy, healthy and strong, whose voice proclaims his right to exist in an unjust world that does not welcome him easily, a Jewish child to replace one of the many thousands that were killed. His screams are defiant, protesting the cold space into which he has been thrust, demanding to be heard, echoing the cries of so many other innocents that did not survive. This child will live. The captain signs the birth certificate and fills in the name that he has chosen, "Bion," a strange name of Greek origin. We decide we will keep the name as a reminder of the circumstances and upheaval that marked his entry into a very imperfect world.

The secret is hardly kept for long. When I have recuperated sufficiently, I go on deck with the baby and he is the centre of a great deal of excitement. Everyone seems to know about the ordeal I endured and the circumstances of the birth. Many on board have tried to cheer us and have offered their congratulations. Vivi is amazed to find that she now has a little brother and wants to hug him and play with him, just as she does with her doll. When we dock in Honolulu, Poldi takes her ashore with him and I stay behind with Bion.

When they return she is full of eager excitement. "Look, Mommy, what Daddy bought for me." Vivi shows me her new Hawaiian doll dressed in a grass skirt. "Her name is 'Aloha' because that's what everyone says here."

"She's beautiful, Vivi," I say with a smile. "Come, give me a kiss."

We have begun speaking English to Vivian although we still speak

German between us. In this way we hope that she won't have an accent or feel strange when she is growing up and that things will be better for her and Bion. Maybe we can shield them from the alienation we have experienced. The ship remains in the port for only a day and then sets off again for the rest of the journey to the mainland.

"Mommy," Vivi says to me one day as I'm nursing the baby, "the water is soapy and we have to drink 'boy' water."

I look at Poldi quizzically. He's smiling at the child's confusion.

"That's right, Poupie," he says, "all the ocean water has foam like bath water and we can only drink boiled water to kill the germs."

She nods her head in serious agreement with her father's explanation. "Boy water, Daddy, not girl water, right?"

"Right." Already she seems a child of the new world, with no memory of what has gone before, only the delight in discovery and observation. I am grateful she can amuse us like this, that she doesn't bear the fearfulness and wariness we see in the faces of many adults on the ship.

As we approach the harbour in San Francisco, we are awed by the sight of the Golden Gate Bridge. We troop down the ship's ramp, now with two children in arms. We have to have all our documents inspected, then go to a hotel where we plan to stay for a few days. Poldi sets out to find a *mohel*, a Jewish doctor who specializes in ritual circumcisions, so that Bion can have a *bris*. We are dazzled by our surroundings, the steeply sloping hills of the city where cable cars rumble up and down. When I look out at the seemingly infinite panorama of the Pacific, I marvel that we have spent so long in the land beyond the horizon.

Finally we are ready for another journey and board the train to start the long ride across the United States, into Canada, and then to our new home in Toronto.

Ships and trains, ships and trains, and a world of sea and land for us to cross since we left Vienna. The journey has seemed endless and fatigue numbs our limbs. The train steams night and day across the terrain, mountains changing to prairies and flat land stretching for seamless, boundless acres covered in snowy drifts and mounds of white. The air is clean and the water is pure. As we travel across the vast land mass, we hear about the Great Lakes, five wide bodies of fresh water, drinking water to last forever. The Canadians we encounter speak with pride about their open spaces and untapped natural resources.

Thick evergreen forests whiz by the windows and we smell only the pure scent of unspoiled Nature. It seems to me that I have searched for a place like this forever. Snow has been a big part of my fondest childhood memories, an essential ingredient in any place that could really feel like home. The subtropical heat of Shanghai is a world away now, and all the years of hardship seem to be slipping behind us with each mile that we travel. We have discovered another homeland, a place like my vision of the Garden of Eden, a frosty white-coated Paradise.

CHAPTER 38

TORONTO FEBRUARY 1949

C runchy and white beneath our feet, the snow continues to fall thickly. It blows and swirls around us like floating eiderdown. Huge drifts are piled at the curbsides. It has been ten years since we last saw such snow, except for our view of the far distant peaks of Mount Fuji in Japan. We have not felt its welcome tingle on our skin or revelled in the icy joy of winter for a seeming lifetime. Although we are foreigners again, facing the uncertainty of a new language and culture, this time there is a feeling of surprising familiarity.

Poldi's cousin, Joe, a tall lean man with a friendly smile, easy manner, and gravelly voice, meets us at the train station and packs us into his car for the ride to his home. There are no soldiers at the station, no trace of the military strife that we have left behind in Europe and in China. The streets are calm. Along the way we are captivated by the winter snowscape, everything coated in pristine white. The spiny boughs of tall evergreen trees are so heavily laden with the thick new-fallen snow that they are bending from the weight. Icicles hang like dripping wet crystal from the eaves of the rows of brick houses along the way, and puffs of smoke are rising in lazy curls from the chimneys.

As we drive along the busy streets, we see people pulling their coats and hats closer to shield themselves from the wind's swirling gusts. Red streetcars, attached to overhead cables, clang past us on metal rails. A milk wagon, pulled by a slowly plodding old horse, munching on its feed bag, clunks by. Children are laughing and throwing snowballs in mischievous glee at annoyed passers-by, or busy rolling the snow into fat balls to fashion snowmen. Other youngsters are on their way to one of the frozen rinks, with skates slung over their shoulders. Shops are brightly lit, filled with an abundant supply of food and all types of wares. The snow turns to grey mushy slush on the much travelled roads and sidewalks. A man in sooty overalls is delivering coal. He is bent from the weight of a lumpy sack carried on his back, his thick boots turning the snow black where he has trod. A pair of uniformed policemen on horseback are clicking nonchalantly along at an easy pace by the curbside of the road. They are smiling and look friendly, tipping their caps politely to an elderly couple making their way, arm in arm, across the intersection. Throughout so many years I have dreaded the sight of men in uniform, first the Nazis, then the Japanese, then the Chinese Communists. Here to my great relief and even surprise, there are uniforms that don't signal alarm or fright but security and comfort.

I'm enthralled by the sights and sounds of normal life, things that I have longed for, but feared I might never see again. The simplicity of the moment is in itself an astonishment. The terror and violence we have known is replaced with sounds of unremarkable life, so real and ordinary that it is shocking. The skies above are quiet, no storming fighter planes or threat of bombs. People are rushing about, newspapers tucked under arms or loaded with brown paper bags filled with groceries to make the evening meal for families coming together at the end of the day. My tears flow but I don't try to hold them back. They are warm and comforting and allow me to release years of sorrow and pain, washing me clean, as pure as the snowflakes floating from the sky. Our children are asleep in my arms as the car rumbles along the city streets. I offer silent thanks to God for bringing us to this place, and for answering my prayers at last, here in this perfect sliver on the Earth where we hope to raise our family in peace.

We arrive at Joe's home after a long drive through the city. The two men have been talking in the front seats and I have been in the back with our sleeping children. It has given me a chance to collect my thoughts without the interruption of conversation. Pulling up to the curb, we stop in front of a store with a door to its left side. Joe and Poldi remove our belongings from the trunk and set them in a heap by the entrance. Poldi helps me and the children out as Joe tells us, "I'll just go and park my car. Wait here inside the doorway for me and I'll be back to take you upstairs."

Joe has an upholstery business in a storefront. In the shop we can see skeletal chair frames, awaiting the stuffing, tacking, and cloth covers to be fashioned from the stacks of fabrics piled on tables and in corners. He works here and lives with his family in the apartment above. We stand transfixed, huddled at the bottom of a high, narrow stairway. Holding our two young children, bundled against the cold, we are momentarily hushed and immobile. Thinking of the great journey we have experienced, a weighty fatigue overcomes us. I feel shrunken and almost invisible, in danger of dissolving into air. We remain motionless in the doorway, stunned and glued to the spot.

Partway up the frame of the door I notice a *mezuzah,* a small ornamental rectangular object, tilted on an angle and nailed into the wood. In it we know there is a small scrap of parchment with a prayer in Hebrew for the safety of the household. It is a startling sight because it proclaims boldly that a Jewish family resides here in freedom. Jews in Canada do not shrink and crouch in fear of discovery. They are able to proudly proclaim their heritage without concern for the consequences. Poldi reaches up to tap the sacred symbol of our people, then touches his lips with his fingertips. The significance of this common gesture holds us suspended, caught in a dreamy trance. We have still not spoken nor moved.

Suddenly, we are shaken from the silence. Joe's wife, Minnie, a woman of generous proportions, stands silhouetted at the top of the high narrow stairway. She calls to us in a hefty, chuckling voice. Her whole body heaves with delight as she shouts down, "Welcome to Canada! The Chinese cousins are here! Come up, come up!" She is obviously tickled with her own wit and laughs uproariously at her joke. She stretches her fleshy arms in welcome.

She appears warm and huge to us, as if she could shelter all the refugees in the world in her outstretched arms and hug them to her bosom. A light comes on at the top of the stairs, and in it we see the maternal roundness of her form. Her dress is cut deeply at the neck to reveal mounds of jiggling soft flesh. She has a brightly coloured apron tied around her middle, decorated with a motif of ripe red strawberries hanging from curling vines along the bottom and up the sides. Each of the two pockets is a huge single red berry patch sewn on either side.

Behind her, her three teenaged children are shouting and poking their heads into the doorway, trying to get a better look: "Why are ya hollerin', Ma?"

They are all chewing gum. The two girls are dressed in sweaters and rolled-up blue jeans. Their hair is tied back in ponytails. The boy has a very short haircut, close to his head. They stare at us in stupefied silence.

Minnie calls to us again and the spell is broken. Delicious cooking aromas filter down to us as we slowly mount the many steps. We are beginning to feel flushed and excited as we near the top. From inside the apartment we hear the sounds of music from the radio and then the ringing of a telephone. When we step over the threshold, we will begin a new life, for ourselves and for our children. Somehow, we have survived to this day, a day filled with hope and possibilities.

We know that the rest of the family is already en route and we are sure we will soon be reunited. If ever there was a true miracle on this Earth it must be the salvation of the whole family. Except for Mama, who perished in China, and the devastating loss of Poldi's parents, we will all make our way to Canada – Erna, Fritz and Lily, Stella and Walter, Dolu and Eva, Willi and Susie, and we four. There were so many, so very many who did not live to witness this day. We have survived our own Exodus, making our way across a great part of the world to arrive at a new beginning in peace.

CPSIA information can be obtained at www.ICGtesting.com
Printed in the USA
LVOW07s1808031214

416973LV00001B/134/P